Writings on War

To E.P.W.

WRITINGS ON WAR

Carl Schmitt

Translated and Edited by
Timothy Nunan

polity

This volume comprises three texts, originally published in German as

"Die Wendung zum diskriminierenden Kriegsbegriff", 4th edition, © Duncker & Humblot GmbH, Berlin, 2007

"Völkerrechtliche Großraumordnung mit Interventionsverbot für raumfremde Mächte. Ein Beitrag zum Reichsbegriff im Völkerrecht", 9th edition, © Duncker & Humblot GmbH, Berlin, 2009

"Das internationalrechtliche Verbrechen des Angriffskrieges und der Grundsatz 'Nullum crimen, nulla poena sine lege', 1st edition, © Duncker & Humblot GmbH, Berlin, 1994

This English edition © Polity Press 2011

Polity Press
65 Bridge Street
Cambridge CB2 1UR, UK

Polity Press
350 Main Street
Malden, MA 02148, USA

ISBN-13: 978-0-7456-5296-2
ISBN-13: 978-0-7456-5297-9 (pb)

A catalogue record for this book is available from the British Library.

Typeset in 10.5 on 12 pt Adobe Caslon
by Servis Filmsetting Ltd, Stockport, Cheshire
Printed and bound in Great Britain by MPG Books Group Limited, Bodmin, Cornwall

The publisher has used its best endeavours to ensure that the URLs for external websites referred to in this book are correct and active at the time of going to press. However, the publisher has no responsibility for the websites and can make no guarantee that a site will remain live or that the content is or will remain appropriate.

Every effort has been made to trace all copyright holders, but if any have been inadvertently overlooked the publisher will be pleased to include any necessary credits in any subsequent reprint or edition.

For further information on Polity, visit our website: www.politybooks.com

Contents

Detailed Contents

Acknowledgments

I owe a great deal to a number of scholars, friends, institutions, and organizations for making this project possible. This book originally began as a much smaller translation project as an undergraduate at Princeton under the supervision of Andy Rabinbach, who, along with Arnd Wedemeyer, was the first person who inspired me to become interested in Schmitt as well as modern German history. I was able to begin the project with Andy, who gave me the opportunity to explore and even professionally translate some shorter Schmitt texts. At Princeton, Mike Jennings, Tom Levin, Nikolaus Wegmann, Devin Fore, Anthony Grafton, Michael Gordin, Stephen Kotkin, Froma Zeitlin, Frank Ordiway, Josh Katz, and William Howarth were all formative teachers and have often been there for me to inflict my ideas on. I might not have ever begun this project, moreover, had I not discovered an original copy of *The Turn to the Discriminating Concept of War* in the open stacks of Firestone Library at Princeton, a resource that was hugely helpful and that I sorely miss.

This project was fundamentally possible thanks to a Fulbright Student Grant and the year of writing and research time it provided. My gratitude goes to both the American selection committees as well as the German Fulbright *Kommission* for their support. At the Georg-August-Universität in Göttingen, Prof. Dr. Bernd Weisbrod pointed me in the way of more Schmitt literature and exposed me to new problems in European history in his seminars, while the Niedersächsische Staatsbibliothek was an ideal atmosphere in which to write, research, and translate. In Berlin, I was fortunate to be able to work at the Staatsbibliothek zu Berlin, an awesome scholarly resource whose resources made writing the introduction to this compilation relatively easy. In Oxford, the resources of the Bodleian Library and the Social Science Library, along with the support of the Rhodes Trust, allowed me to greatly improve a manuscript of this project. In Manchester, Michael Hoelzl and Graham Ward were the best of hosts and made several comments that improved the introduction and translation. Professor George Schwab generously granted the publishing rights for the three texts.

Beyond my time in Princeton, Germany, and England, several other individuals greatly helped with this project. Peter Caldwell was very generous with his time and energy in responding enthusiastically to my inquiries about Schmitt and this project, and his comments significantly improved an early draft of the introduction. John McCormick also encouraged me greatly in my efforts on this compendium, and I am grateful for his efforts in contacting academic presses to move the project along. An anonymous press reviewer's spirited criticism of both the argument of the introduction as well as my translational style prompted me to rethink many questions and helped me to avoid several embarrassments. Likewise, an outside reviewer for Polity provided very helpful commentary that helped to make my introduction more concise and, more importantly, readable. Of course, all the errors that do remain in this collection are my own.

As always, I could not have done without the good advice, close reading, and, most importantly, friendship of Jonny Fluger, Kayvon Tehranian, and John Raimo. My parents and grandparents, though I know there were some concerns when their son and grandson told them he was focusing on German, have always been very supportive of me and provide a better example for me in the way they love my brother, Patrick, than they may ever acknowledge. Porterfield White had the patience of a saint to put up with someone who spent so much time in different time zones from her. I was very lucky to have her as a partner in my life. This book is dedicated to her.

Translator's Introduction

The jurist for the *Reich* remains an enigma. For the reader encounter-
ing the work of Carl Schmitt (1888–1985), a highly original German
philosopher and jurist, for the first time, his oeuvre can seem an eclectic
collection.[1] Some of his interpreters would present him as an "apoca-
lyptician of counter-revolution," someone who sought the coming of a
new global political order to arrest a global wave of cosmopolitanism and
universalism in the twentieth century.[2] Others view him as a writer, who,
however engaged in analysis of the major issues of his day – the League
of Nations, the occupation of the Rhineland, the Japanese occupation
of China, to name a few – can be resurrected as a "diffractive surface for
contemporary political debates"; others, as one whose thought might
buttress ideologies from the European New Right to the American Left
and democratic pluralism.[3] Still others see Schmitt's name as inextrica-
ble from National Socialism: a cynical intellect who furthered his career
with articles on Jewish influence in German jurisprudence and how "The
Führer Protects the Law."[4] These diverse receptions raise two questions:
who was Schmitt, and what can one take from his writings on war for
today?

A very short biography may help with the first question. Schmitt
was born in 1888 in Plettenburg, Germany, in the Rhineland. He led
an academic career as a professor of law at several German universities.
At the same time, he wrote and lectured on a wide range of concerns:
parliamentary democracy, sovereignty, executive power, the League of
Nations, Roman Catholicism, Bolshevism and modernity; and the rise
of the United States. In 1933, Schmitt joined the Nazi Party and was
appointed to a chair in law in Berlin. He became the President of the
Union of National Socialist Jurists and provided legal and intellectual
justification for the Night of the Long Knives as well as the expulsion
of Jews from the legal profession in Germany. After 1936, when he
was sharply criticized by SS press organs, he retained his academic post
but lost prominence within the Party. He devoted himself to a study of

Hobbes and contemporary international jurisprudence. After the war, Schmitt was detained by Allied forces, but never charged with a crime. He did not return to an academic position afterwards, instead corresponding from Plettenberg with a wide circle of European thinkers and continuing to write and publish until his death in 1985 at the age of 96. His critical position towards both Western liberalism as well as Soviet Communism made him a controversial thinker.[5]

As for the second question, all three of the texts presented in this volume might seem obscure documents of interest only to specialists, but they actually remain important for several reasons. Firstly, they give purchase on the major questions of international law that persist today. What is the definition of war? Does neutrality exist? What is the legal difference between war and "interventions," economic sanctions, and troop deployments in foreign lands? On what basis of legitimacy can parties be prosecuted for war crimes? How – and where – should pirates and international terrorists be punished? Is global governance workable?

Secondly, Schmitt's writings provide an original revisionist narrative of interwar European history. Schmitt saw the United States of the 1920s and early 1930s not as an isolationist second-tier power, but rather as the dominant international superpower with legal-conceptual hegemony over both the world and the League of Nations. He presents Hitler's Greater German *Reich* as an emerging European power attempting only to levy the same modern methods of hegemony on Europeans that the British Empire and the United States had applied for decades to Latin Americans, South Asians, Arabs, and Europeans. And Schmitt begins to develop an account of nineteenth- and twentieth-century European history that defines the overseas colony as the central element hindering European internecine war, a narrative he would develop further in *The Nomos of the Earth*.

Finally, Schmitt's life and work represent both a model and a bugaboo for how intellectuals can relate to power.[6] On the one hand, Schmitt remains deeply appealing as an exponent of German Catholic erudition, an intellect as much at home writing on Dante, Mozart, Dostoevsky, Hobbes, ancient philosophy, Catholic legal history, or Spanish imperial history as he was in his juridical critiques of the League of Nations and Versailles. But Schmitt also was an intellect capable of furnishing intellectual support for the Röhm Purge and for Germany's occupation of Eastern Europe. He reported that the dream of his career would have been to represent the Nazis in front of the IMT* at Nuremberg. This nexus between Schmitt's audacious intellectual range

* International Military Tribunal.

and his mephitic relationship with National Socialism makes him a pregnant case study for how twentieth-century intellectuals related to power.

What, then, about Schmitt's relationship with National Socialism? Any honest reader of Schmitt has to bear this in mind while nonetheless recognizing that his thought deserves to be examined. To be clear: it is not a coincidence that this collection covers the dates from 1937 to 1945. The contention raised by the first studies of Schmitt – that 1936 constituted a "watershed"[7] for Schmitt and that after 1937 he merely "turned to international law and international relations, a domain that he thought would leave him out of the limelight" – cannot be seriously maintained in light of the texts presented here and their context.[8] Part of the mind readers have to engage with here is one that could produce an erudite historical treatment of European diplomatic and intellectual history in service of violence and domination.[9] Still, we might focus on how to read Schmitt's writings not looking to pillory him, but to engage seriously with arguments from another end of the political spectrum – a way in which we might seek to imitate Schmitt.

It is in this spirit that I have structured the introduction to these three works, published here as authorized English translations for the first time.[10] While these works hardly form the entirety of Schmitt's output on international law or war, I have selected them in particular as the major book-length texts on international law that Schmitt produced during the years of the Nazi dictatorship have not yet been translated into English – a gap in the story.[11] This collection aims to make Schmitt's thought on that topic during those crucial years, 1933–45, available to English-speaking audiences.[12] I have divided the introduction into three sections, each corresponding to one of the three texts in this volume and providing a cursory summary of the argument of each text. In each section, I offer and answer an interpretative question about each of the texts. The point is not that these short essays be taken dogmatically, only that they raise provocative further questions for readers, some of whom may be reading Schmitt for the first time. First, with regard to *The Turn to the Discriminating Concept of War*, I ask to what extent Schmitt's positions on foreign policy represent a development of his position in his 1927 work *The Concept of the Political*. Second, with regard to *The* Großraum *Order of International Law with a Ban on Intervention for Spatially Foreign Powers*, I inquire as to the relationship between Schmitt's *Großraum* theory and Nazi *Lebensraum* theory.[13] And third, with respect to *The International Crime of the War of Aggression and the Principle "nullum crimen, nulla poena sine lege,"* I ask to what extent that text can be read as Schmitt's apology for his participation in Hitler's Greater German *Reich*.

The Turn to the Discriminating Concept of War (1937)

They intermingle with that wicked band
of angels, not rebellious and not faithful
to God, who held themselves apart.

Loath to impair its beauty, heaven casts them out,
and the depths of Hell do not receive them,
lest on their account the evil angels gloat.
(Dante, *Inferno*, III, 37–42; Robert Hollander, trans.)

The Turn to the Discriminating Concept of War, originally delivered as a lecture to a session of National Socialist jurists in Munich in October 1937, was, as alluded to above, not Schmitt's first foray into international relations.[14] In his previous treatments of the international system, Schmitt had established himself as an acerbic critic of the League of Nations and American imperialism. In a 1925 lecture before a gathering of the Catholic *Zentrums-Partei* in Cologne for the millennial celebration of the Rhineland,[15] Schmitt described the technologies of hegemony that the League had supposedly done away with: American "interventions" in Cuba, the Dominican Republic, Haiti, and Panama; the British "mandate" over Palestine and Iraq; and the "internationalization" of canals, mines, and factories.[16] All of these concepts, he argued, were means for Western powers to suppress these other nations' sovereignty without openly professing to do so. As Schmitt put it with regards to the "internationalization" of coalmines in the Saarland, "thus can a nation literally have the ground taken out from under its feet even though it still bears the name of a free and even sovereign nation."[17] Schmitt would further develop these themes in his 1932 Königsberg lecture, "USA and the Forms of Modern Imperialism in International Law," which elaborated on the Monroe Doctrine, the USA's "official absence but effective presence" in the League and its use of "interventions" to control Latin America.[18] Central to both lectures was the question of how Germany could assert itself as a great power against these new "grammars of imperialism." But Schmitt also vented real anger in his lectures, a moral outrage that even his most ardent prosecutors would have to recognize before denouncing him. "How," asked Schmitt, "is a jurisprudence possible that still dares to speak of 'peaceful occupations' in light of bloody battles, in the face of ten thousands of dead, that hands over the word and the concept of 'peace' to the most gruesome scorn and derision?"[19]

Schmitt's 1932 talk, while superficially about American-European relations, was structured by his thoughts on sovereignty that he had laid out five years beforehand in *The Concept of the Political*. "No human coexistence," he said in Königsberg, "is possible without an open and clear authority."[20] Without a legitimate and transparent authority, members of a community had no higher organ to appeal to in order to resolve conflicts in the community. For Schmitt, "open and clear authority" did not mean "functioning government" or a stable political system: even in situations of vassal states, counter-kings, military occupations, and revolutionary wars, a concept of authority still existed. Civil wars and rebellion against tyrannical rule, for example, could lead to long periods where it remained unclear who factually controlled power, but both rebels and unjust tyrants "present themselves to the world as political eminencies with the entire risk of the political" even as they misused their power.[21] The point was that both legitimate rulers, as well as those with pretensions to rule, would present themselves as sovereign in public: "[They] demand obedience and loyalty, with justice or injustice, but at any event in full openness. [They make a claim] to an eminency and represent it. The publicity that lies in this representation is accepted as self-evident. This belongs, indeed, to the concept of authority." Schmitt also presented a theological version of this argument to his Catholic audience.[22] The aforementioned instruments of hegemony, he argued, forced Christians to abandon their "general duty to be subject to authority,"[23] since 'every authority is from God' (1 Romans, 13)."[24] It was, Schmitt argued, impossible for Christians "to grant respect to authority, and indeed, both external respect, *reverentia externa*, as well as inner respect, *reverentia interna*" if the governmental apparatus was "in the service of foreign powers." In opposing the French occupation of the Rhineland and the abuses of mandates, protectorates, and other forms of hegemony,[25] they could nobly demonstrate their "sense for the fundamental foundations of honesty and candidness for public life" and fulfill their duty as a Christian. In both its secular and theological form, Schmitt's argument was almost the same: modern tools of hegemony, like proxy governments or puppet regimes, were not just sinister tools of *Realpolitik*. Worse, they destroyed the structures of sovereignty and authority necessary for human community.

Given Schmitt's interest in the relationship between theories of sovereignty and international relations, we might ask how much Schmitt's positions in *The Concept of the Political* also structured his analysis in his 1937 lecture.[26] *The Turn to the Discriminating Concept of War* is a review of four contemporary works in international jurisprudence that also analyzes the changes in how the League of Nations defined war for its international system and the potentially catastrophic result. At stake for Schmitt here is the regulation of war. In the opening third of the lecture, Schmitt reviews two works by Georges Scelle and Hersch Lauterpacht.[27] Scelle, a French jurist, saw states as mere "social phenomena" and envisioned a federal world order coordinated by the League of Nations; Lauterpacht proposed that an international court with the League Charter as its constitution could make every conflict between states litigable and thus abolish war. Although these jurists had different approaches, both sought to dethrone the state as the subject of international law and replace it with a universalistic world order. The middle third of the lecture concerns short essays by two British law professors, John Fischer Williams and H.D. McNair, both of whom tentatively identified the problem of neutrality within the League of Nations. Schmitt then proceeds to expand and to articulate the two English jurists' concerns in the third section of the work. Prior to the Treaty of Versailles, so goes Schmitt's argument, war was a legitimate institution of state policy between states that were either ruled by princes who, if not Christian, met a corresponding standard of civilization (the Ottoman sultan). Such an order revolved around a "non-discriminating" concept of war: both warring parties had their reasons for war, but no secular authority on earth could objectively declare one side just and the other unjust. This in turn allowed for the permissibility of neutrality in international relations, since it was justifiable to remain neutral with respect to a conflict where one could not be objectively certain as to which party was in the right.

From Schmitt's point of view, however, Versailles and the League of Nations revolutionized the concept of war, transforming it into a "discriminating concept of war," hence the title of the work. The League – or, in theory, any international organization – claimed not only the universal right to define which side of a conflict was objectively just and unjust, but also, more significantly, the authority to declare this decision binding on all neutral parties. One now faced, instead of wars that were clearly regulated under international law, conflicts rebranded as "interventions" and "pacification actions" on the one hand (when the League approved a war) and as "crimes," "insurgencies," or "acts of terrorism" on the other hand (the terms for the opponents of the League), or even as nothing at all, when the League neither sanctioned nor condemned the action (as in the case of the Japanese invasion of Manchuria). And insofar as one could never remain neutral in the face of crime, the Versailles international system abolished the concept of neutrality. Rather than serve as the building block for a stable postwar order, Schmitt argued, Versailles created the League of Nations as a tool for American, British, and French imperialism to define opponents of their foreign policy aims as murderers, robbers, or pirates and exterminate them in "just wars."

While superficially an in depth literature review and discussion of contemporary problems in international jurisprudence, Schmitt's talk drew heavily on concepts he originally developed in *The Concept of the Political.* That work, which first appeared as a series of lectures in May 1927 and was later modified in 1932 and 1933 republications, had already contained several concrete observations on politics in the real world and international organizations.[28] The distinction between friend and enemy that respective political communities made, Schmitt claimed, was crucial to the very existence of political community as such. Political communities (nation-states or empires, for example) could take any number of measures to condemn or repudiate war as a tool of foreign policy, but it was still impossible for states to "escape from making this fateful distinction between friend and enemy."[29] For such political communities, the alternative to making this decision was either to surrender its sovereignty to another collectivity that would protect it against foreign enemies and make the friend–enemy decision for it (here, Panama or Cuba in the 1920s would serve as an example)[30] or simply to "disappear."[31] The crucial point, however, was that any universalistic organization like the League of Nations would attempt to deny political communities the ability to make the friend–enemy distinction, namely by pretending to encompass *all* countries of the world under the banner of "humanity." Schmitt granted that the distinction between friend and enemy, and hence the concept of the political, would cease to exist "if the different states, religions, classes, and other human groupings on earth should be so unified that a conflict between them is impossible."[32] But this was manifestly not the case in 1927: "if and when this condition will appear, I do not know. At the moment, this is not the case."[33] The real problem following from this was that organizations depicting themselves as champions of mankind (like the League) "generated a murderous self-righteousness," since their enemies, as the enemies of "humanity," were by definition *hostis generis humanis* and had to be exterminated.[34] And even if Schmitt's own friend–enemy distinction explicitly admitted the possibility of physical destruction of the enemy, there remained in his view a certain decorum to the *Kampf.* The enemy, in his view, was an existential fiend to be overcome, an enemy with dignity, something greater than "vermin, a trouble maker, pirate, [or] gangster."[35]

This brings us to one connection between *The Concept of the Political* and *The Turn to the Discriminating Concept of War.*[36] Schmitt's main concern in the text, the discriminating concept of war, with its claim to be a binding decision on the justice of a war for third parties, extends his concern in *The Concept of the Political* with the ability of political communities to make their own friend–enemy distinctions. Schmitt puts this in plain terms:

> Should a neutral state find itself in a position where it must decide on the justice of a war conducted by one state against another, is that third party

free to enter the war on the side on which it thinks justice lies, and hence become a war-conducting party? [. . .] A simple either-or raises itself to be considered; and this is an either-or that has real force: "Either one is neutral, or one is not."[37]

Indeed, given Schmitt's concerns in *Concept*, this question did have real force. The League's claim to decide otherwise-neutral states' positions towards wars in distant corners of the world amounted to nothing less than the wresting away of those states' sovereignty.

Schmitt's analysis of the League's regulation of war in *The Turn to the Discriminating Concept of War* also extended and clarified his analysis of universalistic organizations in *The Concept of the Political*. On the one hand, the attempt of the Versailles Order to criminalize warfare was incoherent. Any attempt to analogize war through crime would fail: one could not plausibly say that a murder victim found him or herself on the unjust side of a crime in the same way one might say that Poland was on the unjust side of a war in 1939.[38] More than that, however, Schmitt extended his remarks to organizations that claimed to represent humanity. He argued that it was impossible to institute a universalistic organization that purported to be a federal organization for all human political communities. Schmitt supposed that a universalistic organization could in theory conquer the world and so usher in an age in which "there would no longer be any wars between the nations of the planet, neither just nor unjust wars." But this could only occur if the League developed a tremendous military and waged a "decisively final war of humanity," "a war of annihilation" against all nations that placed themselves outside of the League's "humanity." In terms of *The Concept of the Political*, the point is that universalistic organizations with a non-discriminating concept of war senselessly ratchet up the friend–enemy distinction. Even if past friend–enemy conflicts between political communities descended into bloodshed and war, Schmitt implies, these wars "owed [their] justice, honor, and worth to the fact that the enemy was neither pirate nor gangster, but rather a 'state' and a 'subject of international law.'"[39] There is, Schmitt suggests, something noble about viewing the opponent in war as an enemy that must be overcome as an equally justified combatant in a battle, as opposed to a bandit. The wars and repressions of universalistic organizations, however, because of their claim to represent all of humanity, made the friend–enemy distinction an extreme one, between humanity/not-humanity, the latter of whom is now "totally morally disqualified [and] no longer recognized as a legitimate form of life."[40]

These, of course, are only some of many concerns one might have with *The Turn to the Discriminating Concept of War*.[41] For instance, even though Schmitt presented the lecture at a time when the Spanish Civil

War was one of the main issues in international politics, he mentions the conflict in the text only in passing: in an ambiguous footnote, he seems to defend the German bombing of Guernica insofar as it demonstrates to liberal commentators precisely what the shift from "war" to "interventions" and "pacification actions" amounts to.[42] Direct evidence for Schmitt's lack of attention to the Spanish Civil War is scanty; he had presented one of his articles at a conference in Barcelona and had many contacts in Spanish right-wing circles, but his only written reference to the war came in 1963.[43] One Schmitt biographer, Gopal Balakrishnan, has made several suggestions: one might posit, shakily, that even in light of Germany's active support of the Nationalist cause, Schmitt wanted to avoid being associated publicly in any way with Roman Catholicism after the SS had denounced him as a Catholic thinker in 1936.[44] Another possibility is that Schmitt simply did not support the Nationalist cause himself and thus wanted to avoid commenting on the war in his public appearances. Another question with the text is why it contains very few anti-Semitic remarks. Schmitt, following the spirit of his suggestion in a 1936 lecture to cite Jews as such in scholarly literature, goes out of his way to mention that Harold Laski, an English scholar, is a "Jewish professor" teaching at the same institution as another Jewish scholar, Hersch Lauterpacht, but Schmitt's tone throughout is measured and professional.[45] The point here may be that *The Turn to the Discriminating Concept of War* was directed primarily at an international audience. While it aimed to discredit an organization, the League of Nations, that Germany had broken with, and while it demanded a new world order, Schmitt's lecture sought to coolly situate these actions and demands in a broader, pan-European scholarly discussion, as well as to normalize and legitimize Germany's actions in a way that might still speak to European lawyers. Indeed, Schmitt's enormous concern in the talk with the rights of neutral countries bespeaks a concern with how *international* institutions should be arranged, rather than simply focusing on Germany's demands regardless of the sovereign claims of other nations.

The Turn to the Discriminating Concept of War was a qualified success. In June 1938, the *Reich* Foreign Minister Joachim von Ribbentrop sent Schmitt a letter thanking him for articulating the German position with regard to the League so convincingly.[46] Swiss reviewers also positively assessed Schmitt's contribution to European discourse on neutrality law and the League.[47] At the same time, the work seemed incomplete: it only criticized the international system of the League and did not propose anything in its place, besides suggesting that the discriminating concept of war be junked – a problem that Schmitt himself later conceded. For the immediate future, Schmitt would devote himself to a study of Thomas Hobbes' *Leviathan*, but less than two years after

Schmitt had criticized the Versailles international order in *The Turn to the Discriminating Concept of War*, he would respond to his critics with his "answer to the question" of what he had to replace the Versailles order.

The Großraum *Order of International Law with a Ban on Intervention for Spatially Foreign Powers (1939–1941)*

That today *Großräume* are forming, and thus a war is flaring up, is in no way worse and more terrifying than other earthquakes in earlier centuries. *Deos video ascendentes*. Why should I fear the Behemoth more than the Leviathan? Your great military and maritime author Castex, whom I read with tremendous pleasure, also says that world history is a battle between land and sea. *La mer contre la terre*. Until Christ returns, the world will not be in order.[48] (Schmitt, Letter to Pierre Linn, 1939)

Schmitt's 1939 lecture *The* Großraum *Order of International Law with a Ban on Intervention for Spatially Foreign Powers: A Contribution to the Concept of* Reich *in International Law* and its subsequent incarnations as a book have a reputation.[49] "Infamous," one Schmitt scholar calls it.[50] A recent history of the Nazi Empire calls it "hard-hitting."[51] Soon after Schmitt gave the lecture, the British press presented him in most sinister terms. "Herr Hitler and Professor Schmitt will now, it is believed, devote themselves to completing the framework of this conception, and the Fuhrer will soon give it to the world as his justification for Germany's relentless expansion," reported the *Daily Mail*. *The Times* reported on the same day: "Hitherto no German statesman has given a precise definition of his aims in Eastern Europe, but perhaps a recent statement by Professor Carl Schmitt, a Nazi expert on constitutional law, may be taken as a trustworthy guide."[52]

And yet Schmitt was hardly the "key man" in Hitler's policy, as the *Daily Mail* claimed elsewhere. He had given the lecture not in front of statesmen, but only in his capacity as a law professor at a pair of three-day conferences at the Christian Albrecht University in Kiel; one was to celebrate the 25th anniversary of the university's Institute for Politics and International Law, the other a gathering for National Socialist law professors. Both were chaired by Paul Ritterbusch, the university rector and legal scholar, a committed Nazi since the early 1920s and Schmitt's friend.[53] This was no policy meeting. Instead, the purpose of the conference was to provide "a model for the way German professors could make themselves useful to the war effort by providing concepts and catch phrases for educated opinion. [. . .] Academics from a whole range of disciplines came together to generate a body of literature which portrayed Germany's war aims in an ennobling, world-historical light."[54] In line with this, Schmitt speaks several times in the text of the danger of his scholarly concepts becoming "talked to death" or "turned into chatter" (*zerreden*).

Schmitt addresses many different themes in *Großraum*, but for the purposes of an introduction, perhaps the best point at which to enter is his discussion of the American Monroe Doctrine in Section II.[55] For Schmitt, the Monroe Doctrine as declared in 1823 was a revolutionary principle in international law because it was the first real *Großraum* ("great space") principle. In the Doctrine, the United States declared not only parts of the Americas but also the entire Western Hemisphere (a planetary way of thinking) off limits to colonization or intervention by the monarchic-dynastical regimes of Europe. The Monroe Doctrine, in Schmitt's mind, was a *Großraum* principle because it connected three things: first, a "politically awakened nation," (the United States of America); second, a "political idea" with "a certain opponent in mind, through which this political idea gains the quality of the political" (democracy as opposed to absolute monarchy); and third, "a *Großraum* ruled by this idea, a *Großraum* excluding foreign interventions" (the Western Hemisphere).[56] Among all contemporary empires, even the British Empire, the United States alone had fully developed a *Großraum*.

Schmitt's primary argument in *The* Großraum *Order of International Law with a Ban on Intervention for Spatially Foreign Powers* is that Germany should follow America's example and develop a *Großraum* principle for Continental Europe. In order to develop this claim, Schmitt introduces the concept of *Reich*, "the leading and bearing power whose political ideas radiate into a certain *Großraum*."[57] Just as the United States of America, with its "ideals of assimilation and melting pots," is the *Reich* of the American *Großraum*, the Greater German *Reich* will serve for the European *Großraum*.[58] Instead of assimilation, however, the German *Reich*'s political idea will be the "the respect of every nation as a reality of life determined through species and origin, blood and soil."[59] Scholars often criticize Schmitt for providing few concrete details here, but his description of the New Order gives the impression that every Eastern European racial group will be encouraged to live as a homogenous group and not be forced in any way to assimilate into a racially foreign nation-state. This, as it seems, is to be accomplished through state-sponsored forced migration, with the forced migrations of 1939–40 involving Germans, Hungarians, Romanians, Bulgarians, and other Eastern Europeans as the model.[60] Still, the Jews are an exception: Schmitt argues that "the Jewish problem" is "completely and thoroughly unique" and that the Jews are racially alien from all other Europeans, but he does not articulate what precisely is to be done with them.

Großraum served many purposes as a text. First, *Großraum* represents Schmitt's sound reading of trends in international politics in the 1930s and 1940s; states as such had begun to seem less important, and the globe was increasingly dominated by entities – the United States and the states of Central America and the Caribbean under its control; the Soviet Union, encompassing the Baltic States, the Caucasus, Central Asia, and the Slavic lands of the former Russian Empire; the British Empire; the "East Asian Co-Prosperity Sphere" – that fulfilled some but not all of the qualities of a Schmittian *Großraum*: political ideas with opponents in mind, "politically awakened nations," and some sense of encompassing the globe. Second, the text amounted to Schmitt moving away from the overly statist principles that had got him into trouble in the mid-1930s; Schmitt replaces the concept of the state he had used in earlier texts like *State, Movement, Volk* (*Staat, Bewegung, Volk*) and *The Concept of the Political* with the more amorphous *Reich*.[61] And third, Schmitt sees *Großraum* as his answer to the conundrum recognized in *The Turn to the Discriminating Concept of War*. In *Großraum* theory, he argues,

> we have the core of a new way of thinking about international law, one that proceeds from the concept of nation and thoroughly allows the elements of order in the concept of state to exist; one, however, that is capable of doing justice to the spatial conceptions of today and the real political vital forces in the world today; one that can be "planetary" – that is, that thinks in terms of the globe – without annihilating nations and states and without, as does the imperialistic international law of the Western democracies, steering the world out of the unavoidable overcoming of the old concept of state but into a universalistic-imperialistic world law.[62]

Schmitt's *Großraum* lecture has to be read within the context of the scholarly and political discussion in the German *Reich* of the late 1930s and early 1940s – a dialogue that used the American Monroe Doctrine as justification for German imperialist policies. Already on March 4, 1939, Foreign Minister Joachim von Ribbentrop had made reference to the Monroe Doctrine in meetings with Sumner Welles, the American Deputy Secretary of State, by claiming that any future partition of Poland was a purely German and Soviet affair.[63] Whereas the other lectures from the Kiel conference were published as a single volume, only Schmitt's lecture was published as a separate book; soon, Nazi theorists appropriated and sometimes criticized Schmitt's concept of *Großraum* as proved useful for their racial-geopolitical tracts. Werner Daitz, a chemical engineer who had become an economic consultant for the NSDAP, attempted to combine the idea of *Großräume* led by the dominant economic and political powers of the day with race theory.[64] In a 1941 essay, he criticized Schmitt's vision of *Großräume* for ignoring the primacy of racial homogeneity:

> The non-intervention principle founded by *Carl Schmitt* is therefore not characteristic for the *essence* of a *Großraum*. The non-intervention principle does not say anything, after all, about the natural essence and the natural content of a genuine *Großraum*. – On the basis of the non-intervention principle a *Großraum* could be filled with peoples of the most diverse families of peoples, with Chinese, Malay, Negros, Indians, and Whites. [. . .] Through the implementation of the non-intervention principle, a genuine *Großraum* with a natural inner cohesion can never be founded and asserted, as one sees with this example.[65]

Schmitt's theory itself, however, had its immediate afterlife in Hitler's *Reichstag* speech of April 28, 1939. After the German invasion of Czechoslovakia, Roosevelt sent Hitler and Mussolini a telegram urging Germany and Italy not to "attack or invade the territory or possessions" of any country on a list of "independent nations" that included all of Europe (except Slovakia), "Russia," Turkey, Syria, the Palestinian Mandate, Egypt, the Arabian Peninsula and Iran until 1949 or, more hopefully, 1964, as well as to participate in American-led talks outside of the League of Nations focusing on disarmament and the lifting of economic protectionism.[66] Hitler attacked Roosevelt's suggestion as hypocritical: Germany, he argued, had never suggested to the United States how it ought to conduct its affairs in the Americas. He called upon the Monroe Doctrine, stating that "we Germans support a similar doctrine for Europe – and above all for the territory and the interests of the Greater German *Reich*."[67] The process by which this reference to the Monroe Doctrine entered Hitler's speech is unclear, but after the speech Hans Frank called Schmitt and told him to remain silent "about the true origin of the concept of a European Monroe Doctrine," noting that "the *Führer* prided himself on his originality."[68]

Schmitt's *Großraum* theory may sound similar at first glance to Nazi *Lebensraum* theory, but the relationship between the two is complex and deserves some consideration.[69] One has to note first of all that the early 1940s were a confusing time for Nazi intellectuals attempting to define the contemporary character of the expanding *Reich* or to suggest how the New Order ought to be ruled. No single Nazi policy of occupation or foreign administration existed, nor did there exist an essential doctrine of *Lebensraum* against which one can compare Schmitt's remarks. On the one hand, theorists like Schmitt, Carl Bilfinger, and (less academically) Daitz sought to define the *Reich* with various concepts. Schmitt, of course, offered *Großraum*. Bilfinger proposed an empire defined by a core of "Germandom" in communion with Hitler surrounded by many European vassals that were "led" but, importantly, not "ruled."[70] Daitz viewed the empire as a project of ethnic cleansing and German demographic expansion to the Ural Mountains that would bring the historic territories of Rus' into a "economic, cultural, and legal" European community and lead to a flourishing twentieth-century version of the Hanseatic League and an "Anti-Atlantic Charter."[71] Not that any of this was a good use of anyone's time: despite the mention *Großraum* received in Hitler's *Reichstag* speech, little suggests that leading members of the Nazi regime were interested in such a formal theory of empire that might do anything to limit the dynamism of expansion and genocide to the East.

At the same time, Nazi administrative elites had their own solutions for empire. At one end of the spectrum was Werner Best, a lawyer for the SS who traveled widely to European capitals to study comparative administration.[72] In a June 1941 essay in a *Festgabe* for Himmler's birthday, Best proposed different categories of German foreign rule for European nations based on the conquered nations' level of civilization and likelihood to resist. He emphasized that each race had and should be allowed to develop its own institutions, but Best was no liberal: the *Führungsvolk* (leading nation), he wrote, might have to "totally destroy (or totally expel) from its sphere undesired groups." The point, however, was that Germany could negotiate favorable trade agreements and leave the policing of Jews, communists, and homosexuals to local national bureaucracies with minimal cost. For instance, while Best was based as the chief administrative officer in Paris, he oversaw the entire French occupation bureaucracy with 200 German officials in the capital and under 1,000 in the entire occupied area. Here was "home rule" for Europe. But Best was also wasting his time, because leading officials such as Hitler, Himmler, and Heydrich had little time for such a policy in National Socialist Europe. In Serbia, for example, Hitler ordered police to shoot 50 to 100 Serbs for every German soldier killed there by partisans, while Himmler later appointed a slavophobe administrator to the country whose watchword was: "I like a dead Serb better than a live one."[73] Heydrich, in the Protectorate of Bohemia and Moravia, had more than 400 Czechs executed in a period of two months after his arrival, and his style of administration was seen as the model for German colonial rule until Czech commandos in the Bohemian countryside assassinated him.[74]

The real question here is therefore not one about the direct link between *Großraum* and an essentialized concept of *Lebensraum*, but rather where to place Schmitt's theory in a wide spectrum of thought. Those who contest the affinity of *Großraum* theory with the more grisly

varieties of German colonial and administrative theory have several arguments. For one, Schmitt posits the essential element of a *Großraum* to
be the "political idea" – not race, nationality, or national culture. Schmitt
intended that the European *Großraum*, borne by an ethnically homogenous Greater German *Reich*, would have the United States of America as
its "opponent in mind" – an opponent, that, to be sure, presented "ideals
of assimilation, absorption, and melting pots," and was home to large
populations of Jews, Slavs, and African immigrants and former slaves,
but also contained millions of first- or second-generation immigrants
of German descent. Second, while Schmitt explicitly excludes the Jews
from his picture of European *Großraum* as "racially alien," he describes
Central and Eastern Europe – inhabited by Germans, Slavs, Romanians,
Roma, Gaguaz Turks, and Crimean Tatars – as a space in which there
live "many nations and national groups that are not racially alien from
one another."[75] This does not exactly conjure up visions of racial rights to
land. Moreover, Schmitt most often uses the word *Volkstum* for "nation"
– a concept that has more to do with cultural heritage, language, and
identity than race *per se*. And third, as the case of Werner Daitz illus-
trates, several contemporary theorists who prided themselves on being
Lebensraum thinkers attacked Schmitt's theory of *Großraum* as insuf-
ficiently *völkisch* (a term that is hard to translate and was often used as a
placeholder for lack of specific criticism, but can perhaps be rendered as
"racialist").[76]

And yet there are several arguments for an affinity between *Großraum*
and *Lebensraum*. Perhaps the most compelling of them is that one has
to look not at an idealized philosophy of *Großraum* but rather at the
policies that Schmitt described in his rhetoric as examples of *Großraum*
policy. Regardless of what he says about the centrality of "political idea"
to a *Großraum* (as opposed to race), the "political" idea of the German
Reich in 1939 was not "the respect of every nation as a reality of life
determined through species and origin, blood and soil" but rather the
cultural genocide of Czechs, Poles, and other Slavic minorities and the
murder and ghettoization of Jews. Schmitt celebrates the forced migration of national groups, even in cases where this forced resettlement was
dependent upon the deportation of Jews and Poles to ghettos or the
General Government, as an example of the new "order based on national
groups."[77] His characterization of the Jews, who "have of course as little
made the hitherto existing spatial theories as little as they have made
anything else," speaks for itself.[78] The extent to which this was Schmitt
really speaking his mind or him adapting to a new rhetorical context –
although one in which he had slim chances of seriously influencing policy
– remains a matter for speculation.

A more fundamental, but also more speculative problem regarding the link between *Großraum* and *Lebensraum* is whether Schmitt's image of America and the Monroe Doctrine in *Großraum* served as an ersatz for a deeper-seated fear of Jews. One major theme throughout the text, indeed, part of its title, is Schmitt's concern with the "interference of spatially foreign powers"; in his view, the United States constitutes a "spatially foreign" (*raumfremd*) (Schmitt does not elaborate on this term) entity that interferes with and so determines European politics. Schmitt's concern with America as an interfering agent is quite similar to, for example, Daitz's anti-Semitic rhetoric. In a 1941 article, Daitz wrote the following about the Jews:

> Only the Jew forms an exception. Different from all other peoples of the earth, the Jew does not own – and does not want to own – his own living space. The biological law within him only permits him to live as a parasite in the living spaces of other peoples. He thrives all the more in them as they become vitally weak or enter into rot either through him or due to any other reason. It is for this reason that the Jew is linked with every kind of imperialism, which is indeed always directed towards the decomposition of natural orders of life; the Jew is interested in imperialism, is its most loyal companion and advocate and encourages it wherever he can.[79]

In both Daitz's and Schmitt's writings there is an obsession with the Jews' lack of ties to the land, with geography, as well as an anxiety towards alien – be it American or Jewish – interference in Europe. This argument does have some weaknesses. Schmitt is content to grant the Western Hemisphere to the United States as its *Großraum*, whereas Daitz postulates that the Jews neither have nor desire any legitimate *Lebensraum*. The United States, moreover, was not only a convenient stand-in for anti-Semitic anxieties but also the major global competitor with Germany in the 1930s and 1940s. Still, Schmitt's linkage of Jews as the "fermenting agent in the dissolution of concrete, spatially determined orders" with the Western powers in *Großraum* suggests that the geopolitical moment may have given Schmitt the chance to repackage his enemy, the Jew, in a discourse of great powers and *Großräume*.

All the same, Schmitt's vision for a European *Großraum* failed. His vision for a German-led European *Großraum* was incoherent within the framework of Schmitt's own *Großraum* construct. "The European Eastern space," as Schmitt called it, was not a clearly defined geographical space in the same way as the Western Hemisphere, and for all of his talk of "thinking planetarily," Schmitt described the European *Großraum* only in terms of Europe, not as the "Heartland of the World Island" or the Northern Eastern Hemisphere. Europe is not a continent. It was only with his 1942 *Land and Sea* that Schmitt attempted to rearticulate his vision of geopolitics. Schmitt based his vision of *Großraum* on a lie: namely, the idea of "mutual respect for nations" in Europe. Even if something like this (with the obvious exception of Jews) existed in Western Europe and Scandinavia under the Nazi New Order, the legacy of the New Order in Eastern Europe both prior to and after Barbarossa was not "a peaceful existence [for nations] corresponding to their *völkisch* unique nature" but rather cultural genocide, deportation, and mass murder for Poles, Serbs, Romani, and others.[80] Schmitt's *Großraum* project responded to real developments and real challenges in geopolitics, and it was the most confident and articulate – if not the official – of the Nazi New Order in Europe. But the difference here between Schmitt's strategy of European *Großraum* on the page and the reality of Nazi rule, of implemented *Lebensraum* that he supported, proved to be an ocean of blood.

The International Crime of the War of Aggression (1945)

I would have gladly died had my August 1945 exposition on the criminalization of the war of aggression been able to be published then or during the trials.[81] (Carl Schmitt, June 20, 1948)

Schmitt's 1945 *The International Crime of the War of Aggression and the Principle* "Nullum crimen, nulla poena sine lege" is an important text for several reasons. It presents an erudite critique of the impending Nuremberg Trials from a German perspective at a time when many Anglo-American jurists were still debating the ground rules of the proceedings. It offers an impressive history of interwar European jurisprudence that anticipates parts of Schmitt's longer 1951 work, *The Nomos of the Earth*.[82] And as Schmitt's first major postwar text, it offers insight into Schmitt's postwar relationship with Nazism.[83] If, by the most conservative standard, Schmitt from 1933–6 was an official counselor of the regime and had to cloak his divergence from Nazism in erudite Hobbesiana and his *Großraum* theory from 1937–45 to continue intellectual activity while avoiding suspicion, then 1945 should mark the watershed year when Schmitt could write and say what he actually thought. At stake is the extent to which one can read the worst of Schmitt's arguments as an extension of his "true" beliefs – or whether the opportunism thesis makes sense.

A very short summary of the text may be helpful. The goal of *The International Crime of the War of Aggression* is twofold. First, through a history of European international law from approximately 1918–39, Schmitt aims to show both that no precedent exists for treating a war of aggression as a crime *ipso facto* (as was done at the Nuremberg

International Military Tribunal) and that doing so would violate the principle of "*nullum crimen, nulla poena sine lege*" (no crime, no punishment without a law) as codified in the tradition of due process in Continental, English, and American law. Second, Schmitt argues that even if wars of aggression are treated as a crime, the "economically active ordinary businessman" – a reference to his client, the German industrialist Friedrich Flick – cannot be made the subject of this crime in light of both the usual primacy of the state in international law, the closed, non-democratic structure of the NSDAP*, and the unreasonable demands this would place on citizens in oppressive regimes.[84] Throughout, Schmitt includes some sharp criticisms of the United States (for decrying Nazi aggressive war as uncivilized and backwards, even though the USA had just dropped atomic bombs on Hiroshima and Nagasaki) and of Great Britain's opposition to intervening in Abyssinia against Italian aggression on the grounds that "it is really no good crying over spilt milk." Still, on the whole the text represents a sober history of interwar international law and an impressive accomplishment of scholarship, given that it was primarily dictated and based only on Schmitt's memory and his home library in the Schlachtensee neighborhood of Berlin.[85]

On a first reading, the author of *The International Crime of the War of Aggression* seems far removed from the man of 1939–41 who wrote of "Jewish authors [who] have of course as little made the hitherto existing spatial theories as little as they have made anything else"[86] and of Hitler's having "lent the concept of our *Reich* political reality, historical truth, and a great future in international law."[87] Schmitt's most striking accomplishment in this 1945 text remains less his mastery of legal history than his protean ability, here on full display, to transform himself from Hitler's *Preußischer Staatsrat* to the hopeful chief defense attorney for the Nazis before the liberal individualistic jurisprudence of the International Military Tribunal. He appears to write with conviction about the atrocities of the Holocaust, whose "rawness and bestiality [. . .] transcends normal human comprehension. They are," he writes, "parts of and appearances of an iniquitous '*scelus infandum*' in the full sense of this word."[88] In an English language note attached to the end of *The International Crime of the War of Aggression* (presumably directed towards Anglo-American jurists), Schmitt states, "it goes without saying that – at the end of this second world war – mankind is obliged to pass a sentence upon Hitler's and his accomplices' '*scelus infandum.*'" He argues that the "monstrous atrocities of the SS and Gestapo" explode the categories of all hitherto existing international law.[89]

And yet several moments in Schmitt's analysis engender doubt as to

* *Nationalsozialistische Deutsche Arbeiterpartei*: the Nazi Party.

whether the jurist has made a break. One problem is Schmitt's tendency to artificially dichotomize the Nazi wars against Poland and the Soviet Union into a "war of aggression" and "atrocities" as if the two were separate acts. This becomes especially clear in his analysis of the citizen's obligation to resist his or her government. In Section IV and V of *The International Crime of the War of Aggression*, Schmitt notes that the judge who intends to prosecute not only the head of state but also private citizens for participation in war crimes faces a major difficulty. If citizens, Schmitt argues, not intimately linked with the execution of aggressive war can be prosecuted after wars for aiding and abetting the crime of aggressive war, then every citizen faced with the injustices of war must rebel against his or her own government if he or she wishes to avoid postwar prosecution as a war criminal. Schmitt argues that this harm is especially pernicious in the case of a "terrorist regime" like the Greater German *Reich*: "the [postwar] punishment of [such] an individual citizen would declare not only the terrorists but also the terrorized, the victim of the terror, a criminal."[90]

Schmitt's analysis is compelling for more conventional wars like the First World War, but it is questionable whether this standard did not historically apply to the Polish and Soviet theaters of war. The Nazi wars of aggression in Poland and the Soviet Union were not wars where atrocities "accidentally" happened alongside warfare that was permitted under the *jus ad bellum* (criteria for a just war), but rather wars where atrocities became the very medium of attack: consider the *Einsatzgruppen* or the Commissar Order on the Eastern Front. If the Nazi war is conceived not as merely another example of a war of aggression but rather as a novel kind of war making atrocities the medium and extermination the end of war, then Schmitt's analysis of civilians' responsibility to resist falters. If one can be held responsible for not resisting in the face of state-sponsored atrocities, then one can also be held responsible for supporting and participating in a war that consciously made atrocities both its means and end.

More broadly, Schmitt's argument here in favor of German citizens' right *not* to resist the Hitler government is conspicuous in light of his 1925 treatment of the occupation of the Rhineland. There, Schmitt argued in favor of both citizens' and Christians' responsibility to resist rulers or systems of rule that lacked "publicity" – "rule that demanded obedience and loyalty" in less than "full openness."[91] As we have seen, in the historical context of 1925, this meant resisting the French and British occupation forces in the Rhineland. While we have to take in mind that Schmitt is writing a legal memorandum for a client in *The International Crime of the War of Aggression*, it is notable that he makes no attempt to subject the Hitler regime to the same kind of analysis;

the implication is that one owed obedience to the Nazi regime either as someone living within German-controlled territory or, more generally, as a Christian faced with the problem of paying respect to secular authority.[92]

Still another question with regard to Schmitt's "apology" in *The International Crime of the War of Aggression* is whether Schmitt fully appreciates the importance of the Holocaust – the understanding of which was of course different in the public consciousness of the summer of 1945 than it is today. It is too much to assert that Schmitt, as a Nazi collaborator and outspoken anti-Semite, could simply never "apologize enough" for the Shoah.[93] Schmitt's earlier remarks may seem sufficient to many readers. But two moments in *The International Crime of the War of Aggression* suggest a kind of flippancy only months after the last camps had been liberated. The first comes towards the end of the text. Concerning the possibility of a miscarriage of justice at postwar tribunals, Schmitt writes:

> If a criminal judicial case proceeding in a solemn form commits such a mistake on a decisive point, that is no everyday error of justice that one can put up with as a human mistake. The injustice and the calamity of such a mistake would correspond to the greatness of the global crime towards whose atonement the great trials were arranged.[94]

Part of the thrust of Schmitt's statement here is linked with his remarks in the "Note" on mankind's obligation to pass a "strict and impressive" sentence on the crimes of Hitler in order to condemn Nazism.[95] One has to remember that Schmitt accorded tremendous respect to the solemnity of an international juridical decision. Still, this statement comes across as similar in effect to Heidegger's 1949 comparison of extermination camps to modern agriculture.[96] Taking the industrial extermination of six million Jews, and turning this fact into an off-hand object of comparison for an elaborate scholarly reflection on judicial procedure, may be the same as ignoring it altogether.

A second major problem with regard to Schmitt and the Holocaust has to do with the term "*scelus infandum*," which Schmitt uses to describe those "planned killings and inhuman atrocities whose victims were defenseless humans."[97] As Helmut Quaritsch has demonstrated, the phrase appears to come from the foreword of an antiquarian eighteenth-century edition of Lucan's *Pharsalia* owned by Schmitt. In that context, "*scelus infandum*" refers to the beheading of Pompey by the boy king Ptolemy XIII, and specifically to the fact that a relative scoundrel murdered a Roman ruler of great prestige.[98] It remains unclear why precisely Schmitt chose this specific phrase for his text: was he seeking to position himself as a senior expert in international law? Did he wish to demonstrate a European or Classical "depth" in his thinking? Still, it remains pretentious and disturbing that Schmitt would take this obscure literary turn when describing the murder of the European Jews.[99]

More concretely, Schmitt's depiction of his client, Friedrich Flick, in *The International Crime of the War of Aggression* and his relationship to Flick and his advisors casts doubt on the sincerity of Schmitt's coming to terms with his connection to Nazism and the Holocaust. Schmitt argues that Flick, an industrialist whose factories made extensive use of slave labor from Nazi concentration camps, ought to be considered an "ordinary businessman of any European state" who "has taken part neither in offenses against the rules of the law of war, nor in barbarities."[100] Even though public knowledge of the conditions in Flick's factories existed by the summer of 1945, Schmitt attempts to paint his client as an apolitical businessman rather than as someone whose exploitation of concentration camp labor constituted a "characteristic expression of a certain inhuman mentality."[101] The analysis of some critics of Nuremberg that this inclusion of industrialists in the circle of perpetrators of war crimes would constitute an "excessive expansion of the Anglo-American concept of perpetration and participation" misses the point here.[102] Even if the prosecution of those who had some *knowledge* of war crimes as perpetrators as such is unjust, this is manifestly not the same thing as prosecuting industrialists whose factories employed concentration camp inmates under this same heading for participation in war crimes and atrocities. It is not fair to expect a defense attorney to reveal incriminating information about his client in a legal memorandum, but *The International Crime of the War of Aggression* completely elides Flick's extensive cooperation with the concentration camp system. Nor does Schmitt's "extraordinarily thankful" acceptance of a 1,000 *Deutschmark* honorarium – funds accrued in no small part from the exploitation of slave labor – in 1951, after Flick had been convicted of war crimes and crimes against humanity, speak convincingly of his coming to terms with the "abnormity and monstrosity" of Nazi war crimes.[103]

The International Crime of the War of Aggression, then, while a brilliant reconstruction of interwar European jurisprudence, was hardly a high point in Schmitt's moral or professional life.[104] But neither is this the whole significance of Schmitt's 1945 legal memorandum. Scholars of international law and the criminalization of war will find that it offers new perspectives on those subjects. For example, Gary Ulmen points out in a 1996 piece on the book how Schmitt's discussion of aggressive war exposes the hypocrisy of the differentiation between just and unjust wars as articulated in Michael Walzer's famous thoughts on the subject – a distinction used to underwrite American foreign policy in the 1990s.[105] At first glance, Walzer's attempt "to recapture the just war for political and moral theory" seems sensible. He declares that the "use of force or imminent threat of force by one state against the political sovereignty or territorial integrity of another constitutes aggression and is a criminal act," and compares American involvement in the Vietnam war to Nazi aggression and the Soviet invasions of Hungary and Czechoslovakia.[106] In later works, however, Walzer begins to write of the necessity of humanitarian intervention: "Old and well-earned suspicions of American power must give way to a wary recognition of its necessity."[107] As Ulmen correctly points out, however, one cannot argue on the one hand for the criminalization of war – the bombing of Vietnamese – and on the other hand for the necessity of "humanitarian interventions" – the bombing of Serbs. Such attempts to discriminate between just wars, unjust wars, and "interventions" lead to a situation – as after the First World War – where defeated warring powers are treated as criminals owing only to the political preferences of the victors rather than any objective standard. Justified "interventions" here serve not morality but rather the imperial interests of the day. At stake is whether the concept of war can be divided or categorized without inevitably being exploited by the concerns of *Realpolitik*. As Ulmen concludes:

> Once war ceases to be a means of rational politics, it becomes a means of ideological (or religious, moral, ethnic, etc.) domination. Once war ceases to be a public contest between recognized political entities, it becomes what Schmitt called an "international civil war." Clearly, the dissolution of old orders and the desire for new types of political collectivities has raised again the central question of international law – the concept of war.[108]

Concluding Thoughts

Schmitt's writings on war present several lessons that are valuable for us today. One is that, as he puts it, "the history of international law is a history of the concept of war."[109] In Schmitt's time, concepts of criminality and universalism had so contaminated the concepts of neutrality and war that, in his view, a robust, fair international system under the Versailles Order had become impossible and made a war of extermination against nations outside the "universal" League of Nations likely. Mixed as they were with his ambitions to position himself as an expert on law for the National Socialist regime, his comments in the 1937 lecture speak pertinently of the danger that a less than rigorous concept of war poses for international law. In our time, we find both states and international organizations, themselves both subjects of international law, waging something – but not formal war – against organizations and individuals such as al-Qaeda and the Taliban that do not themselves appear as subjects of any international law. On a conceptual plane, this amounts to a creep towards what Schmitt called the denationalization of war – doing away with the war of states in order to transform war into an "international civil war." The consequences of this shift in the concept of war for international law writ large can only be anticipated. The case of Anwar al-Awlaki, a radical Muslim residing in Yemen whose assassination was approved in 2010 by the United States, the country of his own citizenship, suggests some of the possible future contradictions in international law. Independent of its own merits, al-Awlaki's case offers a possible glimpse into a new order where the traditionally state-centric concept of war has become fully unhinged, where at least three kinds of conflicts (international, interpersonal, and personal-national) will have to be accounted for. Whether the current institutions of public international law can accommodate such a change, and what effects this might have, remain unclear.

Linked with these considerations is a second lesson that Schmitt offers, namely that "*Caesar dominus et supra grammaticam*" – "the emperor is also the master of grammar."[110] One takeaway from Schmitt is that if you want to understand how a given international system works, you must ask how war is defined, as well as who decides when something is called war and when something is instead called a "counter-insurgency operation," "low-intensity conflict," or "intervention." We may be shocked when Schmitt writes, not long after the *Luftwaffe* bombings of Guernica, that those bombings of defenseless civilians reflected a change in the rhetoric of war – one endorsed by Western nations – that allowed such bombings to be described as a "pacification action."[111] But Schmitt's analysis in 1937 foreshadowed what was in store when Václav Havel, not Slobodan Miloševic, called the bombings of Serbia a "humanitarian bombing."[112] The United States' bombings of Pakistani and Afghan border areas today, as well as its covert operations across the Muslim world, are rigorously designated as anything but formal "war," and it was the United States, not the hundreds of thousands of Iraqis who starved under the Saddam Hussein regime, who defined the American actions of the 1990s as "sanctions." This, or so Schmitt tells us, is the analysis you must make in order to understand who is Caesar of the international system – an analysis, some would argue, that exposes the hypocrisies of imperial foreign policy.

At the same time, there are consequences if one accepts Schmitt's account of politics and international relations. Schmitt casts serious aspersions on universalism and any hopes you may have for a universal brotherhood of mankind. As he wrote in 1927, "rationally speaking, it cannot be denied that nations continue to group themselves according to the friend–enemy antithesis, that the distinction still remains relevant today, and that this is an ever present possibility for every people existing in the political sphere."[113] Nations always have been, still are, and will continue to be different and find ways to see their existential threat in other nations: this is life, Schmitt tells us. "Humanitarian intervention" after intervention in order to pacify those nations not in line with the liberal values of a so-called "universalistic" organization may lead to some gains for the liberal values of "humanity."[114] But this mission, Schmitt underlines, will remain incomplete without a "decisively final war of humanity" to exterminate those parts of the Earth's population less inclined to these values.[115] That's life, one might say. But one can reject Schmitt here by saying, to paraphrase the intellectual Adam Michnik, that Schmitt's vision of permanent friend–enemy groupings is "just life" only in a world of totalitarian regimes.[116] Accept Schmitt's skepticism towards the ability of liberalism to remake the world and you have the gain of avoiding any penultimate and massive "clash of civilizations," of refusing to take part in a potentially never-ending war of converting and exterminating criminals, terrorists, and insurgents who represent a repugnant medieval ideology. The alternative, however, is not necessarily simply accepting Taliban rule in South Asia, female genital mutilation in Africa, or the live boiling of prisoners in Uzbekistan.[117] For Schmitt, far from advocating civilizational relativism, demands that we reevaluate our entire vocabulary of universalistic human rights and humanitarian intervention, declare rights and responsibilities for situations or regions where there exists a concrete authority (like the medieval Roman Catholic Church), and engage our enemies in combat as just that – enemies to be overcome as a challenge to our communities' identities, not criminals or outlaws.

There are also more present consequences when accepting Schmitt's arguments. One appears in the justification that Schmitt makes available to proponents of a strong executive and that was offered by the lawyers of the second Bush administration in relation to torture.[118] Since any terrorist attack is by definition an exceptional event, and the attacks of 9/11 were (according to Bush Administration lawyers) a "situation unprecedented in American history,"[119] the American president "enjoys complete discretion in the exercise of his Commander-in-Chief authority and in conducting operations against hostile forces" – his emergency powers, in other words.[120] Therefore, the President has an unenumerated executive power that is at its height during wartime, and any move towards Congressional legislation to regulate the President's actions would, in effect, violate the authority granted to the President as Commander-in-Chief by the Constitution. These arguments and the subsequent actions of the Bush administration were entirely consonant with the Schmittian doctrine of the exception. The Obama Administration has, in several ways, affirmed the analysis of the Bush Administration lawyers and expanded the scope of extraordinary presidential powers. Since late 2009, the Administration has, with minimal public consultation, expanded clandestine military activity throughout the Middle East and Eurasia.[121] John O. Brennan, Obama's lead counter-terrorism advisor, has spoken of a "multigenerational" campaign against terrorism in Africa and Asia – a vision for permanent war marrying Schmitt's early 1930s conception of executive power with the liberal imperialism he feared in 1937.[122]

Talk of multigenerational campaigns brings us to the final consequence of turning to Schmitt's thought: accepting that we do not know what the new world order will look like. By the time he had begun the final of the three writings on war presented here, Schmitt knew that the *Großraum* structure of the world that he had prophesied would not come to fruition, at least not in the arrangement he had envisioned. Preparing the text that would eventually become his 1950 *The Nomos of the Earth*, Schmitt wrote of the tremendous changes in the way people viewed Earth by the late 1940s: some thought that "the whole world, our planet, is now only a landing field or an airport, a storehouse of raw materials, and a mother ship for travel in outer space." Commensurate with these potential ground rules for divvying up the planet, Schmitt saw three possibilities for new world orders: the domination by the USA or the USSR of the entire planet through technical administration, the rise of the USA as a sort of global naval and aerial policeman, the rise of several *Großräume* "precipitating a new order of the earth."[123] For some time in the 1990s, it seemed as though the second option had been realized.

Today, however, two decades later, things are less certain: it is fashionable to speak of China, India, and the EU as emerging superpowers to rival the United States. There may be significant developments in the realm of energy and sustainability, developments that will affect countries' industrial power and their geopolitical significance with regards to oil and gas reserves. And in light of the financial crisis of the late 2000s, the temples to capitalism stand empty. Skepticism about bankers' bonuses, globalization, and a world view that values economic growth above all else runs high, and fears about a debt-fueled American decline grow.

Schmitt's *Writings on War,* then, while of a different world from our own, also offer a guide to future challenges. No matter what the shape of the coming *nomos* of the Earth, however, it will be crucial both to redefine the concept of war in that system as well as to articulate whether states, *Großräume*, organizations like Hezbollah, the Taliban, or al-Qaeda are the primary subjects of the new international system. Schmitt may remain a problematic thinker due to his support for National Socialism and unthoughtful relation to the Holocaust, but his *Writings on War* were sincere responses to real challenges: global economic crisis and competition; European integration; imperialism – challenges all present with us in our world today. It is my hope that the reader takes Schmitt's writings in the face of a constellation of rising great powers, failing international institutions, and hegemonic ambitions, and uses them to evaluate the responsibility of intellectuals and politics today as well as the failure of the post-World War I new world order. If the attempts of today's generation to build a stable new world order founder in the same way as those of Schmitt's, we may not have the luxury of analyzing that failure in hindsight.

Note on the Translation

Translation is a risky business. Almost any choice of translational style, particularly of an author as erudite and, in some of his texts, prolix as Schmitt, is bound to raise irresolvable choices between fidelity to the source language on the one hand and fluency in the target language on the other. At stake is whether the translator seeks to bring the reader to the writer, or the writer to the reader. Rare is the compelling translation of which even a native speaker of the source language can say that the translator has actually improved on the style of the original, without betraying any of the author's original tone. More often, the most a reader can expect of a translator is for the translator to present their overall translational strategy, justify their choices to the extent possible, and make the reader aware of particularly rich linguistic moments in the text. Such is the goal of this brief note on the translation.

German, and Schmitt in particular, present the English-language translator with several dilemmas. German, in particular the academic German in which Schmitt wrote, is full of long sentences with many clauses. Verbs in subordinate clauses are pushed to the ends of those clauses, sometimes creating a bottleneck of verbs at the end of a sentence, which (if not terribly eloquent German) is understandable, but makes for a difficult translation into the English. While a clear and cogent writer for the most part, in the more technical moments of the texts presented here, Schmitt can lapse into such complicated constructions. While I originally strove towards a more literal – in some sense more faithful – translation of Schmitt's German, many native English speakers who read earlier manuscripts of this project commented that the prose, though faithful to the original, lacked flow, and tended to distort the English speaker's understanding of the text, even if it was accurate in some sense. Therefore, while seeking to maintain Schmitt's word choice as closely as possible, I have taken some liberties in rearranging sentence syntax, dividing long sentences into multiple sentences where appropriate, and moving clauses around in the English in order to produce what sounded to me like the most compelling English-language product. The final goal was readability in the English – hopefully without having distorted too much of Schmitt's rhythm and register in the German.

With regard to specific word choice, here there are a few problematic terms where I have been unable to find a truly appropriate or satisfying equivalent in English. The most prominent cases are *Großraum* and *Reich*, which I have elected to keep in the German rather than rendering as "great space" and "empire," respectively. Current anglophone Schmitt scholarship typically speaks of *Großraum*, and at certain points in the text, Schmitt contrasts his use of *Großraum* with the use of the *Groß-* (great, big) prefix in other phrases in a way that makes his intended meaning for the word more clear. I have decided to follow both convention and Schmitt's intention in the text. As for *Reich*, Schmitt himself places clear emphasis on the untranslatability of the word as well as, in his view, the necessity of describing what English speakers today would call "Nazi Germany" as the "*Deutsches Reich*" – not only in German but in all languages. As Schmitt writes, "word and name are never of secondary importance, not the least with political-historical eminencies that have been determined to uphold international law." The term "*Reich*" and "*Deutsches Reich*" should be distinguished from "empire" and "British Empire," the latter of which Schmitt does not view conceptually as the same as a *Reich* and would not have described as one in his terms. Given Schmitt's insistence on this point, my decision as a translator was to keep *Reich* as *Reich* in order to bring the reader closer to the writer's intentions and linguistic world.

One term that presented special problems for both several native German speakers and bilingual speakers whom I consulted was "*Kleinräumigkeit*," a term Schmitt uses in *Großraum* to describe a kind of spatial myopia when it comes to thinking geopolitically. Depending on the context, I have translated the term variously as "geopolitical claustrophilia," "continental-claustrophilic school," or "state-centric microspatiality." While none of these neologisms make for especially eloquent English, they should make Schmitt's point clear. Another word that was difficult to render was "*Leistungsraum*," which I have translated in the text as "achievement space," though it might just as well have been rendered as "dynamic space" or "performance space." The point Schmitt is making with this phrase is to distinguish between what he views as an old, superseded concept of space – an open space which existed *a priori* to all movement and action – and a new concept of space, one that is itself created by performance, movement, achievement, or action. Schmitt expands on the concept himself in *Großraum*. For these and for other terms that appear less frequently throughout the text, I have added footnotes detailing the German for particularly tricky moments of translation.

Beyond these notes on translation *per se*, a word about the scholarly apparatus. The superscript numbers appearing throughout the body of the text reflect Schmitt's own footnotes to his texts and are set as endnotes in this translation, while footnotes to the text marked with symbols reflect my own notes on the text: primarily biographical information, historical information for more obscure events, translations of foreign-language term Schmitt uses, and, where significant, bibliographical information about works cited by Schmitt.

Timothy Nunan

The Turn to the Discriminating Concept of War (1937)

Notes on the Text

The Turn to the Discriminating Concept of War was originally presented as a lecture on Friday, October 29, 1937, at the 4th annual conference of the Academy for German Law (*Akademie für Deutsches Recht*) on the theme "The Law of *Reich* and *Volk*," a week-long conference at the Ludwig-Maxmilians-University in Munich. The conference had begun on Saturday, October 23, 1937, with speeches by the Academy's President, Hans Frank, and Constantin von Neurath, the German Foreign Minister, and after a Sunday tour of the construction site of the Oswald Dieber "House of German Justice," which was to serve as the home for the Academy's legal research upon completion, the attendees at the conference broke up into separate working groups from Wednesday to Friday focusing on discrete problems of law such as inheritance law, criminal proceedings, and nationalities law. Schmitt himself was presenting his lecture to the Division for Legal Research. *The Turn to the Discriminating Concept of War* was originally intended to be published along with Carl Bilfinger's *The Law of the League of Nations Against International Law* and a contribution by the jurist Viktor Bruns. However, because Bruns failed to provide his text for the compilation on time, the project fell through and Schmitt's text was eventually published as a stand-alone volume.

This text is based on the 1988 edition of *Die Wendung zum diskriminierenden Kriegsbegriff*, published in Berlin by Duncker & Humblot. That edition is an unchanged reprint of the first edition of the book, also published by Duncker & Humblot in Berlin in 1938.

Introduction

For several years now, bloody struggles have been carried out in the varied regions of the earth – struggles to which a more or less common understanding warily avoids attaching the term "war." It may be all too easy to scoff at this observation. In truth, however, it has become all too clear that old orders are unraveling just as no new ones come to replace them. Indeed, the problems surrounding the concept of war reflect the disquietude of the current international situation. What has always been true reveals itself: the history of international law is a history of the concept of war. International law is, after all, a "right of war and of peace," *jus belli ac pacis*, and will remain such as long as it remains a law between independent peoples organized into states – so long, in other words, as war is a war between states and not an international civil war. Every dissolution of the old orders and every attempt at new bonds raises this problem. Within one and the same order of international law, there may just as little exist two contradicting concepts of war as there may exist two mutually exclusive conceptions of neutrality. The concept of war today has, therefore, become a problem. A realistic debate on the subject can only part the haze of illusory fictions that plague current thinking about international law and allow the real state of current international law to be recognized.

The world powers today have good reason to search for provisional terms and concepts between open war and genuine peace. The facts that are implied by the phrase "total war" may make such provisional terms particularly advisable.[124] These provisional concepts are, however, only deferrals and postponements through which the recent problem of the concept of war can in no way be solved. What is decisive here is that the *justice* of a war is, more than anything else, fundamental to its totality. Without the claim to justice, every claim to totality would be but an empty pretension, just as, conversely, the grand-scale just war of today is in itself a total war.

The problem of the discriminating concept of war entered the history of modern international law with President Wilson's declaration of war on April 2, 1917, under which he led his country into the world war against Germany. With it, the question of the just war raised itself in a completely different way than had been thought of by scholastic theologians or Hugo Grotius.* For nations of a certain relativistic or agnostic mentality, today there are no more holy wars, even if the experiences of the world war against Germany have shown that wartime propaganda in no way dispenses with the moral convictions that are normally only acquired from a Crusade. But the modern disposition requires the procedures of legal or ethical "positivization" for a just war. The Geneva League of Nations, if it is anything appreciable at all, is fundamentally a system of legalization, a system that monopolizes judgment on the just war. More than that, it bestows the momentous decision on the justice

---

* Hugo Grotius (1583–1645) was a Dutch natural law jurist.

or injustice of a war – a decision tied with the turn to the discriminating concept of war – upon certain powers. As long as it exists in its current form, the Geneva League of Nations is only a means to the preparation of a war that is in the fullest sense "total:" namely, a war backed by trans-state and trans-national claims to justice.

The following analysis should, combined with a report on a few notable publications from the foreign literature on international law, give a picture of the latest developments in the field since 1932–3. What is noteworthy about this recent stage of the development of international law is that the union of today's Geneva League of Nations with a universal, ecumenical world order – and in particular the achievement of a distinction between just wars and unjust wars – has led to such a crisis (as shown by the events in East Asia, Africa, and Spain) that it is now impossible to distinguish between not only the just and unjust war, but also between "war" and "not-war" – that is, whether war can even be said to exist. Only this crisis could force the champions of a union between the international law of the Geneva League of Nations and universalistic international law to consider a clearer shape for their idea, be it in the form of an institutional-federal or judicial-ethical institution. And yet just as the thoughts behind the Geneva League of Nations have led to a manifest crisis, the Geneva League is at the same time forced through a kind of dialectical necessity into an escalation and deepening of aggression in wars. A hierarchy of mere norms will clearly no longer suffice. Either there ought to be a hierarchy of concrete institutions and authorities of international law,[125] or the discriminating concept of war ought to be accepted. Institutionalization gives the many programs of a "constructive pacifism" just that which one could dub a legal "positivization." It accords, not only in principle but also in practice, the worth of a real, concrete order to the community bound to international law and organized through the Geneva League of Nations. The Geneva League of Nations and the entire "*communauté internationale*" bound therein receives either a true "constitution," through which institutional and constitutional possibilities of an effective "collective" action are guaranteed, or the Geneva League has at least some meaning by representing the "moral" conviction of an authority that decides on the justness or unjustness of a war for the world. The jurisprudential means and argumentation here, as well as both the typically French idea of "institutionalization" and the typically English "concretization" of the legal problem will arise from the following report. These opinions have assumed a fundamentally different and greater level of meaning than the purely literary comments of years past because of the recent intensity of the problem of foreign policy created by the Geneva League of Nations and its international law. To name only a few of these more literary texts:

the efforts through legal-logical reasoning to arrive at a "constitution" for the international law community; the claim raised many times since Wehberg-Schücking's* commentary on the League of Nations Charter that the Geneva League is a "federation of states" in the sense of a conceptual antithesis to the federal state, a federation that has its "own" organs, not just "collective" organs actually administered by member states.[126] The debate today centers, more now than ever, around the question of the just war.

The first decade of the postwar years was dominated by a contractual positivism motivated by a call to the sanctity of contracts and the maxim *pacta sunt servanda*,[†] the entire attitude of which and the only achievement of which was the legalization of the status quo of the Paris Peace Treaties. It was a status quo over which there hung, on the one hand, the ideology of pacifism and, on the other hand, the conceptually empty ideograms and "logical reductions" of a "pure legal doctrine" – two ideologies regarded as essential, but nonetheless less than convincing.[127] But since 1932 – and here the deciding phenomenon is the new problematic introduced by the Japanese assault on East Asia to the League of Nations' concept of war – the dynamic of political events also reflects itself in the theory of international law. The idealess contractual positivism of the status quo not only failed to delay the "collapse of the Treaty of Versailles,"[128] but was also untenable from the perspective of legal theory. The adherents to a new, universalistic world order that was continually expanding had to find the maxim *pacta sunt servanda* an inadequate foundation for a new world order. The concept of "revision" experienced an unexpected expansion. More than the mere "revision" of contracts being recognized, the concept of "collective security" and the necessity of real reform, the effective application of justice, and procedure involving a "peaceful change" were also all taken up. Moreover, this "necessity" was something that could no longer be dismissed as "unjuridical" or "unscholarly" in light of Article 19 of the League of Nations Charter.[129] The chaotic perplexity regarding the concept of war, so tragically documented by the events in East Asia and Spain, brought a new dilemma not yet dealt with by existing international law to the consciousness of the entire world.

Put in this position, the theory and systematics behind the Geneva League of Nations, its goals, and its ideals stand before new tasks and questions. Their relation to the normativism of the first period should

---

* Hans Wehberg (1885–1962) was a German pacifist jurist and law professor. Walther Schücking (1875–1935) was a German jurist, law professor and liberal.

† Pacts must be respected. The idea that non-fulfillment of contractual obligations constitutes a breach of said contract.

not be misunderstood, for systematic thinking and well thought out theories are usually to be found not at the beginning but at the end of an epoch. Therefore, the following works do represent not a conscious turn away from the work of previous years but rather a product of the those times' mode of thinking. Their meaning lies in the fact that they, born as they were through recent developments, enter the new stage of developments in international law containing a different, more serious type of actuality than the preceding body of literature based on the legitimization of an already reached status quo could ever summon up. Whether one finds, as is to be expected, a variety of points of contact, crossovers, and transitory terms in this newer literature with that of the preceding period is irrelevant. On the whole, the unique nature of this new phase of development, characterized as it is by an attempt at a true "institutionalization," has become completely clear in recent years. In particular, the efforts at an "activation" of the Geneva League of Nations against Italy in the fall of 1935 have posed all of the major critical questions: the concept of war; the new concept of neutrality; the juridical nature of the League of Nations. The attempt at sanctions against Italy can virtually be regarded as a "pathognomic moment"; a moment, in other words, that makes the critical stage of the progressive or regressive "institutionalization" or "concretization" of the League of Nations and international law clear for all the world to see, and, in doing so, makes it recognizable to scholars.

It is, on this note, by no means coincidental that the most interesting achievements of this new phase of development belong to the French and English literature. In the first phase of international law in the postwar years, from 1920–32, the activity and efforts of statesmen like Benesch* and Politis† could still be content with a normativism born in Vienna, a normativism that in some regards was only a reflexive reaction against the abnormal situation of international law in postwar Austria.[130] This normativism demonstrated the typical Habsburg quality of abstract art in jurisprudence.[131] Today, however, the horizon is constantly changing and expanding. Most relevantly, the constantly pressing problematic of the international law of the League of Nations associated with the attempts at sanctions against Italy since October 1935 has revealed one fact: this is a debate not about new norms, but rather about new orders – orders whose concrete character international powers struggle with. In this sense, one may say that international legal thought, as manifested in the texts that this report concerns, finds its foil in the collective political

---

* Edvard Beneš (1884–1948) was the Czech Foreign Minister (1920–5), Prime Minister (1921–2), and President (1935–8).
† Nicolaos (Nicolas) Sokrates Politis (1872–1942) was a Greek scholar of international law.

situation of world powers such as England, France, and the United States of America. It is not a coincidence that this brand of thought has shifted the gaze of the world not to Vienna, but to London and Paris.[132]

As soon as scholarly debates between the claims of an institutionalized, trans-national and ecumenical world order and those of the will to self-determination of free nations become more intractable and spirited, there appear numerous questions and problems that would, in other eras, have been left to the philosophy of law or, more simply, the pedagogical realm of education. Today, however, these issues take on a new, practically revolutionary guise. This concerns not only the well-known, age-old question of universal nature: monism or dualism/pluralism; the primacy of international law or national law; a justice of subordination or of coordination; states with or without sovereignty; whether international law ought be of a trans-state or interstate character. At stake here is the question of how the new system of international law should be constructed, and how the "big questions" are to be disposed of. There is, for example, a weighty difference between – on the one hand – viewing colonies as only a projection of state authority, treating them with some qualification as state territory, and regarding them as being under the dominion of states, and – on the other hand – perceiving colonial administration (as has been done recently) as a specific phenomenon of international law, one that finds its legal foundation in a mandate and "delegation" accorded to it by a regional or universal community of international law. In the latter case, this would mean that the idea of the mandate in Article 22 of the League of Nations Charter, which is normally thought to contain a legally positivistic approach, was a new unifying principle that aimed to unify both the regional and the universal of international law. It is, to add another example, not irrelevant how the question of the so-called protection of minorities under international law is dealt with in the total legal system: if minority protection is viewed as a comprehensively intra-state concern, the "*domaine exclusif*" of the individual state, or if it is viewed as the expression of a concept of nationhood that explodes state borders and raises the nation over the state as the decisive subject of international law. It revolves around the question of whether the concept of minority protection expresses an effective qualification in international law to the concept of membership to a state, or if minority protection is the legal mandate of a certain state, group, or perhaps even the entire international community. At stake, in other words, is whether minority protection is a problem of homogeneity,[133] of intervention, or an effect of the stress on the primacy of the individual in contemporary international legal thought. This is a debate, to give more examples, that is not irrelevant to the debate on whether the Free City of Danzig finds its place in international law alongside "states" or elsewhere in the framework provided by the Geneva League of Nations; whether the League of Nations exists as the coronation of international law, or just within the framework of existing contracts of international law. Finally, one ought to recall that the concept of "piracy," which has suddenly become relevant once more, and which has long represented a noteworthy problem in discussions of international law, still may seem a purely theoretical trifle, but actually represents the breakthrough of a completely new type of international law that explodes the concept of the state.[134]

These examples may suffice to point to the practical meaning of the systematics of international law and (if I may call it thus) the "systematic conceptual geography" of the current situation. The fact that a certain question is dealt with in a particular way by the international legal system already anticipates decisive events. The "trajectory of a concept," to borrow the vivid picture of a young Frenchman,[135] the consistency, and persuasiveness of a concept in international law, is determined not only through the content of its isolated conception, but also fundamentally through the position of the concept in a conceptual system.

The following analysis begins, therefore, with a report on two theoretical works from the French and English literature that are in many ways both rooted in the theoretical project of the previous phase of international legal thought. The report then moves on to approach practical and concrete argumentation, particularly that of English authors. This organizational scheme carries no judgment on the greater or lesser scholarly value of these works: rather, all systematic and theoretical legal claims require their expansion through typical argumentation of concrete and practical comments. Only through this method can there arise a complete impression that can aid a correct understanding of the current state of international jurisprudence as related to the Geneva League of Nations and its position vis-à-vis the problem of the just war.

I. A Report on Two Works Concerning International Law

The theoretical works that should be dealt with are: first, the "*Précis de droit des gens*" by the noted Parisian scholar of international law and pioneer of the universalistic current of thought regarding the League of Nations, Georges Scelle.* Scelle's work, which up until now has existed in two volumes, makes a conscious distinction between itself and previous works in speaking not of a "*droit international*" but rather a "*droit des gens*" as a true international jurisprudence. The second work is the 1933 book "The Function of Law in the International Community," devoted

---

* George Scelle (1878–1961) was a French jurist and proponent of legal monism.

to A.D. McNair* and written by the teacher of public international law at the University of London, H. Lauterpacht.† This work, too, merits special attention, for its author continues the line of thought begun in L. Oppenheim's world-famous legal work, "International Law," carrying its arguments through a litany of recent dealings and contracts in international law. Both of these works, both Scelle's and Lauterpacht's, seem to me to be important evidence of the fact that the debate in international jurisprudence, too, has, in a systematic and legal-theoretical way, entered a new and interesting stage of development. Both works supersede the earlier stances of positivism and normativism in their fundamental and systematic concretization. The maxim *pacta sunt servanda* is, in the eyes of both authors, the expression of a still voluntary international law – that is, a law founded on the subjective will of individual states, regardless of whether this will be perceived as – as Triepel puts it – the "common will" arising from a "unification."[136] Both works, then, aim at a universal world order secured by institutions, an order in which the Geneva League of Nations – a universal community of international law, an order for global justice – and mankind mutually work together, expand, and strive for progress. And while Alfred von Verdroß‡ in a recently published textbook on international law[137] treats states as "sovereign legal communities" in spite of the "primacy of international law" and builds his systematic upon states (a systematic that expressly distinguishes between international law and the law of a federal world government), both of the works discussed here show how the dynamics of world events carry the international jurisprudence established by the Geneva League of Nations to a more audacious institutionalization. The distinction between present positive justice and justice to come, just as much as the distinction between the Geneva League of Nations and a universal international community of law, is certainly recognized, but at the same time, its meaning is diminished in a contradictory and unclear way. On the one hand, the construction of the system and the positivization of certain foundations dilutes the meaning of such a distinction; on the other hand, the distinction between *lex lata*§ and *lex ferenda*¶ suffers as part of a tendency towards progress and development, since the positive international law contradicting this progress can only be treated as an abnormality already sentenced to defeat. Thus, instead of a jurisprudence

---

* Arnold Duncan McNair (1885–1975) was a British legal scholar.

† Hersch Lauterpacht (1897–1960) was an international jurist of Galician-Jewish provenance.

‡ Alfred von Verdroß-Droßberg (1890–1980) was an Austrian jurist and professor.

§ The law as it exists.

¶ The law as it ought to exist.

of the mere status quo, a virtually contrarian achievement seems now to have been thrown up: an international jurisprudence of a form of justice that is both revolutionarily new and supports itself on the foundations of justice; one that takes up the progressive dynamic of world events in itself and is still in the process of evolving. In light of Scelle's work, one could go so far for a moment as to believe that Proudhon's* astounding prediction regarding international jurisprudence had been fulfilled: that the twentieth century would be as federalistic as the nineteenth century had been constitutionalist.[138]

Viewed side by side, both works here are distinct from one another, not only in style and their intellectual outlook, but also in their methods towards institutionalization and in the conceptions they make of the structure of the institutionalized community of international law and the institutions that determine its character. Scelle constructs a novel system of international law that, in spite of many contradictions to his earlier remarks on the subject and in spite of tremendous unclarities regarding important issues (the structure of a league of nations, for example), nonetheless functions as a closed entity. Scelle's work dispels the entire systematic of international law determined by the central positioning of the state and causes this conception to seem like an obsolete, virtually medieval matter. Scelle's system is radically individualistic and democratic in the sense of the concrete-real (not just "logical-retractable") primacy of a trans-state, international order of justice. One can dub the work the first completely thought out systematic of the individualistic, liberal-democratic ideology and its application to international law. In dressing political goals and ideals in legal formulations and systematic constructions, Scelle stands in the great legal tradition that began with the Legists of the French medieval period and that has stood the test that each century of modern European history, with their various foreign and domestic challenges, has had to offer. Scelle's juridical outlook is determined by the fact that he makes legislation, the legislature, the decisive institution of institutionalized international jurisprudence and introduces legislation as the "primary function," the foundation, of the system, while international adjudication, itself a "secondary function" of the international system, is to be dealt with in a coming third volume. The legislature, for so long overlooked and just assumed as a trapping of international law, is audaciously reconstructed as the centerpiece of Scelle's international jurisprudence.

Scelle's international legal order, which claims dominion over the entire globe, is merely the trans-state mirror image of a legislative state – France, for example, which has long been regarded as the fatherland

---

* Pierre-Joseph Proudhon (1809–65) was a French politician and philosopher.

of legal codification. In the face of such a world that has the allure of a radical, systematic, and unique creation, H. Lauterpacht's book has a cautious and conservative appeal, but not in the usual English manner. Indeed, Lauterpacht's work does not represent "the typical representative English comments" in the same way that the essays (which shall be commented on later in this work) of such English legal minds as Sir John Fischer Williams and A.D. McNair do. Lauterpacht's non-English nature is easily understandable taking into account his heritage as a native of the Polish region of Galicia. But as a work of jurisprudence, while it may tend more towards legal theory than a systematic approach, it must occupy an eminent place in the anglophone literature of recent years on the topic. Lauterpacht's work ties together with great care the specifically English dispositions with the ways of thinking associated with *common law* and the justice of judges, discusses through painstaking research a tremendous amplitude of preliminary decisions, avoids Scelle's constructivist terms and conceptual debt to the Legists, and, through it all, abides by the recognized principles of commonly accepted legal doctrine. And through its critical analysis, Lauterpacht's work wins, yard by yard, the conceptual ground upon which the state and the nation organized therein can at last be dethroned, the ground upon which a *civitas maximas* with a universal *common law* and an international rule by judges as a specific institution appears. To be sure, the deep polarity between the French state and the English commonwealth, the opposition between, on the one hand, a legal way of thinking based around a "legislature" striving towards a written codification and, on the other hand, a *case law* determined by judicial decisions and universal in application, is reflected in the two works. The constitutionalization and institutionalization of a league of nations and the community of peoples means (as becomes clear when studying these two works) something different depending on the construction and conceptual analogies from the French or English constitution, and depending on whether institutions take their lead from the French or English *Rechtsstaat*.[139] But in spite of these discrepancies, in spite of the difference in their methods, style, and temperaments, both authors succeed at achieving their goal – that of a universal and institutional global legal order. Both authors, in other words, fight on the same front. This fact is the reason for selecting these two most important theoretical works on international law in recent years for a closer inspection. The report here on Scelle is more elaborately composed because Scelle's work represents the first characterization of a liberal-democratic international justice proceeding from pure programs and postulates.

1) *Scelle* has radically dethroned the state from its usual central position in international law. He denies the state any legal personality and

any legal subjectivity. The state person, the "*état-personne*," is, for him, a mere naked fiction. The only real subject of justice is the human individual; everything else is thrown out as unscientific, medieval "metaphysics," or an "anthropomorphism." The norm is an expression of the social solidarity of men who make up collective groups of varying characters: economic groups, religious groups, territorial groups, and other collectives, among which the state is only one among many "social groups." This diversity of groups, Scelle argues, represents in its very diversity the division of human character across many different societies, "*le tableau de la répartition de l'espèce humaine*" among these diverse "*sociétés*." The relation this construction has with the teaching of social pluralism of the Jewish professor Laski* (a professor teaching at the same London academy as Lauterpacht) ought to be at least mentioned, in spite of the fact that Laski, who has created the social theory of the Second International from the pragmatic philosophy of the true Anglo-Saxon, William James, is not especially mentioned by Scelle in his own work.[140] The state of hitherto existing international law transforms itself in this process into a delegated competency bound by international legal norms and entitled to the persons ruling at a given time. The fact that this position of the ruler suffers from an unfortunate duplicity of international and intra-state "function" is explained away as a product of the existing primitivism and imperfection of international institutions. But as Scelle notes, this is no reason to change the already existing and valid principles of that order. Because of this, there suddenly arise "international" instances from institutions that would have regarded themselves before now as unquestionably "national." The hierarchy of norms is, in the easiest way possible – with the help of the concept of "competence" – perfected and elaborated as a hierarchy of international authorities and institutions. In this system, competency controls the international legal order, "*le système juridique mondial du droit des gens*." The difficult question as to the recipient of this norm of international law, just as much as the oft discussed problem of transformation, becomes totally meaningless, for the confines of the state have fallen, while the individual is raised up as the lone subject of law, and therefore international law. He hence becomes the lone recipient of every norm. Duguit's† thought on the objective "social rule" and Kelsen's‡ normativistic contemplations have strongly influenced this way of thinking.[141] But Scelle manages to exceed both of these intellectual legacies in ascribing a "dynamic" to the norm, a dynamic that creates institutions and transforms the "*droit normatif*"

---

* Harold Laski (1893–1950) was an English political theorist, economist, and professor.
† Léon Duguit (1859–1928) was a French scholar of administrative law.
‡ Hans Kelsen (1881–1973) was an Austrian-American jurist and professor.

into a *"droit constructif."* This raising of the objective, social rule above the law-giver is normativistic and objectivistic in the sense of a rejection of every subjective will – and also in the sense of an international "common will" arising from "unification." The legal rule is regarded as something preceding and superior to the law-giver – *"antérieure et supérieure au législateur,"* as Scelle puts it. In opposition to this, then, in the sense of a need for a legislature, is the Legist-style construction of a *"législateur"* through the metamorphosis of the international legal contract into an *"acte-règle."* The seemingly unsolvable problem of "international legislation" is solved by regarding international legal contracts no longer as obligatorily binding legal contracts in the sense of a mere *"contrat,"* but rather as legislative acts. Contracts founded only on the force of obligation and not on the legally objective connective responsibilities of a founded *"contrat"* become something rare in Scelle's system, a mere after-effect of patrimonial theories of state. These contracts were, in Scelle's mind, mere trifling affairs that had to do with money, freedom of movement, transfer of property, and such matters. In contrast to this, that which one termed the international legal "contract" should be not only a "union" in the sense of Triepel's teachings, but also a legislative act, a *"traité-loi."* The binding nature of the international legal contract is, therefore, no longer based on the maxim *pacta sunt servanda,* which was only an expression of the old theory of will anyway, and is therefore vigorously criticized. The lawmaker of international law is every person competent to undertake effective legal acts of international law through which an international legal rule may materialize: the resulting legislative act has, then, an *"effet global et unitaire"* for international law.

After finding a legislature for international law in such a fashion, it no longer appears difficult to construct a constitutional competence and *"pouvoir constituant"* endowed with the appropriate jurisdiction for international law. Through this, the international justice system becomes a monstrously expanded reflection of the constitutional legal order of intra-state constitutional law, loyal down to the smallest detail. The liberal constitutionalism of the nineteenth century is simply carried over to the international community of peoples. The investigation of the *"phénomène fédératif,"* to which the third chapter of Scelle's first book is dedicated in systematic construction, serves to make clear the possibility of an organized federal constitution-making force – something along the lines of other federalist entities such as the English world empire, the Soviet Union, the pan-American union, and the Geneva League of Nations. At the same time, this chapter of Scelle's work serves to guard the transformation of intra-state constitutionalism into an international entity against a centralized universalism. Constitutionalization and federalization turn out to be practical constructive means for institutionalizing both the Geneva League of Nations and the universal international community of peoples. "*Droit constitutionnel international*" is the decisive concept of this entire system, a concept that Scelle has thus made the title of the second part of his work. This constitutionalized international law serves the protection of life, liberty, and individually and collectively owned property just as much as does intra-state constitutionalism. This international law builds itself on the recognized basic rights of the individual: the right to petition, the right to life, personal freedom, freedom of movement, the right to private property, etc. The creation and elaboration of a positive international law is identical to the creation and elaboration of an international legislature that, in the international legal union, in the "*traité-loi*," has reached its still imperfect, but at any rate highest, level of organization for now. The Geneva League of Nations' Charter should, in spite of its contractual origin, be a true federal constitution, a "*constitution*" in the legal sense. Because of this, the Geneva League of Nations becomes outfitted as a true trans-state institution with "constitution-giving authority" as a "*pouvoir constituant*." A constitution constructed in such a way is clearly nothing other than an implementation of the two-part liberal constitutional scheme carried over to the international level: individualistic rights to freedom as the foundation, and an "organization," in particular, a legislature. The "primacy of international law" as opposed to state justice becomes, therefore, a concrete constitutional reality. Contracts of international law, which have now become international "laws," plainly and directly override every state law as well as every intra-state constitutional article. In the event of a contradiction between international law and intra-state law, the latter – as well as any contradicting intra-state constitutional norms – are to be regarded as *ipso facto* null and void. Scelle finds examples and supporting documents for this interpretation in the fact that Article 80 of the Treaty of Versailles contradicted an envisioned Article 61, Clause 2 of the Weimar Constitution that provided for the union of Austria with Germany; he also looks to the invalidity of the Vilnius Proviso of Article 5 of the Lithuanian Constitution and to the protection of minorities in international law. The question of which state organs – more precisely, which persons – are legally competent to conclude contracts of international law is therefore obviously a question for the international law delegating the jurisdiction. It is no longer, as was the case under the current line of thinking, a question for intra-state constitutional theory. What one used to designate "internal" affairs, what one used to dub the "*domaine exclusif*" of the individual state, still exists, but becomes delegated by international law and the "*ordre international*." The same applies to the region in which the state regime was typically autonomous and had far-reaching free reign. This reign now becomes restrained and controlled by international law. The fact, writes Scelle, that the current state of positive international law manifestly contradicts this interpretation only has to do with the fact that international law and the international community of peoples still finds itself in a primitive stage of development. Scelle believes in a historically irresistible development that, in spite of all defeats, in spite of Fascist and National Socialist tendencies, shall lead from a state-centric view to a trans-state view, from anarchy to hierarchy, to an increasingly clear specialization of functions, to a working out of a trans-state, universal, ecumenical order.

Individualism and universalism are the two poles that this international legal system moves between. Its logically consistent individualism balks at nothing: neither when it differentiates between *lex lata* and *lex ferenda,* nor when it feels compelled to deplore the "primitive" imperfection of the current positive legal situation, the residue of state "exclusivity," and the ensuing "anarchy" between states. Decisive for Scelle is that the individual is seen as the lone subject of international law and as a direct member of the international community, the "*communauté international.*" This international community is a community of individuals, not one of states; the Geneva League of Nations, too, exists – like any collectivity – only on the basis of individuals, not on that of states or governments. The League of Nations, in other words, would have two billion members, including those living in colonies and mandated territories, even though these new members are, according to current regulations, unfortunately still not "citizens," (*citoyens*), of the League of Nations by dint of their nationality in these locales. The fact that the so-called international legal right of minorities is also constructed on an individual basis goes without saying. Indeed, the individual should, independent of minority protection treaties in international law, be entitled as a subject of public law to the internationally guaranteed right of petition against intra-state instances of his own state. It is for this reason that the "*beau cours*" of Nathan Feinberg* is referred to.[142] This right of petition of every single person under international law should, according to current international law, already be a "*compétence immédiate*" of the individual, "*conférée directement par l'ordre juridique international.*" Unfortunately, here the positive intra-state law of all current states again contradicts such a right to petition, although Scelle believes that in principle it should nevertheless be recognized as a positive right. This logically consistent individualism goes further in claiming that every individual ought to have the direct right to choose his nationality and citizenship at any given moment, for one could not expect it of the

---

* Nathan Feinberg (1895–1988) was an international jurist of Lithuanian-Jewish provenance.

individual to belong to a given state against his own will. Scelle continues: a true individual freedom exists only where the economic, moral, and emotional interests of the individual are protected. The individual should, therefore, also have the right to maintain his citizenship when he does not want to give it up; the German law of July 14, 1933 on the cancellation of naturalizations* is posed here as an example of discrimination and arbitrary rule contrary to all international law.[143] Every individual is, in other words, simultaneously a world citizen in the full legal sense of the word and also a state citizen.

In support of the life and freedom of these individuals – and of the citizens of affected states – other governments, but especially those of the Geneva League of Nations, should possess the jurisdiction of the intervention in international law. The intervention becomes the normal and central legal institution of Scelle's system. He writes that the League of Nations would have been allowed to intervene in Germany in 1933 on the grounds of the treatment of the Jews "*à juste titre.*" The efforts towards an intervention against National Socialist Germany were just as "*juridiquement fondés*" as they were against Bolshevik Russia and Fascist Italy; unfortunately, politics still rules over the guarantees of international law. This individualism reaches its zenith in claiming that a legal *right to resistance* is granted to every individual, national citizens included, to resist internal decrees that violate international law. Here, for a moment, the deeper meaning of this new international law becomes visible: that of the metamorphosis of the state war into civil war. Every individual who receives the order to mobilize in a war not allowed by international law should have the right to regard this order as null and, in a totally regulated procedure, demand the annulment of the mobilization order. Scelle rejects on practical grounds a direct legal *duty* of the individual to resistance against a war not permitted by international law, as the famous pacifist Hans Wehberg has claimed.[144] But he does take this occasion to condemn the inadequacy of positive law, and, in this respect, that of international justice itself, which has not sufficed to achieve significant protection of this individual right to resistance within individual states. And yet it must go without saying that a *Rechtsstaat* (*État de droit*) is compelled to protect the life of the individual after it has made legal guarantees of protection of personal freedom and property. For this reason, an international authority that can call upon the individual to act against his use in the service of state authorities in cases of mobilization is encouraged, provided that the decision on this question

---

* The Nazi Law on the Revocation of Naturalization was a 1933 law that made it legal for the German government to annul the citizenship of any German citizen who had been naturalized between November 9, 1918 and January 30, 1933.

is "not beyond all suspicion." A common right of self-determination is granted to all collective groups – even the right to secede is granted. The given rulers of a state no longer have the right to maintain the unity of their state with authority.

The new system of international law that Scelle constructs for this theory makes the practical meaning of these legal systematics and systematic placing of individual questions of international law vividly clear to any jurist. Both the fact that the so-called minority problem of international law only appears as a case of the implementation of the smashing of stately "exclusivity" and the position of the individual in international law have already been mentioned. That the legal situation of Danzig has already been handled by the League of Nations is used as an example for the fact that this true governmental authority bears a "*pouvoir gouvernemental.*" The universal community of peoples grants colonial authority to the individual state. The revolution of the entire previous conceptual system becomes especially clear in this regard. The entire second volume of Scelle's international law, which is dubbed an "international constitutional law" ("*droit constitutionnel international*"), is, as shown here, only a magnified mirror image of liberal constitutionalism reflected into the universal international realm. It attempts to transform the world into (in the deepest sense of the world) a global *Rechtsstaat.* This second volume is divided, as a result, into two parts that correspond to the two parts of the constitutional constitution scheme: rights to freedom and "organization," in particular the "legislature," since this "*Rechtsstaat*" is, in all truth, only a legislative state. The systematic constructed by Scelle in the first part of this second volume is, however, no less tumultuous. This part of the work carries the heading: "*Le milieu intersocial,*" for in the sense of previous interstate justice, international law appeared only as a part of *intersocial* justice. This part of the book is divided into four chapters, whose titles and succession say it all, especially when compared to the previously common systematic:

1. *Le phénomène étatique* (pp. 73–141)
2. *Le phénomène colonial* (pp. 142–86)
3. *Le phénomène fédératif* (pp. 187–287)
4. *Le phénomène social extraétatique* (pp. 288–312)

The fact that the "colonial phenomenon" is introduced directly next to the "state phenomenon" as something on the same level expresses the idea that both state authority and colonial authority depend on the universal order of international law. Today, every colonization receives its legal foundation from the "*société internationale globale*" just as, in previous ages, it was legitimized by papal bestowal and, later, through European conference committees. The determining of mandates, described in Article 22 of the League of Nations Charter, becomes but a mere case of applying this universalistic interpretation to the colonial problem, a piece of evidence for the universalistic point of view. The implementations of the third section here on the "federative phenomenon" serve to make clear the concept of a trans-state constitution with the help of the concept of a federal constitution. Such federalistic analogies are, too, a viable lever to lift the individual state out from the depths of international legal theory and insert it into a trans-state system. The so-called "extra-state phenomenon" of the fourth chapter then furnishes the most vivid example of Scelle's methods to relativize and degrade the state using international law. The Catholic Church does not exist, as in previous textbooks on international law, as a singular power in international law explicable only on historical grounds; rather, the Church becomes only the case of a new category in international law, the "extra-state social" power; a power, that, like the colony and federation, is ordered on the same level as the state, the power that stands on the same systematic level as the state in international law. Alongside the Catholic Church, the "national homestead" of the Jews in Palestine is treated as a further example of an extra-state social power – and also as a type of international device that should guarantee "the material and intellectual interests of such parts of the population that have no sufficient fulfillment of their justified efforts within the framework of the state institution, or that find no sufficient guarantee for their security." These types of extra-state social institutions should be developed further, Scelle argues, especially through the Geneva League of Nations. It is in this connection that he deplores the fact that the Geneva League of Nations did not succeed in rescuing the Armenian nation from persecution. This lack of success should, however, not deter one from further efforts towards construction of this fourth, extra-state social category.

A detailed report of the two volumes of Scelle's work is provided here – taken aside from the author's unusually numerous other publications – because his system of international law has, for the first time, brought the connection of liberal individualism with international legal universalism to a new systematic of international law with logical consistency. In his legal construction, that which one called a "state" until now is universalized to a "social phenomenon" alongside other social phenomena; legally speaking, the state is transformed into a mere "jurisdiction" of certain men acting in a double role of international and national function. The fact that reality yields an entirely different picture of international law is well known to the author of this system. But in such aberrations, he sees only the residue of the overcome anarchy of the life of nations, residues of medieval conceptions of the "exclusivity" of the clan. That current trends seem to be taking another direction under the influence of Fascism and National Socialism will not jar Scelle from his belief in progress. This, he says, only reflects trends that admittedly occur but eventually pass; this, he claims, cannot in the long run delay the political and legal organization of mankind into an ecumenical whole. International law is incidentally by its own nature so strongly permeated by common principles, Scelle argues, that in most important cases in the current legal situation, a point corresponding to this individualistic interpretive framework has already been reached. Owing to the unique state of international law as an "imperfect law," it is not difficult to find constructions with whose help ideological postulates can appear as already valid, positive law. Only in cases where the situation of positive law finds itself openly in conflict with a practically insurmountable resistance is the difference between *lex lata* and *lex ferenda* expressly mentioned.

Such methods, of course, make it easy to "institutionalize" the Geneva League of Nations. The Geneva League is mentioned once as an "intermediate construction between a federation of states and a federal state" that excludes the right of secession, later directly referred to as an entity "related to a federation of states." But it is also raised to the status of a trans-state federal system that today may proportionally solve problems, although Scelle notes that the existing tendency towards more closely bound trans-state organizations plays a dominant role in the formation of the League. The League, he argues, has a *"pouvoir constituant"*; the League of Nations Charter is, as already mentioned, a real "constitution"; admission into the League of Nations means, contrary to current interpretation, that even those members of the League that voted against admission of a new member must recognize the new member from a legal perspective. Prevailing conceptions of contracts are described as a distressing legal error. Scelle notes, however, that the legislative acts of the current organs of the League of Nations represent only "material" legislation – that is, they lack a *"force exécutoire,"* and that every government is free to decide whether a legislative act of the League of Nations applies to its citizens. The fundamental principle of unanimity, which is unfortunately still recognized, influences that federative system so strongly that it is finally described not as trans-state, but as *"inorganique ou interétatique."* But this idea of the League of Nations – marked as it is by a totally unclear blending of current and future justice and a raising of the institution to a federalist institution – is distinguished from that of a universal global order of justice. In Scelle's international legal system, the Geneva League of Nations takes its place next to other federative legal institutions such as the English imperium, the Soviet Union, and pan-America. In spite of this, Scelle remains a representative and pioneer of the universality of the League of Nations; he must, therefore, unhesitatingly affirm the question of whether this "League," if it is to truly become universal, is identical to the universal global justice order of the "*société écouménique du droit des gens*." As to whether this ecumenical global legal order is a "world state," Scelle has provided only contradictory opinions.[145] According to the work we are examining here, the unified world order is thought of as a "world federalism" of deeply different "societies." The current legal situation is constructed in such a way that the system of trans-state competencies that the Geneva League of Nations presumably represents today should be inserted into the currently anarchic situation of the global legal order, and that this system is to be permeated, expanded, and controlled by the global legal order. This historical development, writes Scelle, is only obscured today through dictatorships and states that are not liberal democracies. In the meantime, analogies with federalistic constructions serve as the lever that serves a universalistic construction of international law and raises the old world from its old legal depths. Alluding to his federalistic ideas, Scelle easily overcomes the objection that he might strive for a centralized world state.

And yet the distinction between universalism and centralism is deeply current for Scelle – this should go without saying for this Frenchman, whose thought stems from Duguit and who is familiar with Proudhon. The actual difficulty here lies in the fact that a "federalistic universalism" is today a contradiction in itself, at least by contemporary terms of international law. This self-contradiction becomes recognizable upon a consideration of the concept of war. War has, nonetheless, no place in Scelle's system; within Scelle's type of international law, war has, in the deepest sense of the word, become "inconceivable." For a conflict is either justice – and hence not a war – or unjustice, in which case it is a mere crime; consider, for example, the war of aggression described as an "international crime." This problem of the concept of war will be discussed further in a coming chapter because of its fundamental and totally decisive character.

2) In an introductory section to his work, H. Lauterpacht discusses the historical development of the doctrine of the "limiting of the judge's function in international law" dating from the application of this doctrine to the legal arbitration agreements of the Hague Convention (1907) to the many treaties of recent years. A second part of the work concerns itself with the relationship of the jurisdiction of international law with the totality of international law; this second part of the work also discusses the problems of the "gaps in international law," filling in these holes, and the permissibility of a *non liquet* in international jurisprudence. The third part of the work discusses the distinction between judicial and

state disagreement and the non-partisanship of the judge. The question of the adaptation of international law to the changes in the political situation dominates the fourth part of the work. The following issues are also considered: the unique situation that has arisen from the lack of an adaptation through legislative regulation; the diverse adaptation through legal praxis or comparison; the judicial application of the principle *clausula rebus sic stantibus*;* the doctrine of the abuse of justice (*abus de droit*) in international law and the extent of judicial competency as regards recommendations and decisions *ex aequo et bono*,[†] through which the judicial decision becomes a part of the international constitutional machinery. Conflicts of justice and interests, coercive comparison, and disagreements of interests are discussed in the fifth part of the work. The sixth and final part of the book speaks of the specific character of international law as "imperfect" justice. The common problem of justice of international law (Is international law justice or morality? Is international law a type of especially weak justice?) along with the question "Coordination or subordination?" and the "Rule of justice in international law" stand as the central problems of the work, while the result of the work, as already mentioned, is that international law is law in the full sense of the word. Therefore, international jurisprudence faces the task of developing this form of justice as a trans-state norm of the community of nations – not through the will of states, not through the maxim *pacta sunt servanda* which, after all, only begs the question of this will, but rather through the principle *ex fine civitas maxima*[‡] as discussed by Grotius. The primary question as to the limits of the judge's function in international law is answered, then, in the following way: law exists without the legislator, but not without the judge. The question is, therefore, not whether clear and sufficient rules exist; instead, everything depends on granting the judge the task of deciding matters of dispute and endowing the community with peace. A *legislator* of international law would himself become a trans-state; he would constitute a super-state. In contrast with this, a *judge* of international law would, in the framework of current praxis and doctrines of international law, restore the rule of justice without his own existence encouraging a trans-state organization. The task for

---

* Things thus standing. The idea that a treaty may become invalid owing to a fundamental change in international circumstances, provided that such a nullification of the treaty is not declared unilaterally.

† According to the right and good. The idea that arbitrators, when ruling on a case, may dispense with consideration of the law and rule on what they personally consider right, just, and fair in that case.

‡ To the end of a great political community. The idea that international law should be developed with the goal of laying a legal foundation for an institutionalized international community with the aim of promoting the common good.

scholars of international relations stems from recognition of this fact. The value of international jurisprudence resides in its task of raising the standard of international justice, while not lowering it to the rudimentary praxis of the current period. The attempt at a distinction between political and juridical questions turns out to be a dead end. All important questions are juridical questions. For this reason, an arbitrated decision of all international legal questions along with a fundamental securing of peace becomes possible. Arbitration neither can nor should replace war, but it is a condition *sine qua non* of the normal means of maintaining peace. "Peace" by far prevails as the leading encouragement of justice; seen from a legal point of view, however, this encouragement is only a paraphrasing of the unity of the judicial system. "Peace" contradicts the idea of self-help and, at the same time, that of war. Legal positivism, says Lauterpacht at the end of his work, has become unscholarly within international law because of its own tendency to overreach. Positivism finally only desired to register the praxis of states, and, in doing so, to paralyze every attempt at a higher principle and the concept of international law itself. But Lauterpacht writes that a scholarly and critical jurisprudence is capable of reaching this wholeness of international law.

This work, too, ends with the notion of the "wholeness of international law," of "states in their totality" in the sense of an already existing *civitas maxima*. It is more restrictive in its argumentation than Scelle's book and avoids speaking openly of a trans-state organization or even legislation. This becomes especially clear in the practical result of its universalism. By posing international law as a consistent, gap-free whole, Lauterpacht constructs a (supposedly) already existing, legally traceable international legal community, a *civitas maxima* with the help of the maxim: *ubi jus ibi societas*.* "International law is made for states in their totality," not for the fleeting interests of individual states. The decision on the question of how this lasting interest of collectivity exists cannot be made by the individual state, for this would contradict the simple legal principle of *nemo judex in causa sua*.† There must, therefore, exist an international jurisdiction independent from the states. But the fact that the universal legal community is to be constructed on a justice free of gaps and determined by judges, along with the fact that the legislative analogies so typical for the continental state are avoided, creates an enlightening connection with the legal condition of Anglo-Saxon *common law* and judiciary, based not on the state but on the law – a doctrine that contrasts with the French doctrine of the primacy of the state. What is unique about Lauterpacht's

---

* Where there is law, there is society.

† No one judges in their own case. The idea that no one can judge a case in which they are party.

train of thought is not that he constructs any new system of international law. Rather, he analyzes the often contradictory principles of superseded international law as borne by the state so typical for the argumentation of legal theory in general. In the end, he finds the true principles of justice that stand beyond individual cases – *the law behind the case*. Lauterpacht declares valid the universally recognized principle "*nemo judex in causa sua*" that the Permanent Court of International Justice expressly recognized in the Mosul Affair* (B12 of November 21, 1925) – a principle which even Hobbes allowed to be valid for the natural state of "*bellum omnium contra omnes.*"[†] He views it as valid against many other principles: the principle, for example, following from the sovereignty and equality of states that no state can be subjugated to a foreign jurisdiction against its will *(par in parem non habet imperium); or the principle deduced from par in parem non habet imperium* that "*omnis judex in causa sua.*"[‡] The concept of the judge presupposes his non-partisanship; the only party qualified to be a judge is he who is not bound to any of the quarreling parties. In other words, without developing a totally new system, without deploying the flamboyant juxtapositions and frontal attacks so typical for Scelle, everything is recognized in Lauterpacht's system – but at the same time both relativized and problematized. The previous theory of contractual positivism is, through common legal principles, tirelessly carried through to absurdity. At the same time, the previously dominant, essentially state-based theory of international law is junked as "metaphysics" and "unscientific." As opposed to the insufficient and primitive distinctions of justice and politics, Lauterpacht correctly recognizes that every international issue, just as much as it contains the possibility to be political, has, at a certain point, a legal side and can potentially be litigable. With the help of common legal principles and concepts, every gap in justice can be filled in; in spite of the recognition of the particular difficulties and shortcomings of international law, its weakness remains remediable, although there is just as little reason given here for the authorization of a *non liquet*[§] within an international judiciary as there is for such an authorization for the intra-state judge. For this reason, nothing more stands in the way of a universal international legal community determined by judges.

---

* The Mosul Affair was an international crisis in 1925–6, the basis of which was a disagreement between Turkey and Britain about whether the city of Mosul should be included in Iraq or Turkey. Following war scares, the League of Nations Council declared that Mosul would remain in Iraq and that the Brussels Line would form the basis of the Turkish–Iraqi border, as it continues to do today.

† The war of all against all.

‡ Everyone judges in their own case. The idea that anyone can judge a case in which they are party.

§ It is not clear. A situation where there is no applicable law.

Institutionalization is thus already achieved here. The only change here from Scelle's model is that the central, structure-determining institution is not, as in Scelle's case, a legislature, but rather (in a way typical for the English) a community of judges ruling on the basis of an international common law.[146]

To be sure, there exist all sorts of disagreements and even oppositions between Lauterpacht's system of international law and Scelle's system. But as concerns the practical result of both systems, they are in total agreement: both find concrete institutions to support a law that dethrones the state as legal institution. There exists here such a juxtaposition of disagreement in argumentation and yet at the same time a concord in the practical final result of both men's works – one that becomes most clear through Lauterpacht's position regarding the concrete questions of the League of Nations' sanctions in autumn 1935. At that time, Lauterpacht wrote an essay for *The British Yearbook of International Law* on the question of whether the League of Nations Charter represented a "higher law" as contrasted to other contractual norms of international law. This question became prominent for the many member states of the League of Nations taking part in the so-called League of Nations "sanctions" against Italy with respect to the question of the practical decision of how valid existing trade treaties (treaties that were to the benefit of most parties involved) were to be handled with respect to Article 16 of the League of Nations Charter. The "Legal Sub-Committee" established on the recommendation of another cobbled-together committee, the "Coordinating Committee," certified the primacy of the League of Nations Charter. What is of interest as regards Lauterpacht's legal argumentation is that he makes Article 20 of the Charter – an article that has played little role in such disputes until now – the centerpiece of his argumentation.[147] He comes to the conclusion that, as a contract, the League of Nations Charter, insofar as it is a contract, is founded on stronger ties of connection, and, in this sense, represents a "higher law" than other international contracts. For this reason, Lauterpacht writes caustically against the attempt – so typical for someone like Scelle (who is not mentioned here) – to give the Charter a legislative and even constitutional character. Such constructions of a legislative character are, for Lauterpacht, mere empty "incantations of a higher art." Lauterpacht stands firm in the position that, as regards the League Charter, the debate centers on contractual and obligatory – and not legal or constitutional – responsibilities. But this lone connection is enough for Lauterpacht to reach the conclusion that the League Charter has a position of "higher law," in the spirit of the fundamental principle of all legal doctrine: contracts that contradict an already valid contract are non-binding. For Lauterpacht, Article 20 of the League of Nations

Charter is but the expression of the common legal principle of the nullification of contradictory contracts. The expression "abrogates to" used in Article 20 proves, says Lauterpacht, his contention that the Charter is "superior to" other contracts. For this reason, it makes no difference whether the responsibilities of member states towards the League of Nations are expressly reserved or whether such an explicit reservation is lacking from the Charter.[148] The League Charter is avoided, but the practical result is the same as that of the more recent doctrine of non-recognition,[149] achieved here with the help of commonly held principles. It is expressively highlighted that in such a way the League Charter becomes "a purposeful instrument in the process of political integration of mankind."

II. A Report on Two Essays From The British Yearbook of International Law

A complete picture of the most recent stage of development of the jurisprudence of the League of Nations cannot be gleaned only through a consideration of systematic-constructive or legal-theoretical endeavors like those of Scelle and Lauterpacht. A reasonably exhaustive picture becomes visible only through adding representative comments from those authorities who have, in a topical way, taken a position on the decisive problem of any international jurisprudence – namely that of war and neutrality. Perhaps what most distinguishes these authors is the way their works avoid being governed by, on the one hand, common theoretical argumentation, and on the other hand, cynical and tactical argument. Approaching the problem from this viewpoint, two works from the far-reaching legal literature that has arisen since the attempts towards sanctions against Italy are particularly worthy of consideration. Both of these essays, which are of tremendous meaning, were published in the most recent volume of *The British Year Book of International Law* in response to the action by the League of Nations of 1935: the tract "Sanctions Under the Covenant" by Sir John Fischer Williams, and the essay "Collective Security" by McNair. Both works are, as evidenced by the names of their authors, representative for the English way of thinking with regards to these important questions of international law. As a practical matter, they represent a part of the efforts to use the occasion of the so-called sanctions against Italy in order to prove that the Geneva League of Nations is true community. To put it as we see it, they attempt to "federalize" the Geneva League of Nations. But even though these works do not concern themselves with an actual institutionalization in the French sense, their achievements are indeed weightier than the majority of similar French legal opinions on the same subject. These

French works tend, as a result of their state-based conception of law, to become bogged down in legal concepts and logicisms, as seen in the essay by Charles Rousseau.[150]* Rousseau's is a work, that, while interesting in all other parts of its discussion, unfurls on this occasion the entire opposition between voluntary and objectivistic international law, between *"individualisme contractuel"* and "objective norm." It is a work that desires to make more precise the legal nature of the conceptual positions of the League of Nations and to examine the entire problem of a "third state" in order to strengthen the *"caractère sociétaire"* of the League of Nations. The English scholars of law, who are marked in their jurisprudence not by a distinction between State and Law, but rather by Common Law, avoid these conceptual antitheses. Instead, they argue effectively through the practical-concrete nature of their argumentation. But when it comes to the most decisive point – that of the question of the just war – they are no less decided than the two English analyses discussed here, both of which end with an unusual, practically alarmist, forcefulness.[151]

1) The essay by Sir John Fischer Williams on the sanctions of the League of Nations discusses, under the name of "further development," a change in the constitution of the League of Nations that is fundamentally what this report has dubbed a "federalization" of the Geneva League of Nations. The essay concerns a legal problem relevant to the League of Nations that became acute in October 1935 – that of a common collective action of League of Nations member states on the grounds of Article 16 of the Charter against a member of the League who violates the Charter. Analyses of this problem both retain today and will retain in the future their meaning, even if the further course of events, along with Italy's victory in and conquest of Abyssinia, renders them politically irrelevant. Fischer Williams speaks of the war not as an "international crime," not of punitive actions, since both concepts – crime and punishment – are used not for actions of state or nation, but only of individuals. Along this same line, he points out that Article 16 of the League of Nations Charter knows nothing of the word "sanctions." What one is to understand from Article 16, what the Article really means, is only that it intends to hinder the success of a war contrary to the Charter such that members of the League will, contemplating the hindrance of such measures if they *do* launch such a war, abide by the terms of the Charter. The application and the further development of Article 16 is, of course, further debated, especially regarding how discussion of the Article 16 arose surrounding the Italian–Abyssinian conflict in the first place. The sanctions against Italy did not come about, as is generally thought,

---

* Charles Rousseau (1902–93) was a French international jurist.

through a decision of a Council of the League of Nations;[152] in the Council meeting of October 7, the individual members of the Council, with the exception of Italy, expressed the opinion that Italy had "taken the step towards war," showing contempt for Article 12 of the Charter. The President of the Council meeting noticed the fact "that fourteen of the representative members of the League of Nations Council are of the view that we find ourselves confronted by a war that was begun in contempt of the responsibilities of Article 12 of the Charter." In connection with this comment, the President also declared that a report which had come to identical conclusions had reached him from a Committee of Six of the Council. The President also recommended that a protocol of this October 7 meeting be sent to all members of the League of Nations and reminded everyone of the common meeting of October 4, 1921 on the "economic weapons of Article 16." He also added that "the Council [must] take up its responsibility towards coordination with respect to actions against Italy." This action was, according to Fischer Williams, no longer an application of the League of Nations Charter, but a necessary and legitimate "further development." A second "further development" followed: an assembly of the League of Nations, not mentioned in Article 16, was included in the procedure. But this assembly made no decision; instead, each member expressed his position on the earlier expressed opinion of the 14 Council members. But here the principle of "silence means consent" was applied in a few cases. More than that, three states – Austria, Hungary, and Albania – issued dissenting opinions, as is well known. Proceeding at any rate, a "recommendation" was made, a "*vœu*" of the assembly from October 10, 1935 was issued that invited members to form a so-called "coordination committee" for the common consulting and "facilitation" of measures considered by participating states.

   This procedure of a "further development" of a collective treaty is of great interest to anyone who has any interest in federal constitutional law and its history. The difficulties that are associated with the demand for unanimity in order to authorize a common action are overcome through a typically "federal" expansion of the treaty by treating the federation as a "community." A "general sentiment" arises from the positions of the individual member states and the "recommendations" that arise from simple majorities; this "general sentiment" is then taken as a sufficient foundation for common actions on the part of the League, and thus is the (to use a term of Williams') "built-in difficulty of the principle of unanimity" cancelled. And a further, by no means "merely" built-in, difficulty is brought to order in a similar "federal" way. Article 16 gives every individual member of the League the right – but not the responsibility – to conduct war against a violator of the League Charter, for the violator has, according to Article 16 (which is itself the relevant heuristic to determine that the violator has gone to war in the first place), committed *ipso facto* an act of war against every member state of the League. But this right to conduct war would contradict the "general implications" and the "spirit" of the Charter were every individual League member to conduct war; a "legally permissible war should not be conjured up as a medium to the hindrance of another war, especially not another legally permissible war." This right to war corresponds, in other words, to the spirit of the League of Nations Charter – a spirit to first limit oneself to economic methods of coercion. More than that, the right to war echoes the spirit of the Charter even more in that while these coercive actions are undertaken by individual member states, they are done so as a common, collective action, so that, according to Fischer Williams, they represent League measures and not just mere individual actions of the individual member states. It does not bother this Englishman that the point of departure for League sanctions – the establishment of a breach of the League Charter – is itself not an act of the League of Nations as such, but rather of individual states. Whatever action, meanwhile, these individual states should undertake in the spirit of their freedom of decision against a Charter-violating state, should take place in the framework of a collective League action explicitly undertaken by the League itself. The resolutions, too, of the assembly of the League of Nations from October 4, 1921 on "economic weapons" are but "recommendations" and not of the same primacy as the League Charter. But were all members of the League of Nations to mutually agree on a given interpretation of the League Charter during an assembly in front of the entire world, it would be "difficult to not consider these member states as united through their own declaration"; were they not considered so, a "solemn act would be robbed of any sense it could possess." Thinking of a possible legal motivation here, one is reminded of the English legal principle of the "estoppel,"* although such analogies should not be decisive. The history of law, in particular the history of English law, is rife with many examples of successful legal extrapolations and reforms through other instances than the legislator, should a sovereign legislature not be in the position to undertake necessary expansions. Thus, the Geneva League of Nations becomes a "collective" entity capable of action; not truly "institutionalized," its Charter remains

---

* Estoppel is a legal doctrine in common law that bars a party in a contractual relationship from claiming an argument on an equitable ground. In general, it protects an aggrieved party, if the counter-party induced an expectation from the aggrieved party, and the aggrieved party reasonably relied on the expectation and would suffer detriment if the expectation were not met. For example, if a creditor unofficially informs a debtor that the debt has been cancelled without any formal documentation, the creditor may later be "estopped" by a court from collecting the debt, since the change would be unfair.

a contract, but the League becomes federalized in an effective way, even though the word "federalize" is never used. And in doing so, its dispositions and procedural policies receive a concrete "federal" efficacy. For it is only on account of these dispositions and procedures that the fundamental question is determined: that of the justice or injustice of coercive military or economic measures against a state.

The last part of Williams' essay amplifies and deepens this non-institutionalized federalization of the Geneva League of Nations to a fundamental debate on the new problem of "neutrality." Here, too, the central issue is a typically communitarian-legal and federative-legal clause: within the Geneva League of Nations, there cannot exist a legal indifference towards wars – a stance that the previous concept of neutrality amounted to. Here, neutrality is even less possible insofar as the League Charter, as opposed to the Kellogg Pact, expressly arranges for counter-actions against the member state that breaks the League Charter and moves towards war. It is obvious that the right of neutrality cannot contain the execution of valid determination of statutes. The well-known government statement by Mr. Eden from October 23, 1935 attests to this fact. There, Eden emphatically rejects the idea "that any covenant-breaking state had any legal right to require observance by other members of the League of any of the laws of neutrality." There is no neutrality towards a violator of peace. But in spite of this, during the League's actions against Italy, the English government applied the rules of the Hague Neutrality Convention to Italian warships and support ships, treating, in other words, Italy not as an international "lawbreaker" but in a "non-partisan" fashion that seemed to correspond with the old right of neutrality. Fischer Williams explains this conspicuous inconsistency by saying that there exists no legal responsibility to disregard the most necessary action in the event of a League action. The legal-logical difficulties become even greater, though, when Williams poses the question of how permissible a blockade of a Charter-violating League member state would be when undertaken against a non-member state (assuming that a state of war does not exist). According to the previous right of neutrality, such a blockade would certainly be construed as contrary to international law. To attempt to construct this act as something in line with international law would be an act of conceptual sophistry, a sophistry that would contradict the common sense of English jurists. But Williams sees that something entirely different than the old question of blockades during peacetime is at stake here, for the League blockade against a member state takes place with the authorization of a treaty of the League Charter, to which the affected party agreed prior to his offensive actions. Could non-member states retain their right to uninhibited commercial trade with respect to the affected blockaded member state, even given the League action against the blockaded state? This remains an open question. By the same token, the question of the validity of a declaration of contraband permissible only in war is left for further development. Granted: the fact that though war is avoided, a war in progress is effectively at hand may be seen as just a legal construction. Still, this would be a war in which League powers are seen as "quasi-trustees" of the future legal partner in war, a war in which League powers can perceive all of their rights.

This part of Fischer Williams' exposition is, therefore, especially important to us because of the way it reveals the difficulties and contradictions that any attempt at a concretization of the Geneva League of Nations must lead to. In reality, there remains no other way out of this predicament than that of the old concept of neutrality, itself depending on the obsolete non-discriminating concept of war. This is, then, the revolving result that changes the face of international law, the result to which the English jurist has solemnly avowed himself in the impressive closing sentences of his essay. He gives here an outlook on the future that reveals the seriousness of the question and brings the central issue of the current stage of development of international law more clearly and sharply to one's awareness than could any other speech or argumentation. He says: the coming generation will probably consider the responsibilities of neutrals more strongly than their rights. Moreover, wars might arise in which not taking a position – whether in terms of military commitments or just thought – would be seen as impossible for any morally conscious person. In such a world war as one that would be no mere "dogfight," one would be led with all possible moral energies (to use the common current expression: a "total" war); neutrality, respectable though it may be, could be not respected. Dante, closes the famous English scholar, bequeathed a unique contempt and punishment on the angels who remained neutral in the great struggle between God and the Devil: not only because they committed a crime by breaching their responsibility to fight for justice, but also because they misunderstood their most personal, truest interest.* The neutral party in such a struggle would, in other words, meet such a fate of which not only Dante but also Machiavelli would approve.

Thus, the old warning of *Vae victis!*† finds itself replaced by *Vae neutris!*‡ The legal grounding of this exhortation is based on the fact that the Geneva League of Nations is implied as a real community in which distinctions between legal concepts such as federation, community, and

---

* Fischer Williams was referring here to lines 25–51 of Canto III of Dante's *Inferno*.
† Woe to the vanquished.
‡ Woe to the neutral.

society do not really matter. For the Geneva League is at any rate, not a "society" whose mere existence makes it legally impossible that member states remain neutral and unbiased towards other member states in the event of a breach of the Charter. It is not a "society" that requires *eo ipso** every member to conduct its business in such a way that it can expect trust from the other member states and that a "spirit of community" is possible. Concepts of the "general sentiment" and the common "spirit" are, in the argumentation of Fischer Williams, the analogy to that which the constitutional doctrine of German federalism dubbed the "foundation of contractual trust and the conviction of federative brotherhood," or the "common federative legal rule of federative and friendly behavior," an analogy with which this doctrine happily overcame the formalism of a supposedly "purely legal" method.[153] The introduction and concretization of such typically "federal" conceptions contains the most effective and most consequential federalization of the Geneva League of Nations, for it makes existing establishments, in particular the Council, into true federal powers with all of the necessary federal jurisdiction. As soon as a true federation is at hand, everything will develop by itself. And in doing so, Williams' essay avoids all conceptual-constructive questions such as "Federation of states or federal state?" Fischer Williams has elsewhere compared the Charter of the Geneva League of Nations to an Impressionist painting: to be regarded not with a legal microscope, but rather with the eyes of a practitioner.[154] For this reason, it is irrelevant to Williams whether the League Charter is a constitution or a contract. He reasonably sticks to his goal of enabling effective actions against a Charter violator without giving up the individual member states' freedom or right to decide more than is necessary. And it is in this accomplishment that one finds the unique style and preeminence of this unusually important essay on international law. Its deeper, implicit central thought is that it is not important to force every League of Nations member state to participate in common actions of the League. Rather, it emphasizes that what is important is that all "third states," be they member states or non-member states, consent to the justice of this action.

2) The unusual importance of McNair's essay is to be found in the fact that he directly attacks the final and decisive question here – that of a new concept of war and neutrality. McNair cites here his predecessor of Cambridge's Whewell Professorship, Brierly,[155†] and reminds his reader of how Grotius approached the question of distinguishing between just

---

* By that very fact.

† James Leslie Brierley (1881–1955) was an English scholar of international law.

and unjust wars. McNair shows how this distinction nonetheless eventually totally disappeared from international jurisprudence to the point that the unconditionally dominant paradigm perceived war as "extralegal," no longer posing the juridical question of its "illegality." The flip side of this non-discriminating concept of war was a certain concept of neutrality that bounded non-warring states to a responsibility of complete non-partisan behavior without consideration for the justness or unjustness of a warring party. This concept has, however – so believes McNair – become something completely different, at least for the larger part of the world. In light of the behavior of League of Nations member states in the face of the Italian–Abyssinian War, he sees evidence that the League of Nations Charter, at least in the form it has existed in until now, with its demand for non-discriminating non-partisan behavior, has superseded the right to neutrality. For those states that are not members of the League of Nations, the demand of distinguishing between just and unjust wars ought to arise from the Kellogg Pact, which, save for a few unremarkable exceptions (Tibet, for example), remains valid for all states on earth. The new concept of neutrality arises through this process. The new order of the planet becomes determined through the piece-by-piece development of methods of "collective resistance against the aggressor." The tendency towards federalization uses the services of the word "collectivization." McNair expressly points out the fact that new collective methods for the revision of the status quo and for the collective enforcement of such revisions become necessary with the collectivization of the action against the aggressor. McNair sees in the attempts to date towards the organization of a common mutual support mechanism (one thinks here of the 1923 draft, the Geneva Protocol of 1924, the General Act of 1928, among others)[156] evidence of the fact that mankind finds itself on the path towards new forms of an effective collectivization. Coercion and violence are not abolished, but rather "collectivized" and "denationalized." This is not to happen through the construction of an independent, international regime – as some have suggested – and not through a new international power distinct from individual international regimes. The application of power must remain in the hands of the individual state governments, which decide on the condition and type of such an action in the framework of a common council and teamwork. The federalization of the Geneva League of Nations is to take place, as with Sir John Fischer Williams, through a practical and judicious incorporation of federalistic conceptions, but without the antithetical escalations and without the institutionalization that are typical of the French. These reforms, he notes, are to be carried out under the protection of contractual foundations and with painstaking consideration for the independence of individual states.

No member of the League of Nations is to be forced to participate in a military action, but the League of Nations Charter empowers that member to participate, should it consider such an action the right move. On that note, every member has, quite reasonably, the right to consult with and, in the event that the aggressor is suspected to take aggressive action with its armed forces, decide to offer resistance along with a sufficiently powerful number of cooperating powers. But more important than anything else is the distinction between just and unjust wars, and the practical enforcement of this distinction against the aggressor – against, in other words, a state conducting war in an unjust fashion. McNair sees in Articles 10 and 16 of the League of Nations Charter the legal foundation valid today for practical conclusions drawn from the distinction between just and unjust wars. He hopes of the United States government that it follows the necessary conclusions from its participation in the Kellogg Pact, and that it does not hold fast to the superseded concept of neutrality when faced with an aggressor state – even though the President of the United States, as he notes, still did not make the necessary distinction between aggressor and object of the aggressor in the Italian–Abyssinian conflict.

These analyses are, in spite of their short length, of immense consequence for international law; in their pregnant concentration on the fundamentals, they contain the most thorough perception yet of the most decisive question of the current stage of international law. With impressive straightforwardness, they place the problem at the correct level: that of the concept of war. The closing paragraph of McNair's work reminds one of the close to Sir John Fischer Williams' essay. McNair begins with a comparison, which, for an easily swayed reader, might seem to open up virtually fantastic aspects to the essay. He points out that the wealthy English state, faced with the necessity of a revision of the status quo, may find itself in the role of a young teenager blundering into the Gospel; a teenager who, despite his best intentions, "left the whole affair with sadness" once he learned that it was actually expected of him to renounce all of his earthly wealth. Unfortunately, this lovely and probing comparison is touched on only for a moment; the picture of the young adolescent is but fleeting, barely met, shunned, and from then on, there is no mention of following this metaphor to any concrete consequences or practical details. The reader is instead reminded that England has already achieved an important contribution towards collective actions through its cooperation on the formation of an international troop in the event of the Saarland plebiscite and through its conduct in the League of Nations during September 1935. Because England has already taken these steps, concludes McNair, other states must also be prepared to take the encumbrances and the risk of new methods upon themselves if they wish to participate in the blessings of collective security – if they wish that the condition of lasting peace gradually comes to bear.

III. A Critical Discussion of The Recent Shift of International Law to a Discriminating Concept of War

The two essays from *The British Yearbook* that concern themselves with the concrete question of the so-called "sanctions" are much stronger and more compelling works than Scelle's systematic-constructive work or Lauterpacht's undertaking of legal theory. For both McNair and Williams show that today – as in every intensive moment of the history of international law – the *concept of war* stands at the center of all debates and has become the touchstone of all international law. For Scelle, war is on the one hand a mere "international crime," on the other hand a police-able action and, therefore, a legal procedure. This, however, would all be perfectly realized in a trans-state organization.[157] One may, not without anticipation, wait and see just how this French jurist systematically maps out the legal problem of war in the continuations to his work – or if he, with his courage and logical consistency, views this problem as already settled and no longer mentions it. Lauterpacht, for his part, regards the issue of war as an open question in his legal-theoretical work. In his edition of L. Oppenheim's *International Law*, Lauterpacht proceeds from the obsolete concepts of war, attempting to justify the changes in the right to neutrality effected by the Kellogg Pact and the League of Nations with these superseded concepts. He does this because he believes to have found these changes to the right to neutrality contractually secured through the League Charter and the Kellogg Pact. It is for this reason that a discriminating procedure against a violator of the League Charter should not be regarded as a breach of the responsibility to non-partisanship demanded by the right of neutrality. According to obsolete treaties of international law that abdicated from the claim to neutrality and consented to discriminating behavior, this behavior is permissible. Members of the League of Nations would have declared themselves to be in a state of mutual understanding from the start, since they agreed to Article 16 of the Charter. All other states, writes Lauterpacht, agreed to discriminate against the treaty violator in advance through their signing of the Kellogg Pact. While this argumentation ignores the recent questions of the concept of war and neutrality raised by Fischer Williams and McNair, it seems to have reached practically the same result.

The most recent textbooks on international law – in particular those by A. von Verdroß[158] and E. Wolgast[159*] – still adhere to the obsolete

---

* Ernst Wolgast (1888–1959) was a German legal scholar.

non-discriminating concept of war and neutrality, though not without a few reservations. The same can be said of the most recent, somewhat larger monograph by Josef L. Kunz.[160]* The treatment of the right to neutrality by E. v. Waldkirch† and E. Vanselow‡ in the *Handbook of International Law* (published by G.A. Walz§) nonetheless remains stuck to these obsolete foundations.[161] But in spite of this, one cannot deny that the legal concept of war, marked by its growing strength and incalculable importance, has dominated today's development of international law. The question of the "just" war has raised itself.

It was courageous and candid of McNair to pose with such clarity this all-decisive question. Has the new legal concept of war, founded by the Geneva League of Nations and the Kellogg Pact and distinguishing between the just and unjust war, caught on in international law? Compared to the claims made during the world war, is this new concept of war an effective element of the new order, more effective now than it was in the years from 1917 to 1919? Should one wish to affirm this question, the expositions of McNair and Sir John Fischer Williams seem to me, like so many other efforts in the same direction, to provide only a weak and problematic piece of evidence in favor of this idea; both seem to presuppose the Geneva League of Nations as an already existing community with a federal character. And I would never misjudge the international legal meaning of the fact that powers like England, France, and the United States of America have an interest in a discriminating concept of war. But I cannot believe that the demanded and monstrous turn has already occurred in reality, or that the mere program behind such a shift is adequately clear and free of contradictions. The systematic and legal-theoretical attempts towards an institutionalization of the League of Nations and the community of nations require a legal clarification based on the concept of war just as much as do the practical-concrete arguments of Fischer Williams and McNair. As our demonstrations thus far should have shown, at stake is no mere conceptual or theoretical controversy, but a question of the most elementary, practical meaning: namely, the question of neutrality in a possible coming war.[162]

It is correct that Grotius speaks of just and unjust wars: he calls the unjust war "*latrocina*" and even says that there exists no legal responsibility for the subject to follow his prince into an unjust war. But Grotius clearly concerned himself not with an international law based around the

---

* Josef Kunz (1890–1970) was a German legal scholar.

† Eduard Otto von Waldkirch (1890–?) was a legal scholar.

‡ Ernst Vanselow was a German naval officer present at the signing of the World War I armistice and a scholarly collaborator of Waldkirch's.

§ Gustaf Adolf Walz (1897–1948) was a German scholar of constitutional and international law.

idea of nations organized into states, but rather with a virtually feudal commonwealth ruled by common law tinged with medievalism and natural law. It is for this reason that Grotius still speaks of private wars, a concept that ends in itself and morphs into the "facts of a crime, punishable by law" as soon as there begins to exist a closed state order that concentrates and monopolizes the *jus ad bellum* within the state itself. The extent to which the modern state forms itself clarifies the unique style of an international law borne by such states and explains the non-discriminating concept of war specific to this form of state. In the eighteenth century, this non-discriminating concept of war was defended by Vattel* in his *Droit des gens* (1758). And while this concept of war may have been seen from the point of view that every independent nation ought to decide on the justice of a war in doubtful cases, Vattel speaks at length on the just and unjust war – and even the private war, though here he mentions it only as an instance of the "state of nature."[163] According to Grotius, the unjust war is of course still a war, and something different from, on the one hand, executions of sanctions, and, on the other hand, murder, robbery, or piracy. Grotius expressively notes: *Justitiam in definitione (sc. belli) non includo.*† His *jus belli ac pacis* can of course still speak of just and unjust wars just as much as can recent international law once valid but now obsolete. His *jus belli ac pacis* can, however, neither absorb the concept of war nor the related concept of neutrality without destroying not only this concept of war as such but also the entire structure of the order of nations.

In praxi the real question is whether every state can make the decision, can have the *jus supremae decisionis*‡ of the justice or injustice of a war, or whether another state or group can make the legal decision on the justness or unjustness of a war in such a way that this decision becomes valid for a third party.[164] Faced with this basic question, it is irrelevant how war is constructed from a legal-theoretical perspective, how war is delineated. It is irrelevant whether war is an "action" or "status," a legal procedure, a legal institution, self-help, or just an action not contrary to but rather something outside the legal order. It is irrelevant whether the "will to war" or "objective" facts are the deciding factor in the justice or injustice of a war.[165] All questions of this sort simply do not matter. The fact that every state at war ever has, of course, posed its actions as just, and those of its opponent as unjust, is inconsequential to our question here. As regards third parties, neither is it relevant that some have

---

* Emerich de Vattel (1714–67) was a Swiss philosopher, legal scholar, and diplomat.

† Justice does not belong to the definition of war. The idea that war must not definitionally be just.

‡ The right to a final or supreme decision.

attempted to modify neutrality with suffixes like "benevolent neutrality," "armed neutrality," "conditional neutrality," and so on. The practice of neutrality has always been full of many nuances. But such attempts at nuance never claimed to be bound to the decision necessary for third-party states or the community of nations on the justice or injustice of a war. Should a neutral state find itself in a position where it must decide on the justice of a war conducted by one state against another, is that third party free to enter the war on the side on which it thinks justice lies, and hence become a war-conducting party? Even if this is the case, this third party cannot make this implicit declaration of the justice or injustice of a war universal and forceful in international law. In the decisive moment, and with respect to the question of how much contemporary international law recognizes just and unjust wars, a simple either-or is raised. This is an either-or that has real force: "Either one is neutral, or one is not."[166] Neutrality may be nuanced, but never bisected. Neutrality cannot be separated either from the concept of state and nation, or from the current order of international law.[167]

When today a state or a group of states gives up this fundamental non-discriminating behavior, and takes steps to war in such a way that distinguishes just parties from unjust parties in the eyes of a third party, the claim is implicitly made that one acts not only in one's own name, but also in that of a higher (in other words: trans-state) order and community. The claim is hence made to do something totally different than that which was understood by the phrase "the conduct of war." And this is something that simply cannot be called a "war" in the contemporary sense of that word in international law. As soon as the conception of possible neutrality and the possibility of a non-partisan "third state" is negated, a claim is implicitly made to universal or regional authority. When an order of international law built out of nation-states and founded, on the one hand, on the concept of the *state* as the final decision-maker when it comes to the state's *jus belli* and, on the other hand, on the logically consistent non-discriminating concept of war and neutrality exists, then the introduction of an authoritative policy of discrimination fundamentally questions the validity of not only the non-discriminating concept of war, but also *any* concept of war. In reality, the question is no longer: just war or unjust war, allowed or forbidden war. Rather, it becomes: war or no war? The great "planetary" quarrel of nations runs so deep that it touches upon the final fundamental concept and the real dilemma here: war or no war? As concerns the concept of neutrality, this development has also led to a similar alternative: Does neutrality still exist? The remarkable behavior of the United States of America from 1914 to today – characterized by the path from a rigorously passive, logically consistent, non-distinguishing concept of neutrality, to the abolition of the concept of neutrality and finally turning to a discriminating concept of war that made the decision on the justice or injustice of war – can only be explained by these previous reflections.

All attempts to introduce a discriminating concept of war into international law through the Geneva League of Nations therefore run into *two great contradictions* today: on the one hand, the irreconcilability of every concept of war with the League of Nations' claim to a new order; on the other hand, the irreconcilability of universalism and federalism in the current crisis of international law.

1) The concept of war that has prevailed until today makes it possible, through non-discrimination and the importance it lays on parity for both parties involved, that a mutual armed conflict can legally stand as a unified legal concept. The assumption of such a system is non-extension to third states, in other words, the waiving of a legal distinction between just and unjust wars valid for third states. As soon as a decision that regards the legality or illegality of wars or the permissibility of wars is taken to apply to third parties, the unity of the concept of war is exploded, leaving behind it on the one hand the just war permitted by international law and, on the other, the unjust, impermissible "war." These two concepts actually represent two wars, each of which means something totally different and contrary and therefore cannot be described with the same term – "war" – as each other's counterpart. Justice and injustice cannot be legally bound to the same concept. A recognized legal act and a recognized illegal act cannot, within the same legal order, constitute one and the same legal concept. That would be just as unthinkable as if a state attempted to classify the fight between the police and the criminal, or the illegal military attack and the act of justified self-defense, as a unified legal construction that had a "legal side" and an "illegal side." By the same token, as long as a legal order allows an act like the duel or recognizes it as a legal construction, this same legal order can perceive certain disputes as "non-duels"; this same legal order could, for example, designate a dispute as a mere punishable act of bodily harm. But what this legal order *cannot* do is, insofar as duels exist, distinguish between "just" and "unjust" duels. As soon as an order of international law – in other words, a trans-state order of international law that can distinguish between justified and unjustified wars in a way authoritative for third parties – makes this sort of distinction between the "just" and "unjust" duel, or the "just" and "unjust" war, an armed action on the side of justice is nothing else than the realization of justice. This is true whether this takes shape in the form of an execution, sanction, international justice, police, or whatever the case may be. On the unjustified side of the war, however, such acts are rebellion against a legal action: thus rebellion or

a crime, and certainly something else than the obsolete legal institution of "war."[168]

The Geneva League of Nations has taken no decision with respect to the concept of war. In Article 16 of the League Charter, military action on the part of a Charter violator is described as "war," just as much as counter-strikes against the same violator are also "war." Paragraph 7 of Article 15 still envisions wars in the old style (on the part of both parties *"pour le maintien du droit"*). Similarly and on this note, the jurisprudence of the League distinguishes between "allowed" and "unallowed" wars with two different concepts of neutrality: the new concept for the unallowed war; the old one for the allowed war.[169] Both types of war should, however, remain unified as one legal concept under the name of "war."[170] Here, the indecisive half-measures of the League Charter become clear to all, for it introduces new distinctions without being able to carry them through and, in doing so, combines the two most contrary legal acts in one and the same concept: "war." In truth, the Geneva League Charter describes three types of "war": wars of sanctions or of impounding, tolerated wars, and forbidden wars. This *ought* to correspond to three different concepts of neutrality. The fact that the League Charter does not concern itself with its own combining of an "impounding act" – in other words, a legally forbidden act – with an act already declared as illegal – in other words, a forbidden act – into one and the same legal concept needs no further discussion.[171] During the implementation of the sanctions against Italy, one attempted in a legalistic, most cautious way, to avoid the question of the concept of war and posed to the states the question of the so-called "sanction measures" within the framework of freedom of decision. The action was to have been "denationalized." But in doing so, the inner contradiction became manifest. It remained totally unclear what "League actions" were as opposed to "actions of individual states." Scelle speaks of the fact that an *"action collective de la Société"* lay before all *"en un faisceau d'actions parallèles étatiques."*[172] In his aforementioned essay, Sir John Fischer Williams strives to produce the connection between individual decision and collective community. But at the end of the day, these attempts at harmonization only show that the Geneva League of Nations neither remains tied to the obsolete concepts of war and neutrality nor replaces these old concepts with truly new ones. Faced with the dilemma: "League impoundings against a violator of the peace, or mere procedures of consultation to facilitate various individual actions of the former style?" the League has neither dared to confess its universal claim to the global order by abandoning the previous concept of war, nor has it summoned up the courage to simply relinquish its pretensions.

We ought to mention a further disastrous effect of the "denationalization" of war and of the introduction of a discriminating concept of war:

the partition of the previous legal assumption of an *inner*, closed unity of nations organized into states. Fischer Williams seems to have noticed this partition, although he seems to miss the point in avoiding making the connection between actions against a Charter violator per Article 16 and concepts like sanctions or simply punishment. More than this, he avoids describing these Article 16 actions as what they are – the objective form of such punitive concepts. Scelle, who speaks of the *"crime international,"* is not so reserved. It is only Hans Wehberg, who, with great candor has followed the consequences through and suggested that the author of an "unjust" war must of course be tried before an international court as a "war criminal."[173] Moreover, the domestic penalties for such crimes are also necessary. Fischer Williams rightfully cites the sentence: "You cannot interdict a nation." Hobbes once formulated this same thought in the following way: "When a Pope excommunicates a whole nation, methinks he rather excommunicates himself than them."[174] Admittedly, it is conceivable that an international action could be led against states and nations as such. But these entities of state and nation are seldom so totally criminal that a nation in its entirety must be turned into *"hostis generis humani"* and a "peaceless" nation. When sanctions or punitive measures are undertaken with trans-state authorization, the "denationalization" of war thus usually leads to a distinction between state and nation: while the two normally possess a closed unity, a discriminating partition is introduced from outside between the two. In other words, international coercive measures – or at least the permission of such measures – are directed not against the nation, but rather against the contemporary regime and its followers. But in drawing a line between state leadership and the nation, such measures imply that a regime has ceased to represent its state or people. The rulers become, in other words, "war criminals," "pirates," or – to cite the modern metropolitan form of the pirate – "gangsters." These terms are, more or less, the dialect of a vicious propaganda. Such are the legal and logical consequence of the denationalization of war already embodied in discrimination. The concept of piracy raises the question of the universalistic and ecumenical side of today's debate. Indeed, the concept of the pirate is marked, more than anything else, by the fact that he is "denationalized" and allowed to fall by the wayside of the state to which he presumably belongs. And through this fact there arises a practically important and most expansive break of trans-state, universalistic conceptual creations. They make it possible to treat entire states and nations as pirates and to evoke anew the concept of the rogue state (itself a term thought for a century to have become totally obsolete) at a level of increased intensity.* All such

* See also notes 178 and 179 on page 218 of this text.

explosions and partitions of the state between a (criminal) regime and a (guiltless) people (in the sense of those outside of the regime as not guilty) represent, in all truth, nothing else than the detonation and dissolution of the concept of war. And this destruction of the concept of war is bound with nothing else than the introduction of the discriminating concept of war to international law.

In the world war against Germany we have ourselves experienced the ramification of the attempt to introduce a discriminating concept of war. To the same extent to which the world war was posed by our opponents as a legal action against a violator of international law, it was also posed as a punitive action *not* against the German people but rather against their government. Both entities, however, stand together in an inseparable connection. This was documented once and for all by the fact that President Wilson's declaration of April 2, 1917, which broke from the obsolete, non-discriminating concept of neutrality, began to mention the partition of the closed state unity of Germany by proclaiming, in obvious connection to the abolition of the non-discriminating concept of neutrality, that "We have no quarrel with the German people." The practical consequences of this stance are to be seen in Part VII of the Versailles Treaty under the heading "Determinations of Punishment:" Germany's former *Kaiser* is, "owing to the worst breach of international morals and the holiness of treaties," "under open accusation"; the German government should turn in the so-called German "war criminals." If Scelle approves of the idea of humanitarian intervention against Fascist or National Socialist states, and wants to raise this idea to the level of an institution of international law, then he belongs to the same tradition and same logic that "denationalizes" war – that, in other words, does away with the war of states in order to "internationalize" war; in other words, to transform war into a tremendous civil war. Sir John Fischer Williams and McNair are, for this reason, completely correct when they allude to the tremendous importance of the turn from a non-discriminating to a discriminating concept of war. They overlook only the fact that this turn is even more consequential in that as a consequence of its discrimination, not only is every concept of war annihilated; along with that, the possibility of a perhaps weaker, but certainly franker, more realistic, school of thought apropos international law is destroyed, with nothing more than a state- and nation-destroying universal pretension entering to take its place. Through the fact that the discriminating concept of war is at least rudimentarily institutionalized with the help of a distinction between a legally permissible and forbidden war courtesy of the League of Nations, the entire current international order becomes unhinged with nothing new coming to take its place. A new claim to world domination is raised – a claim that only a new world war could realize.

2) Federalism and ecumenical universalism cancel each other out in the current crisis of international law. The authors mentioned in this report proceed without any further reflection[175] from the assumption that while the Geneva League of Nations may not yet be universal and ecumenical, it must eventually be so and at least recognize universalism as the final goal. At the same time, these authors attempt to turn the League into a truly federalistic entity through various methods of concretization. Here, again, the question of the collective armed action raises itself. In other words: the problem of the concept of war as the most secure touchstone. War cannot exist within a federation of any type as long as the federation exists. This notion, indeed, is inarguably the core of Sir John Fischer Williams' essay. But the difficulties that arise for him and other authors of the same persuasion become insurmountable as soon as the question of the inclusion of non-member states in this federalist system appears: as soon, in other words, as the problem of ecumenical universalism appears. According to current, non-universalistic international law, an inclusion of non-members is impossible, for the concept of war always demands a simple decision. If I may call it such, the logical dignity of the concept of war is so strong and decisive that the only real dilemma that arises from it is a simple one: war or no war? One must always define their concepts with the concept of war as the baseline. Whatever is not "war" is "peace." If "collectivization" actually brings about a true federation, this logic will have run its course. *Within* the federation one will no longer decide between just and unjust wars; rather, there will no longer be any wars. Then, only executions will exist. "Allowed" wars are still conceivable, but only in the form of non-dangerous small wars, as *dogfights*, as Fischer Williams says. These wars could be tolerated within the federation, just as, for example, the order of the modern state can tolerate duels. But *outside* of the federation, wars are still totally possible. These wars, however, fall under the old, non-discriminating concept of war. And should a closed group of states belonging to the federation make the claim to conduct a just war, this claim is, from the standpoint of international law, unauthoritative to the non-member state. This would seem just as unauthoritative as a state attempting to decide on justice and injustice outside of its own purview – in other words, outside of its borders. But the remedy of the concept of war does not, as McNair wishes, stand in for existing contractual bonds in the way that the Kellogg Pact does. It proceeds instead through the institutional, organized context into a federation. It is fundamental to previous conceptions of international law that war was the stronger concept, that it annulled all treaties between warring parties, and that this breach of contract inherent to war does not do away with the war as a war for neutral third states. Those authors who wish to draw the conclusion of a true "con-

stitution," rather than a contract, from the League of Nations Charter attempt to build a real federation with the help of the concept of institutionalization. And insofar as they give the community of nations such a constitution, they also give it the radical abolition of the hereto existing, fundamentally non-discriminating, concept of war based on parity. Today, neither pacifistic jealously nor antipathy towards the atrocities of war can help the fact that a war today between two states is something other than murder, robbery, or piracy. Before the concept of war can be done away with and turned from a state war to an international civil war, first the peoples of the earth organized into states must be done away with. According to now obsolete international law, war owed its justice, honor, and worth to the fact that the enemy was neither a pirate nor a gangster, but rather a "state" and a "subject of international law." This idea remains valid as long as there exists a political organization equipped with a *jus belli*. But the concept of the federation presupposes the renunciation of the *jus belli* within the federation. And should one attempt to do away with the *jus belli* in such a way that affects not only members of the federation but third-party states outside it, the implicit claim of such a federation is no longer one of international law, but rather one of universalistic rule over the new world order. And in light of such pretensions of global justice, should the case of a total world war arise, one with a sufficiently strong opponent who leads an "unjust" war, then this opponent would achieve the perpetuation of the old international legal concept of war – that of legal non-discrimination. In such a case, a war legitimized through the League of Nations would remain a war in the style of previous international law, in the style of the world war. This would be a war that, just as then, in spite of all efforts to transform the war into an "execution" of international law against a regime distinguished from the German people, and in spite of all the various acts of discrimination against Germany, would remain a war. In the case of the world war, this only happened because of the German nation's strength of resistance. But in other cases – those where such a resistance was not achieved – a universalistic claim to world domination would come closer to its final goal. And were the final goal of universalism ever to be reached, there would no longer be any wars between the nations of the planet, neither just nor unjust wars. But as long as this final goal remains unachieved, the federalistic and universalistic concepts and methods of international law remain mutually exclusive.

In the current stage of the development of international law, federalism and universalism may perhaps normativistically and logically harmonize with one another. But as soon as one approaches an institutional and concrete realization of a federation, their incompatibility becomes immediately clear for all to see. A federalization of the Geneva

League of Nations today necessarily requires firmer centralization and collectivization with an eye on the event where one must count on a considerable military resistance against the League. One must, in other words, fortify for the case of war. As long as the situation persists, the introduction of the distinction between just and unjust wars means *in concreto* only the introduction of Geneva League wars and other wars and, by this token, an intensification of war and enmity. And our experience of the world war would, based on the strength of the behavior of President Wilson, only repeat itself. In this situation, federalization serves as a means of intensification as it attempts to turn the League of Nations into an even more "effective" organization – one that gears itself more towards the event of war. And here the only result can be that the distinction between just and unjust wars leads to a deeper and more intense distinction between friend and enemy. And in the time between the achievement of the final goal of such a plan and the reality of today, surely another war would arise, a "decisively final war of humanity" – at any rate, a deeply hostile "total" war. In this respect, the close to Sir John Fischer Williams' essay – *Vae neutris!* – leaves no doubt. All types of federalization contemplating the possibility of such a war must separate themselves from the universalistic ideal should they still wish to be justified when they claim to strive towards the goal of one humanity and the abolition of all further hindrances to this unity. Everything that today means an effective federalization of the League of Nations creates, in the best possible case, only another federation. And the more perfectly these new federalistic institutions are to be built up, and the more logically the federation distinguishes between just (in other words, its own) wars and unjust (in other words, its opponents') wars, the more serious becomes its distinction between friend and enemy. The Geneva League of Nations, in other words, faces not only the dilemma: "federation or alliance?" posed by Viktor Bruns.[176*] More than that, its mixing of the League of Nations and the idea of a universal community of nations poses the no less difficult alternative: should there be an institutionalized federation or an ecumenical order for the world and mankind?

At the end of the day, these two tendencies of federalism and universalism work contrary to one another. One cannot hope that this stage of a federalism that leads to an intensification of war be skipped and that it would be possible to proceed directly to ecumenical universalism via institutionalization. Those who strive for this path to a universalistic final goal through the means of a federalization of the Geneva League of Nations will surely assume that the contradiction between federalism and universalism will remain valid only for a short, unavoidable interregnum.

---

* Viktor Bruns (1884–1943) was a German jurist and professor.

But this interregnum is, at least seen from the perspective of human prescience and planning, indeed a new epoch of history, one with new and more intensive wars. This new epoch is, for all mortal men, an incalculable period of time with unpredictable results. It was, indeed, a consequential act, when, during the world war against Germany, President Wilson and the United States made the claim of having inaugurated a new era of international law through their rejection of the obsolete, non-discriminating concept of war and neutrality. They claimed to inaugurate an era in which they could determine the justice and injustice of war-conducting parties outside of their own territory. And should one feel that this report returns too much to this tremendous precedent, then this is not because the author wishes to churn up old controversies of international law, but only because he does not wish to see one of the most important – if not the most important – experiences of the history of international law pass into oblivion. We have already discussed the politics of the United States of America, swinging as they were between a passive neutrality that almost held its breath, and an interventionist stance that made the decision of justice and injustice for others. That country's policies have already revealed themselves in the world war. At the beginning of the war, Wilson was the herald of a rigorous, even scrupulous, interpretation of the non-discriminating concept of neutrality. His speech from August 19, 1914 is a prime example of this point.[177] And through the fact that in his declaration of war from April 2, 1917, he thoroughly changed the American position, implying that neutrality was no longer practicable and no longer desirable with regard to world peace and peace for nations, Wilson introduced a fundamentally new problematic to international law.[178] This new problematic has come to light because of the questions surrounding the right to neutrality. But this is not just about the right to neutrality, which cannot be isolated. Rather, this has to do with the concept of war, and, therefore, the entire structure of the order of international law. All attempts to improve international law after the world war revolved around this question. All efforts towards the definition of aggression and the aggressor, towards the strengthening and positivization of Article 16 of the League Charter, the many plans towards collective security and mutual aid, and even the application of the English concept of piracy to the Nyon Conference from September 1937 are determined through the fact that they attempt to abolish the previously held, non-discriminating concept of war through legal criteria that concern the just war.[179] The result to date has been nothing short of the total jolting of the old concept of war, made worse by the complete lack of an illuminating new concept of war. In practical terms, this means: war and yet no war at the same time; anarchy; and chaos in international law. It is only today that we can recognize the importance of the abolition of the old concept of war, an act born in the world war against Germany. Indeed, the chaos of today is only the rotten fruit born of a seed planted in 1917.

Conclusion

To conclude, a word about our own position. The critical discussion of a few particularly noteworthy publications from the foreign literature attempted here in light of international law's concept of war does not rest on the position that one ought to strive to maintain the concepts of an earlier time, be they conservative or reactionary. We know that the eighteenth and nineteenth centuries' concept of war cannot remain unchanged, that new organs and communities of international law are both necessary and unavoidable, and that, in particular, a true community of European nations is the precondition of a genuine and effective international law. An analysis like that of Sir John Fischer Williams', with his reasoned considerations on pseudo-juristic conceptual sophistry and his good sense for the necessities of federalism, would be considered an exemplary argumentation about international law and the paradigm for a convincing argument on this topic – but only if the League of Nations were a real federation able to live up to its responsibility as a community to lead progressive institutionalizations and federalizations. This, however, is not the case. The best attempts at forming a federation and establishing procedure are not only worthless but also harmful and a hindrance to the desperately necessary new order if they are built upon a fictitious community. Our criticisms, therefore, are directed not against the idea of fundamental new orders and work towards this goal. What we oppose is not the goal of a genuine community of peoples, but rather only a certain method towards this goal marked by an unclear and naïve mixing of the League of Nations and a universal world order. The goals of this method – the institutionalization, federalization, and concretization of the decision on the justness or unjustness of a war – are, we think, only a tangent to the ultimate goal that we can agree upon. They are, then, for us, not just "better than nothing." Worse than nothing, they stand in the path of a true community of nations.

The Großraum *Order of International Law with a Ban on Intervention for Spatially Foreign Powers: A Contribution to the Concept of* Reich *in International Law (1939–1941)*

Notes on the Text

The Großraum *Order of International Law with a Ban on Intervention for Spatially Foreign Powers: A Contribution to the Concept of* Reich has a complicated publication history. On April 1, 1939, Schmitt gave a lecture at the 25th anniversary of the University of Kiel's Institute for Policy and International Law called "*Großraum* Principles of International Law," which only encompassed the first five parts of the book and was later published under the full title above in early 1939. Schmitt also independently published Section V, "The Concept of *Reich* in International Law," in the April 29, 1939 issue of the journal *Deutsches Recht*. That article is identical to Section V printed here but for the fact that it ends with the Latin phrase "*Ab integro nascitur ordo*" – "From integrity is born order." The section "*Reich und Raum*" was attached to close a third edition of the work appearing in 1941 that also featured an addition to the section "Minority and National Group Law in the Central and East European *Großraum*" as a paragraph (here the final paragraph in that section) concerning the German–Soviet Friendship Treaty of 1939 and several other treaties in Eastern Europe in 1939–40. The fourth and final edition of *The* Großraum *Order of International Law*, which was published in the summer of 1941, included a final new section on "The Concept of Space in Jurisprudence" and retained the paragraph on the German–Soviet Treaty, even though the German *Reich* had already invaded the Soviet Union shortly before the publication of the fourth edition. Schmitt added a preliminary remark, written on July 28, 1941, to this version of the text that comments obliquely on this fact.

The basis for this translation is the 1991 edition of *Völkerrechtliche Großraumordnung mit Interventionsverbot für raumfremde Mächte: ein Beitrag zum Reichsbegriff im Völkerrecht*, published in Berlin by Duncker & Humblot. That edition is itself an unchanged reprint of the 1941 fourth edition of the book as published by the Deutscher Rechtsverlag in Leipzig and Berlin. Dirk Blasius comments further on the publication history of the book in *Carl Schmitt. Preußischer Staatsrat in Hitlers Reich* (Göttingen: Vandenhoeck & Ruprecht, 2001) 184–202, while Günter Maschke provides both his own annotations as well as an exhaustive history of the text in Carl Schmitt, *Staat, Großraum, Nomos: Arbeiten aus den Jahren 1916–1969* (Berlin: Duncker & Humblot, 1995) 321–51.

Note

The "Institute for Policy and International Law at the University of Kiel" observed its 25th anniversary in 1939. As a result of this occasion, the Institute held a working conference from March 29 to April 1, 1939. The following paper is one of the seminar papers of this conference and represents its authentic position. – The first edition of this writing appeared in April 1939 as Volume 7 (N.F.) of the "Writings of the Institute for Policy and International Law at the University of Kiel." An Italian translation published by His Excellency the Ambassador Count Vannutelli Rey appeared in 1941 in Rome (Biblioteca dell'Istituto di Cultura Fascista) with an afterword by L. Pierandrei. Section V (on the concept of *Reich*) has been published in the Spanish magazine "Revista de Estudios Políticos," Madrid 1941 (translated by F.J. Conde). A French, Japanese, and Bulgarian translation have also appeared or are in preparation.

Preliminary Remark

The present fourth edition of "The *Großraum* Order of International Law" contains, some relatively small improvements aside, a new concluding section on "The Spatial Concept in Jurisprudence." With this new conclusion, a comprehensive, scholarly total contextualization should be presented in the effort to avoid misunderstandings and misinterpretations. In international law, a new thought of world-political consequence is always exposed to the double danger of, on the one hand, of being droned into a hollow slogan, and on the other hand, of being talked to death through excessively critical fault-finding. There is no protection from this other than to think the thoughts further and not to allow the set of problems to become superficial as they grow alongside events.

The paper must remain what it is. It arose early in 1939 with certain theses and points of view in a certain situation. Through the course of events, it has experienced some meaningful confirmation. This is its value as a document. It should not, however, take up a foot race with the events themselves. I cannot simply attach the results of further research to the paper. Great new questions, such as the new problem of the Western Hemisphere and the relation of land and sea in international law, require their own treatment. As a start to this purpose, I can point to the exercises I conducted before the university teachers of history on February 8, 1941, which have in the meantime appeared in the volume of collected works "The *Reich* and Europe," published by Koehlher and Amelang (Leipzig, 1941).

May the reader understand when I give this writing the following motto: "We resemble navigators on an unbroken voyage, and every book can be nothing more than a logbook."

Berlin, July 28, 1941
Carl Schmitt

Preface

International law is, as *jus gentium*, as a law of nations, first and foremost a *personal* concrete order – an order, in other words, determined on the basis of belonging to a nation or state. The principle of order assigned to the concept of nation in international law is the right of national self-determination. This is recognized as a principle today.

Every order of settled nations that live next to and with one another, that mutually respect one another, is, however, not only personally determined; it is also a territorially concrete *spatial order*. The indispensable elements of a spatial order have until now been found primarily in the concept of state, which, more than a personally determined area of rule, means first of all a territorially limited and territorially closed unity. The concept of state that crept over from the eighteenth and nineteenth century was unsettled through the personal aspect of the concept of nation. This will be commented on further in the text (under IV and V). At any rate, it is necessary not only to revise the existing international legal theory through the concept of nation but also to regard it from the point of view of a spatial order. In keeping with this, I find it necessary to go beyond the abstract thoughts of territory lying within the universal concept of "state" and to introduce the concept of the *concrete Großraum* and its related concept of a *Großraum order* to international jurisprudence.

The change in the dimensions of the earth and in the way space on earth has been conceived – a change that dominates current global political developments – is articulated in the word "*Großraum.*" While the word "space" contains, besides all of its different specific definitions, a universal, neutral, mathematical-physical meaning, *Großraum* for us is a concrete, historical-political concept of the present. The origin of and original occasion for the word *Großraum* lie, so far as I have been able to confirm, characteristically not in the domain of state but rather in the domain of technics, industry, economics, and organization. Thousands of word combinations are in principle possible with the prefix *Groß*- and have been used for some time: great power (*Großmacht*), great organization (*Großverband*), great business (*Großhandel*), etc. Friedrich Naumann's* famous book *Mitteleuropa* (1915) contains a number of such word combinations: great state (*Großstaat*), great firm (*Großbetrieb*), great body (*Großkörper*) (p. 177), etc. Naumann already sees that this all concerns an industrial-organizatorial process, through which the individualistic stage of capitalistic organization is overcome; that this is, as he expresses it, a "a state process, an economic process of expansion" (p. 173). The word "*Großraum*," however, received its concrete (and therefore, as far as its conceptual formation is concerned, compelling) realization first *after* the world war, indeed, in the construction "*Großraum* economy." Thus began the history of a beloved buzzword – but also the concrete concept of the present that we need.[180] More than anything, the specific forms, the typical arrangements, and the organizations of the energy economy that arose in connection with the progressing electrification and long-distance provision of gas through metallurgical and coked coal gas were what determined this term.† The first steps in this development fall in the time around the turn of the century, when great power plants and energy distribution centers were built around 1900, when, already around 1913, the proprietary electrical works of small cities and communities were made obsolete. Shortly before the outbreak of the world war there began, too, the inexorable electrification of agricultural and thinly populated regions. Just as in other fields, the world war of 1914–18 only increased the power and tempo of this development. But it was really first with the astonishing achievements of German large-scale industry after the world war, after rising from the collapse of 1918–19, out of Communist revolution, inflation, and French invasion, after the so-called youth movement and rationalization of 1924–5 that "*Großraum* economy" became specifically clear as a word and fact for the first time, all as a result of the cooperation of distant electrical power and gas line networks stretching across great distances, and owing to an "associative economy" – in other words, the rational exploitation of the diversity of energy production plants, rational division of different loads, a return to reserves that assisted one another, and an equilibrium between secured and unsecured outputs and of peak loads. With all of this there arises a technical-industrial-economic

---

* Friedrich Naumann (1860–1919) was a German politician and author known for his book *Mitteleuropa*, a work on Central European geopolitics.

† In German: *Hütten- und Zechenkokereigas*.

order in which the spatially small isolation and separation of the previous energy economy is made obsolete. The economic formation of a *Großraum* can arise from below when spatially small districts more or less "organizationally" merge themselves into larger complexes; it can, however, also take place, as was more the case for the long-distance provision of gas through metallurgy and coked gas, from the top down, through planned *Großraum* networks covering great distances to which the small networks then connect themselves.

But further expositions on technical and organizational economic specifics are not pertinent to our theme. The purpose of our mentioning the developmental context of *Großraum*, *Großraum* economy, and long-distance energy provision is not to limit the word to the realm of economics, industry, and technics. On the contrary: it was only that in this area, in a time of an impotent state, that an organizational process of universal importance was carried out, a process whose principle we now lay bare in order to make it fruitful for the new order of international law. It is, of course, no coincidence, that the theoretical and practical realizations of the concept of the *Großraum* (which are important for international law) lie first of all in the economic-organizational sphere. The practical work and publications of the Reich Office Leader and Envoy Werner Daitz[181]* and the State Advisor Ministerial Director Helmuth Wohlthat[182]† must, therefore, be especially and expressly named here. The wide-reaching geographical work of Captain Ritter von Niedermayer‡ should also be mentioned.[183] As far as our theory of *Großraum* is concerned, it becomes at any rate clear that the mathematical-neutral, empty concept of space has been superseded and that a qualitative-dynamic greatness takes its place: *Großraum* is a comprehensive modern tendency of development of arising areas of human planning, organization, and activity. *Großraum* is for us above all a connected achievement space.[184]

I. Examples of Inauthentic or Obsolete Principles of Space

Many conceptions of space and (correspondingly) conceptions of *Großraum* have been effective at all times in both state law and in international law. In the age of colonial and imperialistic expansion, all kinds of "spheres of interest" were formed. To these belong territorial claims and preferential rights as have been raised for the back country, the territorial contiguity or propinquity, and, finally, for the Arctic in the

---

* Werner Daitz (1884–1945) was a German chemical engineer, economist, and author.

† Helmuth Wohlthat (1893–1973) was a German politician and economic advisor.

‡ Oskar Ritter von Niedermayer (1885–1948) was a German general, adventurer, and scholar.

so-called "sector principle."[185] And yet such a territorial claim is still not a principle of spatial order.

The treatment of the important question of principles of spatial order has been totally neglected in the systematics and conceptual formation of international jurisprudence over the course of the past century. This can be explained through the rule of an empty legal and contractual positivism that was nothing other than the juridical instrument of the legality and legitimacy of the status quo, and indeed, primarily the status quo of Versailles. The demarcations of the Paris Treaties of 1919 were so antithetical to any sense of order that jurisprudence had to abdicate into a contractual positivism, without any ideas, if it was to confine itself to the mere systematization of the contents of these treaties. One understood under the term "natural borders" not conceptions of inner dimensions as a guarantee of peace, but rather only the case where a river, a mountain, a railroad, etc. coincidentally constituted the border in positive border demarcations.[186] And a so-called "space theory" ruled in legal theory. In spite of its name, this assumed the opposite of a concrete conception of space and regarded country, soil, territory, and state territory as a "space" in the sense of an empty dimension of planes and depths with linear borders.[187]

In the international law of the nineteenth century, the idea that the equal weight of states was, if not the real foundation, then a substitute and coincidental guarantee of international law; it was still presented as a theory of international law.[188] This thought, moreover, doubtlessly contains elements of a certain order of space; at the least, it did not simply exclude the idea of concrete spatial relations as unjuristic. We will have more to say about this below, under the discussion of the total structure of hitherto existing international law as conceived as a phenomenon of state (Section V). Nonetheless, a true principle of space is not contained in the conception of equal weight. Another principle, that of "natural borders," spatially determined, is expressed more strongly and more directly. This principle served as a curtain for French expansionary policy for centuries. It was, moreover, widely recognized at the end of the eighteenth century as a "rational" legal principle and made sense to the young Fichte as such. This principle of "natural borders" had to lose its plausibility through France's obvious misuse of the idea, especially with regard to the acquisition of the left bank of the Rhine, and since 1848 it has lost all validity as a real principle of international law. Nonetheless, it again and again plays an important role with respect to important changes of borders, in the negotiations concerning cession of territories in peace agreements, and with respect to similar occasions in connection with strategic, economic-geographic, and other conceptions.[189] Several of its arguments and points of view appear to have a new meaning for us today in light of the new geopolitical scholarship led by Karl Haushofer.[190]* Still, in the form that French expansion policy attempted to make it valid, this principle has been without a doubt abolished. Indeed, two leading French scholars, Th. Funck-Brentano† and Albert Sorel‡ have fundamentally criticized it in an excellent outline of international law awarded a prize by the Académie Française.[191]

The theory of natural borders was determined overwhelmingly from the point of view of geography and geopolitics, and above all by the state. From the point of view of the nation and the growing population of a country, however, another principle, the right of nations to space and soil, especially the right of more population-rich countries with respect to less population-rich countries, has been often named. This principle was especially made valid in the course of the last century by the Italians and Japanese. From the literature on this subject I would like only to name the short, but still rich and engrossing treatise of an Italian scholar, the Dante researcher Luigi Valli,§ "The Right of Nations to Land."[192] Valli describes this claim as the "demographic right." The objective considerations upon which this claim rests are most striking. They cannot be dismissed in the way a well-known American scholar, W.W. Willoughby,¶ did so recently in response to Japanese claims when he said that industrialization, which leads to a growth in population, also educates nations to a higher standard of living, and that the birthrate should sink by itself until this standard of living becomes sustainable.[193] Such an argument seems to us practically immoral and inhumane, and yet it is characteristic for a certain liberal-individualistic ideological behavior. In connection with our discussion, this "demographic" right to land can be seen as a universal foundation for a justification of territorial demands; it cannot, however, be seen as a concrete *Großraum* principle of international law in a specific sense that contains recognizable limitations and standards in itself.

The so-called "regional pacts" that arose in the framework of the Geneva League of Nations and the Versailles System remain out of consideration here. This designation comes from Article 21 of the Charter of the Geneva League of Nations that permits "*ententes régionales.*" The policy and jurisprudence of the Geneva League of Nations recommended

---

* Karl Haushofer (1869–1946) was a German geographer and geostrategist.

† Théophile Funck-Brentano (1830–1906) was a Luxembourgian-French sociologist and academic.

‡ Albert Sorel (1842–1906) was a French historian of eighteenth- and nineteenth-century French diplomatic history and a consultant to the French government throughout the late nineteenth century.

§ Luigi Valli (1879–1930) was an Italian philosopher, poet, and Danteist.

¶ Westel W. Willoughby (1867–1945) was an American political scientist.

treaties named after these pacts as "an excellent means towards the security of the European peace." The so-called Little Entente* between Czechoslovakia, Romania, and Yugoslavia, which gave itself a special organizational pact (of February 16, 1933), is certainly the most important example; this pact even became the archetype of such a regional pact. According to the French aide-mémoire from August 14, 1936, "under the expression 'regional Entente' is to be understood every grouping of powers whose community is founded upon their geographical position or (!) a community of interests."[194] According to this, the word "regional" designates only a general, superficially geographical connection. It does not contain the demand for a new, sensible spatial order, but rather only foresees assistance pacts, confederations, or other political treaties of the old style, which only really serve to maintain the (from the point of view of a spatial order) senseless status quo of the Versailles system in all "regions." From the German side, three leading jurists of international law – Paul Barandon,[†] Freiherr von Freytagh-Loringhoven,[‡] and Asche Graf von Mandelsloh[§] – have demonstrated the inner contradictions and the lack of any real conception of order of these kinds of treaties, which have primarily arisen only out of French security needs.[195] This kind of treaty has, along with the Versailles system and the Geneva League of Nations, been made historically obsolete, but has also been dispensed with as uninteresting from the point of view of international law. Only the Treaty of Locarno from October 16, 1925, is worth a further word of mention. This could have become an approach to a pacification of the region based on the idea of good neighbors, and even if it had not been a real principle of spatial order, it could have contained elements of such an order if the unilateral demilitarization of the German Western border had been abolished. The German government made the honest attempt to make all of these other elements of the Treaty of Locarno designed to content the Western European powers valid. But France's alliance with the Soviet Union destroyed the regional-neighborly Locarno Community.[196] In conclusion, one has to conclude that these regional pacts barely earn their name for superficially geographical reasons,[197] and it is far harder to conclude that they should be seen as the expression of a new concrete conception of a spatial order. The political thought behind them has not the slightest in common with the original basic thoughts

---

* The Little Entente was a mutual assistance pact between Czechoslovakia, Romania, and Yugoslavia and supported by France in 1921–2.

† Paul Barandon (1881–?) was a scholar of international law.

‡ Axel August Gustav Johann Freiherr von Freytagh-Loringhoven (1878–1942) was a jurist and nationalist publicist.

§ Asche Graf Mandelsloh (?–1939) was a scholar of international law and scholarly collaborator of Schmitt's.

of the American Monroe theory. These regional pacts of the Versailles system could only be brought into connection with the Monroe Doctrine at all because in Article 21 of the Charter of the Geneva League of Nations the Monroe Doctrine is named as an example of an "*entente régionale*" for the superficial reasons typical of the juridical formalism of Geneva jurisprudence.[198]

II. The Monroe Doctrine as the Precedent for a Großraum Principle

The American Monroe Doctrine proclaimed in 1823 is the first and, until now, most successful example of a *Großraum* principle in the modern history of international law. It stands for us as a unique and important "precedent." If the legal concept of a *Großraum* principle of international law is up for discussion, then we must proceed from the Monroe Doctrine, not from the theory of "natural borders" or the "right to land" or any of the mentioned regional pacts.

To be fair, the Monroe Doctrine has often been endowed with varying content at different stages in its development. Its history knows periods of obfuscation and even the falsification of its original meaning, which is marked with three key phrases: the independence of all American states; non-colonialization in this space; non-intervention of extra-American powers in this space. The many expansions and changes in the course of later developments do nothing to change this original meaning and the power of precedence of the Monroe Doctrine. The fact, moreover, that such a great German statesman as Prince Bismarck expressed himself so indignantly about the Monroe Doctrine and spoke of American hubris and an American specter does not necessarily hinder us from investigating the fruitful and meaningful (to international law) core of the "Doctrine," which is as remarkable as it has been successful. Bismarck's statements should deter us even less insofar as they fall at the time of the beginning of the imperialistic corruptions of the Doctrine towards the end of the nineteenth century (1898).[199] In recent decades, several important and enlightening attempts towards both a "universalization" of the Doctrine as well as its translation to certain other regions of the earth, like Australia and East Asia, have appeared – attempts about which we will have something to say below. Nonetheless, our attempt to introduce the concept of a *Großraum* principle of international law into international jurisprudence finds its best approach and point of departure in the Monroe Doctrine itself.

In keeping with this, it should be stressed from the beginning that we are not concerned with something along the lines of taking the Monroe Doctrine as such and translating it to other countries and times. Rather, our task is far more directed towards making the core thought contained in the Doctrine, a core thought that can be of use to international law, visible, and, in doing so, making this core thought fruitful for other living spaces and other historical situations. The point here is not to increase the already expansive literature on the Monroe Doctrine by one more treatise. We would hope not to sink into discussing the core problem of this Doctrine to death, or to lose sight of its meaning under a mountain of historical and juridical materials and sources. A clarification of a jurisprudential concept, which is what we aim to tackle here, must make its way through the expansive material and the numerous historical and juridical controversies in order to produce the core of a *Großraum* principle of international law in all of its simplicity and greatness.

What is certain about the Monroe Doctrine is that it, as it says in the common formulation, is "a part of the traditional policy of the United States with reference to the American continent." Many have raised and discussed the question of whether the Monroe theory is a real "legal principle" or "only a political maxim" of the government of the United States. If the question is posed with this typical alternative of law and politics, then the meaning of such a principle has been mistaken. There then remains nothing else but to place the countless statements of American statesmen next to one another. These statements, of course, sometimes proceed from the Monroe Doctrine as a principle of American "public law," as a legally meaningful reservation that is understood in all treaties signed by the United States; at other times, they stress again and again that the Monroe Doctrine is not a real legal principle of international law.[200] The effort to deny the real legal character of the "Doctrine" explains itself through the fact that the doctrine remains unilaterally in the hands of the United States and remains independent from the agreement of other states.[201] If one adopts the style of questioning mentioned above, one can, besides the declarations of American Secretaries of State, count off a great number of names of scholars of international law who have expressed themselves with regards to this question – some scholars under "Pro," others under "Contra."[202] Such a controversy that stems from a falsely posed question results in the evasive answers that the Monroe Doctrine, while it may not exactly have a legal character, has at the least a "*quasi*-legal," or, as C.G. Fenwick* says, rather Solomonically, "at the least a *semi*-legal" character.[203]

In order to not remain stuck in such falsely posed preliminary questions, it makes more sense to heed several simple and uncontroversial facts that I wish to briefly list under three points here.

---

* C.G. Fenwick (1880–1973) was an American political scientist.

1) Virtually all important textbooks and dictionaries of international law treat the Monroe theory without regard for the question of whether its "legal" character is approved or not. The theory appears in every meaningful system of international law. It is an illuminating further question to ask what place the theory is given in the system – if it, for example, is treated (in a way that corresponds to the American tradition) along with the right to national existence and self-defense (for example, Calvo,* §143; Fenwick, p. 169); or alongside the theory of intervention (for example, Despagnet,† §208); or alongside state connections (Santi Romano,‡ *Corso di Diritto Internazionale*, p. 79). For a new "school" of international law as formidable as the one led by the famous Chilean jurist Alejandro Álvarez,§ the Monroe theory has even become – although still only in its genuine and original, in other words, not yet imperialistically corrupted form – the legal foundation of a unique Continental-American international law.[204]

2) Since the First Hague Peace Conference (1899),[205] the United States has succeeded to great effect against primarily English resistance at seeing to it that the "reservation of the Monroe Doctrine" always be either expressly or tacitly valid in the praxis of international treaties. This is, therefore, of decisive meaning for any realistic jurisprudence, since international law is to a high degree a law of reservations. Reality's real place in international law, regardless of normativistic universalizations and universalistic resolutions, is in such reservations. Upon the signing of the Kellogg Pact of 1928, the United States may not have expressly added the reservation of the Monroe Doctrine, even though this was demanded in the Senate; there was, however, no doubt that this reservation, just as in every treaty concluded by the United States, here, too, was understood *sub silentio*, since the Monroe theory is valid as an expression of the inalienable right to self-defense. The Secretary of State Kellogg even said in a speech before the American Society of International Law on April 28, 1928: "This right (that is, the right to self-defense contained within the Monroe theory) is inherent in every sovereign state, and is implied in every treaty." The English reservations regarding the Kellogg Pact, which are still to be mentioned below (under III), are even called a "British Monroe Doctrine."

---

* Carlos Calvo (1824–1906) was an Argentine historian of international law known for his development of the Calvo Doctrine.

† Frantz Despagnet (1857–1906) was a French jurist.

‡ Santi Romano (1875–1947) was an Italian jurist especially well known for his 1918 work *L'ordinamento giuridico*.

§ Manuel Alejandro Álvarez Jofré (1868–1960) was a Chilean jurist and diplomat.

3) The Charter of the Geneva League of Nations awarded the reservation of the Monroe Doctrine a primacy before its own norms in Article 21. The consequence is that the Geneva League of Nations, out of respect for the Monroe theory, "limps towards the American side."[206] This is most remarkable, since the League of Nations and especially Article 21 of its Charter was wrested from the (at the time) European victor powers by President Wilson under the threat that if the Article were not included, the United States would not accede to the League; then, however, the United States did not join the League, even though Article 21 remained in the Charter.[207]

These three points suffice in order to ground the formidable presence of the Monroe Doctrine in international law for our examination. The objections and inhibitions that result from the seemingly shoreless mutability of the Monroe Doctrine's content are more difficult than the pseudo-juridical controversy about the question of whether the Monroe theory is a legal or only a political principle. Around the turn of the century, the Monroe Doctrine became an aggressive, imperialistically interpreted principle of expansion for reasons of fending off the intervention of spatially foreign powers, only for this imperialistic character to be curtailed, at least officially, since 1934. The Monroe Doctrine turned from a principle of non-intervention and the rejection of foreign interference to become a justification for imperialistic interventions of the United States in other American states. It has been desired to be used both for a policy of the most strict isolation and neutrality of the United States as well as for a policy of global interference, for a policy of world war. Americans argue over the question of whether they should regard the doctrine as the foundation or, on the contrary, the main hindrance, to a solidarity encompassing the American continent.[208] Since the end of the nineteenth century, a special "Caribbean Doctrine" concerning Cuba and the West Indies, whose relation to the Monroe Doctrine is not entirely clear, has developed out of the doctrine's great framework encompassing the entire Western Hemisphere. The tremendous variety of such different and contradictory possibilities of application and interpretations give the "doctrine" such an elasticity with respect to changing political situations that it often has the appearance that everything and anything could be read into or out of it, all depending on the situation. The author of a thorough historical treatment of the Monroe Doctrine, Dexter Perkins,* is of the view that the doctrine is obsolete today, that it is no longer "relevant" ever since the United States became a world power and since Europe found itself in a lasting crisis. To this, however, Perkins rejoins that not since a century ago has the Monroe Doctrine been so

---

* Dexter Perkins (1889–1984) was an American historian of the Monroe Doctrine.

necessary and so popular as it is today.[209] The aversion of all "positive" jurists to such a "theory" may be well understood; faced with such an indeterminacy of normative content, the positivist has the feeling of losing the ground from under his feet. But the lack of certainty as to the content of the doctrine resembles, as often occurs in life, to an unusual degree a dialectical transition into a purely decisionist certainty – a decisionist certainty where the genuine positivist feels the ground beneath his feet once more. In 1923, the Secretary of State Hughes responded to the question on the real content of the Monroe Doctrine in such a way that represents a practically classic example of the purest decisionism: only the government of the United States of America "defines, interprets, and sanctions" what the Monroe Doctrine really bespeaks.

The fact that the original Monroe theory of 1823 is the first declaration in the history of modern international law that speaks of a *Großraum* and erects the principle of the non-intervention of spatially foreign powers is decisive for us. The theory refers expressly to the "Western Hemisphere" of the earth. When Talleyrand or Gentz* from the governments of the Holy Alliance speak of "Europe," they mean more to speak of a stately power relation system.[210] The American declaration of 1823, however, thinks of the planet in spatial terms, in a modern sense. This is in itself something totally extraordinary and worthy of special attention in international law. This, admittedly, would not have sufficed to constitute a *Großraum* principle of international law in our sense. Throughout history there have been claims of all kinds of interest spheres. The so-called sector principle practiced by Russia and Canada for the Arctic space is not a *Großraum* conception of international law in the sense of a principle of order determined by its content.[211] A purely geographical conception may have a great political-practical meaning, but alone it does not represent a convincing legal principle. The strength of the great powers that can overcome space is too great for this approach; the master of geopolitical scholarship, Karl Haushofer,[212] stressed the meaning of such powers. Seen from the standpoint of international jurisprudence, space and political idea do not allow themselves to be separated from one another. For us, there are neither spaceless political ideas nor, reciprocally, spaces without ideas or principles of space without ideas. It is an important part of a determinable political idea that a certain nation carries it and that it has a certain opponent in mind, through which this political idea gains the quality of the political.[213]

The genuine and original Monroe Doctrine had the monarchic-dynastic principle of legitimacy as its counter-doctrine in mind. This gave the status quo of European power division of the time its sanctification

---

* Friedrich von Gentz (1764–1832) was the Secretary of the Congress of Vienna.

and holiness of justice. It elevated the absolute and legitimate monarchy to the standard of the international order and justified on this foundation the interventions of European great powers in Spain and Italy. Logically, it would have had to lead to interventions in the revolutionary processes of state formation in Latin America. At the same time, the leading power of this Holy Alliance, Russia, sought to establish itself with colonies in the far north of the American continent. The peoples of the American continent, however, no longer felt themselves to be the subjects of foreign great powers and no longer wanted to be the objects of foreign colonization. This was "the free and independent position" of which the Monroe Dispatch spoke, of which it was proud, and which it posed in opposition to the "political system" of the European monarchies. The peoples of the American continent declared that they did not want to interfere in this European "system," fundamentally different from their own, and they refused to tolerate any "interposition" and any transfer of power that proceeded from this European system. The European system was not to intervene on the grounds of the status quo and its tenured land holdings into a political *Großraum* that had awoken into self-consciousness. This is the political idea that is connected in the Monroe theory with the *Großraum* "America." Here is the core of the great original Monroe Doctrine, a genuine principle of *Großraum*, namely the connection of politically awakened nation, political idea, and a *Großraum* ruled by this idea, a *Großraum* excluding foreign interventions. Not the Monroe Doctrine, to repeat ourselves, but this core, the concept of a *Großraum* order of international law, is translatable to other spaces, other historical situations, and other friend–enemy groupings.

The cases of a translation of the Monroe Doctrine to date have been different from one another and require a special investigation. Two sentences of the Australian Prime Minister Hughes, for example, are called an "Australian Monroe Doctrine." On April 7, 1921, Hughes gave the two conditions under which Australia could agree to a renewal of the alliance between England and Japan: 1) No alliance may have an effect against the United States; 2) No alliance may endanger the principle that Australia belongs to the white race.[214] We have to speak of the so-called "East Asian or Japanese Monroe Doctrine." It should be expressly underlined that we are not suggesting here a "German Monroe Doctrine," but rather only the justified core thought of the original Monroe Dispatch, namely the thought of the impermissibility under international law of interventions of spatially foreign powers in a *Großraum* ruled by a principle of order. This *Großraum* thought – not the Monroe Doctrine itself – may not be arbitrary, but it is reasonably translatable based on the state of political reality. Its applicability to Central and East European space is not abolished through the fact that since 1823 the state of affairs in Europe and in America have fundamentally changed and that, with respect to the character of the political ideas borne in a space, the fronts have practically reversed themselves. The liberal freedom of thought of Western democracy is today historically obsolete. It now serves to legally sanction the mere status quo and to grant the sanctity of law, the consecration of legality and legitimacy, to a set of global possessions. The Western democracies are today in the position of the European powers of the Holy Alliance in the early nineteenth century. A liberal democratic-capitalistic principle of legitimation became a monarchic-dynastical principle. Already, the world war of 1914 to 1918 was a war of intervention of this liberal democratic legitimacy.[215] At the time, this war could still, however, pass itself off as a war against reactionary powers related to the monarchical Holy Alliance, while the liberal democratic Holy Alliance of the Western powers is today clearly on the side of the past and stands on the side of the sanctity of the status quo, and seeks to suppress both new political ideas as well as new, growing nations.

The justification of a capitalistic imperialism, for which President Theodore Roosevelt used the Monroe Doctrine at the turn of the nineteenth and the twentieth century, is a special section in the history of this doctrine. It has been taken, with justice, as a self-contradiction and the most conspicuous example of the change in meaning of such a principle: the fact that an originally defensive concept of space that defended against the intervention of spatially foreign powers could be made into the foundation of a "dollar diplomacy." In all the historical treatments of the Monroe Doctrine this imperialistic-capitalistic reinterpretation of the original meaning of the doctrine stands out as a deep change in meaning. Alongside it, we have to keep in mind another, perhaps still deeper, and, for our examination of *Großraum* principles of international law, still more illuminating kind of change and change in meaning: namely, the reinterpretation of the Monroe Doctrine from a concrete, geographically and historically determined concept of *Großraum* into a general, universally conceived principle for the world that is to be valid for the entire world and demands "ubiquity." This reinterpretation stands together in close connection with the falsification of the Doctrine into a universalistic-imperialistic principle of expansion. The reinterpretation is of special interest for us because it makes clear the point at which the policy of the United States leaves behind its continental spatial principle and binds itself with the universalism of the British world empire.

In 1905, President Theodore Roosevelt is said to have said to Viscount Kaneko* that the Monroe Doctrine must encompass all of Asia, and that

---

* Kaneko Kentaro (1853–1942) was a Japanese statesman and diplomat in favor of peaceful Japanese–American relations.

Japan should proclaim such an Asian Monroe theory. With this he meant, to be sure, the proclamation of an "open door policy" and the "equal chance" of all powers in China. Even when the text of his statement can no longer be literally and exactly pinpointed, the statement is clearly to the effect that Asia and especially Japan should involve itself in the economic imperialism of the Anglo-Saxon world system. An Asian or Japanese Monroe theory, an "Asia Monroeshugi," that had this meaning would have been just as desired by the United States and England as a "Japanese Monroe Doctrine" was unpleasant when Japan conquered Manchuria.[216] President W. Wilson suggested in his message to the Congress on January 22, 1917 that all nations of the world should accept the theory of President Monroe as a "world doctrine," with the meaning of the free right to self-determination of nations for nations both great and small. Article 10 of the Charter of the Geneva League of Nations was even given as an expression and case of the application of this Monroe Doctrine for the world.[217] These are typical and telling changes in the meaning of the doctrine.[218] Their methods consist in dissolving a concrete, spatially determined concept of order into universalistic "world" ideas and, in doing so, transforming the healthy core of a *Großraum* principle of international law of non-intervention into a global ideology that interferes in everything, a pan-interventionist ideology as it were, all under the cover of humanitarianism.

III. The Principle of the Security of the Traffic Routes of the British World Empire

Universalistic general concepts that encompass the world are the typical weapons of interventionism in international law. One has to pay attention to their connection and combination with concrete, historical, and political situations. An important case of such a combination will face us under the topic of minority law (Section IV). Here, however, one should first handle a "doctrine" that is often treated as a parallel to the Monroe Doctrine: the doctrine of the "security of the traffic routes of the British world empire." It is the counter-image of everything that the original Monroe theory was. The Monroe Doctrine had a coherent space, the American continent, in mind. The British world empire, meanwhile, is no coherent space but rather a political union of littered property scattered across the most distant continents, Europe, America, Asia, Africa, and Australia – a collection that is not spatially coherent. The original Monroe theory had the political meaning of defending a new political idea against the powers of the contemporary status quo through the exclusion of interventions from spatially foreign powers. In contrast to this, the principle of the security of the traffic routes of the British world empire is, seen from the point of view of international law, nothing else than a classic case of the application of the concept of the legitimacy of the mere status quo. This principle can be nothing else and is, therefore, in no higher sense a "doctrine,"[219] like, for example, a "Disraeli Doctrine" that declared that the continued holding of Turkey was a question of life and death for the British world empire.

The juridical way of thinking that pertains to a geographically incoherent world empire scattered across the earth tends by its own nature towards universalistic argumentation. This way of thinking must equate such an empire's interest in the unchanged holding of its territories with the interest of humanity in order to have any rationale whatsoever. Such a way of thinking directs itself not towards a certain coherent space and its inner order, but rather, above all else, towards the security of the connections of the scattered parts of the empire. It is more common for the jurist, especially the jurist of international law, of such a world empire, to think in terms of roads and traffic routes than in terms of spaces. The statement of a leading English expert in this field, Sir William Hayter,* is characteristic for the unique style of the British way of thinking when he says that the English government can permit revolutions in Greece and Bulgaria; in Egypt, on the other hand, quiet and order must rule so that the great connecting artery of the British Empire, above all the route to India, be not disturbed. A very well-known English response to the question of whether England should annex Egypt originates from the same way of conceiving the world. This question is answered in the negative, since he who regularly has to make a long trip from his home to another region, while he certainly has an interest in there being a good hotel in the middle of his journey, does not have an interest in being a hotelier himself, in becoming the proprietor of this hotel. Mussolini, in his speech in Milan on November 1, 1936, reminded his audience of the deep opposition between the fact that while for England the Mediterranean Sea is only a road, one of many roads, indeed, only a shortcut and a canal, for Italy it amounts to its living space.[220] The opposition of road and living space becomes clear here in all of its profundity. It was rejoined from the English side that the Mediterranean was not a shortcut but rather a main artery, that for the British "Commonwealth of Nations" there existed in the Mediterranean a vital interest in the full sense of the word.[221] The vital interest of the widely scattered English world empire in sea routes, air routes, pipelines, etc. is incontestable from this point of view.[222] But in accepting this, the difference and opposition of spatial thinking in international law as opposed to route- and

---

* William Goodenough Hayter (1906–95) was a British diplomat active in many European capitals and the Soviet Union in the 1930s.

road-thinking in international law is neither abolished nor overcome, but only confirmed.

While the problem of the American Monroe Doctrine has been treated in countless publications, there is hardly any specific scholarly literature on the great problem of the security of the connecting arteries of the British world empire. This may be partly due to the fact that it does not correspond to the British method to make vital questions of British global policy into the object of scholarly discussions or, indeed, genuine controversies. The English vital interest in the security of traffic routes manifests itself most openly and most clearly in the reservations that are inserted into important treaties of international law. Here, too, our thesis that current international law is fundamentally a law of reservations finds confirmation.[223] The English government abolished the unilaterally declared English protectorate over Egypt in 1914 through its own unilateral declaration recognizing Egypt as a sovereign state, but only under four conditions that were left to the discretion of the English government prior to any further agreement between England and Egypt. As the foremost of these four reservations – before the protection of foreign interests in Egypt, the protection of minorities, and the general reservation regarding the Sudan – stands the security of the traffic routes of the British Empire in Egypt.[224] The later Anglo-Egyptian Treaty of August 26, 1936[225] rests on the exact same stipulation. This treaty determines in Article 8: "in view of the fact that the Suez Canal, whilst being an integral part of Egypt, is a universal means of communication and also an essential means of communication between the different parts of the British Empire," it is stipulated that England take over the protection of the Canal until Egypt is in a condition to do so. This connection of a "universal" world interest with an "essential" British interest is typical and of great meaning for our analysis.

The British stipulation of the security of traffic routes was raised upon the signing of the Kellogg Pact in 1928, too; this time, however, in a way that expressed itself not in terms of roads but in terms of space, whereby reference was even made to the American Monroe theory. The English reservation to the Kellogg Pact is called the "British Monroe Doctrine,"[226] even though the difference, indeed, the opposition of the interests and ways of thinking is immediately recognizable if the genuine concept of space is retained. The formulation of the reservation is so characteristic that the authoritative position from the note from the British Secretary for Foreign Affairs to the American ambassador in London from May 19, 1928, should be cited here verbatim. There it says (under number 10):

> The language of Article 1, as to the renunciation of war as an instrument of national policy, renders it desirable that I should remind your Excellency

that there are certain regions of the world the welfare and integrity of which constitute a special and vital interest for our peace and safety. His Majesty's Government has been at pains to make it clear in the past that interference with these regions cannot be suffered. Their protection against attack is to the British Empire a measure of self-defence. It must be clearly understood that His Majesty's Government in Great Britain accepts the new Treaty upon the distinct understanding that it does not prejudice their freedom of action in this respect. The Government of the United States has comparable interests, any disregard of which by a foreign Power they have declared that they would regard as an unfriendly act. His Majesty's Government believes, therefore, that in defining their position they are expressing the intention and meaning of the United States Government.[227]

The formulation of this reservation contains a clear and intentional reference to the Monroe theory. But it also liquidates its concrete spatial thinking with the help of the universal concept of the "right to self-defence." In spite of this, the difference between original American-continental spatial thinking and the British-imperialistic route- and road-thinking should not go unrecognized here.

As concerns the Suez Canal, English policy achieved a regulation under international law that corresponded to its interest in this traffic route. As long as the Canal was not yet in English hands, the English government argued with entirely universal principles. The statements from this time are documents of the unshaken, practically naïve Victorian belief in the harmony of England's political interest with the interests of mankind as stated in these universal principles. When Lord Salisbury* protested against the monopoly granted to the original builder of the Canal, Ferdinand von Lesseps,† by the Khedive,‡ he called upon the "natural right of all other nations" that, in the interest of global commerce, excluded such maritime arteries from a concession or a monopoly.[228] After English troops had occupied the Canal, it was internationalized and neutralized through the collective treaty of October 29, 1888, whereby England made its universal reservation of freedom of trade during the English occupation of Egypt.[229] The above-mentioned treaty with Egypt from August 26, 1936 already belongs to a third stage of this development, namely that of an argumentation obviously based on the mere status quo, one

---

* Robert Arthur Talbot Gascoyne-Cecill (Lord Salisbury) was a British statesmen and Prime Minister.

† Ferdinand de Lesseps (1805–94) was a French diplomat and developer of the Suez Canal.

‡ Sa'id of Egypt (1822–63) was the *Wali* (Governor) of Egypt under Ottoman rule who granted Ferdinand de Lesseps the concession to build the Suez Canal in 1856. "Khedive" is a Persian word meaning "Lord" or "Viceroy."

whose watchword is "security." Between that initial call to a universal natural right and today's mere securing of a status quo, there lies an intermediate stage worthy of attention. During this stage, the efforts of English international legal policy operated to the effect of making the internationalization and neutralization of the Suez Canal as effected by the 1888 treaty into a prototype for an "international legal system of inter-oceanic canals and maritime routes" for all important maritime routes that were not in English hands.

Upon attempting to achieve this goal with respect to the Panama Canal, however, English policy ran into a resistance organized by the United States in the name of the Monroe theory. The opposition of two worlds came to light in this question concerning the Panama Canal. The struggle ended with a total victory on the part of the United States and, therefore, the Monroe Doctrine, which showed itself superior to England's universalistic claim as a concrete great order principle. A third case that is important for us as Germans concerns the Kiel Canal. Here, too, a chain of argument pertaining to the English world empire attempted to achieve the acceptance of a unified and universal system of international law encompassing the three great inter-oceanic canals and to subject the Kiel Canal to a "regime of the great international maritime routes" allegedly recognized by international law. In the *Wimbledon* trial (1923), the English representative, the counsel of the Foreign Office, Sir Cecil Hurst,* represented the "Three Canal Argument" with great energy. The judgment of the Permanent International Court in The Hague from August 17, 1923 contains in its rationale for the decision a recognition of the English tendency to attempt to implement the principle of the internationalization of all the great maritime routes, including the Kiel Canal, into international law. Ernst Wolgast, whom we must thank for his monograph on the *Wimbledon* trial, has, with the help of his talent for seeing the true meaning of cases, worked out this aspect of the *Wimbledon* trial.[230]

The "freedom" that is spoken of in numerous English arguments regarding international law belongs by its very origin to the natural law of the seventeenth century.[231] These arguments reached their high point in the freedom of global commerce in the nineteenth century. This century is, therefore, the period of time in which there reigned a wonderful harmony between, on the one hand, the political and economic interests of the British world empire and, on the other hand, the recognized rules of international law. In the politically decisive case, "freedom" means a rewriting of the conceptual, specifically British global imperial interest

---

* Cecil James Barrington Hurst (1870–1963) was a British international lawyer.

as concerns the great traffic routes of the world. "Freedom of the seas," in other words, means, according to a formulation of Wheaton-Dana's* that became famous through its citation in the Miramichi case (English prize court decision from November 23, 1914):† "the sea is *res omnium*, the common field of war, as well as of commerce." As long as England had dominance on the seas, the freedom of the seas received its borders, indeed, even its content, through the right and the freedom of war-conducting states to police the commerce of neutrals. "Freedom of the Dardanelles" means unhindered use of these straits by English naval boats in order to be able to attack Russia in the Black Sea, etc. The real context that drives the especially developed interests of a geographically incoherent world empire to universalistic universalizing legal concepts is always evident behind the freedom-oriented, humanitarian, universal interpretation. This cannot be merely explained as cant and deception. It is an example of the unavoidable link between ways of thinking about international law and a certain kind of political existence.[232] The question now, incidentally, is only how long that wonderful harmony of British interest and international law can guard its existence into the twentieth century.

The Monroe Doctrine, too, experienced a reinterpretation into a universalistic-imperialistic global doctrine through Th. Roosevelt and W. Wilson. In spite of these attempts, both principles – the American Monroe Doctrine and the security of traffic routes of the British world empire – have remained distinct from one another. The universalism of the principle of the security of traffic routes today no longer has its wrapping of natural law and freedom; it is the open expression of the interest of a world empire in the status quo – an empire that believes itself already to contain enough legitimation in itself. The universalization of the Monroe Doctrine through Roosevelt and Wilson, meanwhile, was the corruption of a genuine *Großraum* principle of non-intervention into an interventionism without borders. The moment when this universalization was declared in its entirety, President Wilson's above-mentioned dispatch of January 22, 1917, marks the point where the policy of the United States turned away from its home soil and entered into a union with the British Empire's imperialism of world and mankind.

---

* Richard Henry Dana Jr. (1815–82) was an American lawyer and author who specialized in maritime law.

† The Miramichi case was an English prize court case decided in 1914 asserting the right of Britain to seize enemy goods carried in British merchant vessels during times of war.

IV. Minority and National Group Law in the Central and East European Großraum

Our discussion of the Monroe Doctrine and its counter-example, the principle of the security of the traffic routes of the British world empire, should bring to scholarly awareness the difference between an international law grounded in concrete *Großräume* and that of a universalistic-humanitarian world law. Not only the original genuine Monroe Doctrine, but also almost all important fundamental questions of modern international law, are threatened by the hegemony of this universalism in its most authentic sense. The Geneva League of Nations Pact had to fail because of this very universalism. The League of Nations Pact also turned the international legal regulation of so-called minority protection, which was attempted in 1919, into an unanchored and self-contradictory illusion. The minority protection of the Versailles–Geneva system can be best recognized in its concrete character from the points of view of the problems we pose here.

Of course, this system with its minority protection is today historically obsolete. But the ways of thinking about international law that manifest themselves in this system, this system's world of pertinent principles and conceptual formations of international law, still affect events today and have in no way disappeared. They were carried further by the powers of the Western democracies and are a part of the intellectual and moral armament towards a new, total world war, to a "just war" in grand fashion.[233] It is for this reason that the critical work that German international jurisprudence achieved against the universalism of the League of Nations, against the attempted identification of international law and the law of the Geneva Federation,[234*] and especially against the liberal minority protection system has in no way become meaningless.

In the 20-year history of the Versailles–Geneva minority protection system, the German school of national law and national group law elucidated the antithesis that separates a national group law built on the concept of nation and national group from a minority protection scheme constructed on the basis of individualistic liberalism. The diligent work of the German preservers of law in this field – I shall name only a few leading names: M.H. Böhm,[†] W. Hasselblatt, Hans Gerber, C. von Loesch, K.G. Hugelmann, G.A. Walz, N.Gürke, H. Kier, H. Raschhofer, K.O. Rabl

---

* Schmitt is referring to the League of Nations when he writes "Geneva Federation."

† All of the figures whom Schmitt mentions here were German jurists, most of whom focused on nationalities law: Max Hildebert Böhm (1891–1968); Werner Hasselblatt (1890–1958); Hans Gerber (1889–1981); Karl Christian von Loesch (1880–1944); Karl Gottfried Hugelmann (1879–1959); Norbert Gürke (1904–41); Hermann Raschhofer (1905–79); Kurt Rabl; Georg H.J. Erler (1905–81).

– proved fruitful. Its total victory, also as an event of jurisprudence, is no longer doubtful. The juridical and logical muddle that lies behind a universal term like "minority" is today clear to all. In political and social reality, such obviously different and contradictory circumstances – questions of the cleansing of borders, questions of cultural and *völkisch* autonomy, the completely and thoroughly unique Jewish problem, which is comparable with none of these other questions – so obviously conceal themselves behind the empty word "minority" that I only need briefly to remind the reader of this fact in this context. Georg H.J. Erler recently summarized the result well: "In the reality of life this creature 'minority' does not exist. In reality, there are living communities of the most different kind, and even these *völkisch* minorities are very different from one another."[235]

The question of the so-called minorities requires a further clarification from the point of view of *Großraum* orders of international law, the real theme of our investigation. Many opposed tendencies at odds with one another intersected in the minority law of the Treaty of Versailles. In the foreground there stands the universal liberal-individualistic thought that equality and equal treatment are guaranteed to whomever coincidentally belongs to a "minority." Liberal individualism and transnational universalism turn out here to be the two poles of the same ideology. The equality of state citizens and the rights of freedom of liberal constitutionalism are presupposed here as the genuine and basic domestic norm of European civilization. They represent the domestic "standard" of the members of the community of international law, a standard upon which the homogeneity of the members of the community of international law should rest. The further, implicitly understood presupposed thought tied to this is, as shown at the Berlin Conference in 1878,* that the Western democratic great powers, first of all of course England, are leading and exemplary in this regard.[236] Because they stand as true free legal and constitutional states, no minority protection under international law may ever be brought to discussion against them; among the Western democracies, there conceptually cannot exist any minorities in need of minority protection. Along with this structural connection of domestic liberalism and the international hegemony of Western democracies,[237] the minority protection of the Versailles system contains a further element that has purely to do with power politics, an element that articulates itself with cynical openness in Clemenceau's famous letter of June 24, 1919 to Paderewski:† the victorious great powers of 1919 claim a right of

---

* The Conference of Berlin (1878) was a conference of the major European colonial powers that politically reorganized the Balkans.

† Ignacy Paderewski (1860–1921) was the Prime Minister of Poland from January 16–December 9, 1919.

control and intervention against the states of the European East that resulted from or were enlarged through their victory. Moreover – and this is in open dissonance to the claim on control and intervention made by the spatially foreign Western powers – a third conception of space is effective. The geographical zone of the expansion of minority protection under the international law of Geneva and Versailles is limited to and runs from the Baltic Sea to the Mediterranean in a belt of land that resulted from a certain historical development; indeed, a belt that amounts to an arena of interests and claims.

Already in the negotiations of the Paris Peace Conferences in 1919 the contradiction that exists between the universalistic thought of a universal, individually constructed minority protection and this limitation to a historical-politically determined space became clear. The representative of the South African Union, General Smuts,* who, after the American President Wilson, most fervently represented the thought of a universalistic League of Nations, wanted to give the League of Nations a great program of humanitarian tasks and principles, and to include all of this in the League Charter. The current Charter Article 22 (mandate) and 23 (humanitarian and similar tasks of the League of Nations) were thought of as only a part of this comprehensive program. Freedom of religion and the protection of national, religious, and linguistic minorities were to be especially anchored in the League of Nations Charter. The Jewish Question was seen as a question of religion. The Japanese representative demanded that the principle of the equality of races be articulated in the League of Nations Charter. The equality of races was, however, rejected, particularly by Australia. To this, the Japanese delegate responded that Japan would be opposed to the inclusion of a protection of freedom of religion were the declaration on the equality of races not included. As a result, both points – freedom of religion as well as the equality of races – eventually were dropped from the program. The resistance that especially Poland and Romania held against a minority protection system that was not universal but rather only affected their space counted for nothing.

The underlying liberal-individualistic and therefore universalistic[238] construction of minority protection became the foundation for the spatially alien Western powers' exercise of control and intervention in the European Eastern space, a development anticipated by the universalistic Geneva League of Nations. This construction was connected with a limitation of the same order's idea of universalistic minority protection in the European Eastern space in a clearly contradictory way. The Polish government was, therefore, completely right when, on September

---

* Jan Smuts (1870–1950) was a South African statesman and Prime Minister of South Africa from 1919–24 and 1939–48.

13, 1934, it refused any further cooperation with international organs and the controls of the Versailles minority protection system "until the implementation of a common and uniform system of international protection of minorities." After all, the limitation of such a liberal-individualistic, essentially universalistic minority protection system only to certain states amounts to insulting discrimination against these states. To the same extent that the Polish delegate was justified, the Brazilian delegate Mello Franco* had no right to effect a geographical limitation of the Geneva minority protection to the Eastern Europeans and to inter-fere in European affairs with his un*völkisch* ideas of assimilation and the melting pot. At the 37th Conference of the Geneva League of Nations Council on December 9, 1925, Mello Franco gave the much discussed definition that there could be no minorities in America in the sense of the Geneva minority protection, since the term "minority" in the Versailles minority protection system referred to a historically unique development. This is, to be fair, correct insofar as the geographical zone drawn up in the Versailles minority protection system belongs to a *Großraum* that has developed in a particular way, a *Großraum* in which certain viewpoints of international law are sensible, and in which the protection of the unique *völkisch* nature of every national group from the Western ideas of assimi-lation is necessary. But the erection and execution of principles that are not valid for such a *Großraum* is no matter for spatially alien powers that interfere in this space from outside; these are neither the matters of the Western European democracies nor of an American government, but rather of the stately and *völkisch* powers that carry this space; it is, in particular, an affair of the German *Reich*.

Since the declaration that the *Reich* Chancellor Adolf Hitler gave in the German *Reichstag* on February 20, 1938 there has existed a German right of protection for German national groups of foreign state citizen-ship, all on the foundation of our National Socialist national idea. A genuine principle of international law is erected through this policy. This principle is part of the larger principle of mutual respect for every nationhood, which is also solemnly recognized in the German–Polish declarations of November 5, 1937, and which amounts to the rejection of all ideals of assimilation, absorption, and melting pots. This is the political idea that has the specific meaning of a *Großraum* under inter-national law elucidated here; the political idea for the Central and East European space in which there live many nations and national groups that are, however, not – apart from the Jews – racially alien from one another. This is no "German Monroe Doctrine"; it is, rather, an applica-tion of the idea of spatial order in international law appropriate to the

---

* Afranio de Mello Franco (1870–1942) was a Brazilian statesman.

current political and historical position of the German *Reich* and the East European space. The justified success of the American Monroe Doctrine, proclaimed in 1823, rested upon this idea of a spatial order in international law, too, as long as this doctrine was preserved from universalistic-imperialistic corruption and remained a genuine *Großraum* principle of international law repelling the intervention of spatially alien powers. The fact that, aside from this *Großraum* principle contained in the declaration of February 20, 1938, the remaining universal rights of protection of the *Reich* remain in effect for state nationals and racial comrades goes without saying and is its own problem unto itself, one that neither abolishes nor impairs the specific concept of the *Großraum* principle of international law.

The German–Russian border and friendship treaty of September 28, 1939 (printed in the *Zeitschrift für Völkerrecht*, Volume XXIV, p. 99) already uses the concept of *Reich* in an official text. The treaty stipulates the border of "both sides' *Reich* interests" in the region of the former Polish state. Any interference on the part of third party powers is expressly rejected in this accord, and in the treaty's introduction it is emphasized that its purpose is to guarantee to the peoples living there a peaceful existence corresponding to their *völkisch* unique nature. The Versailles system of so-called minority protection for this part of the European space was therefore concluded. The German population of the Baltic countries was resettled into the area of the German *Reich* in the context of the political new order in the East (German–Estonian Protocol on the Resettlement of German National Groups from October 15, 1939 and the German–Lithuanian Treaty from October 30, 1939).* In addition to this, one can point to the remigration of Germans from Volhynia and Bessarabia. The Second Vienna Award of the German and Italian Foreign Minister of August 30, 1940 brought the new border region between Hungary and Romania from the point of view of a just national order for the Danube space.† At the same time, agreements were concluded between the *Reich* government and the Hungarian and Romanian government on the protection of the German national groups in both countries in such a way that here, too, the liberal democratic, individualistic Versailles minority system was superseded and replaced by the concept of an order based on national groups. The Romanian–Bulgarian Treaty of September 7, 1940 foresees the

---

* Both of these treaties, concluded following the German invasion of Poland and the Soviet invasion of the Baltic countries, aimed at resettling Baltic Germans in the Warthegau area of Poland.

† The Second Vienna Award was an international agreement concluded on August 30, 1940 negotiated between Hungary and Romania that awarded Northern Transylvania to Hungary.

mandatory resettlement of both sides' national groups from Northern and Southern Dobruja as a solution for that region.* In all of these cases, the principle of non-interference of spatially alien powers has triumphed as the valid principle of current international law with respect to national group law.

V. The Concept of Reich in International Law

A *Großraum* order belongs to the concept of *Reich*, which should be introduced into the scholarly discussion as an eminence specific to international law. *Reich*s in this sense are the leading and bearing powers whose political ideas radiate into a certain *Großraum* and which fundamentally exclude the interventions of spatially alien powers into this *Großraum*. The *Großraum* is, of course, not identical with the *Reich* in the sense that the *Reich* is not the same as the *Großraum* protected from interventions by that *Reich*. Not every state or every people within the *Großraum* is in itself a piece of the *Reich*, just as little as one thinks of declaring Brazil or Argentina a part of the United States with the recognition of the Monroe Doctrine. But to be sure, every *Reich* has a *Großraum* into which its political idea radiates and which is not to be confronted with foreign interventions.

The connection of *Reich*, *Großraum*, and the non-intervention principle is fundamental. It is through this connection that the concepts "intervention" and "non-intervention," which are indispensable for any international law based on the coexistence of different peoples – concepts that are today terribly confused – receive their theoretical and practical utility. In hitherto existing international law as constructed by states, Talleyrand's famous quip that non-intervention meant roughly the same thing as intervention was no exaggerated paradox but rather an everyday experienced fact. But as soon as *Großräume* of international law with bans on intervention by spatially alien powers are recognized and the sun of the concept of *Reich* rises, a fenced-off coexistence on a sensibly divided earth will become thinkable and the principle of non-intervention may unfold its developing effect into a new international law.[239]

We know that the designation "*Deutsches Reich*" is untranslatable in its uniqueness and magnificence. It befits the historic moment of every genuine political eminence that it brings not just any subsumable, but

---

* The Dobruja is the area of land shared by Bulgaria and Romania along the Black Sea Coast to the south of the Danube River delta. Schmitt is referring here to the Treaty of Craiova, a treaty signed on September 7, 1940 between Romania and Bulgaria under which Romania ceded Southern Dobruja to Bulgaria and agreed to a population exchange of Romanians and Bulgarians.

its own designation with it and asserts its own unique name. *Reich*, imperium, and empire are not the same and are not comparable with one another when viewed from within.* While "imperium" often has the meaning of a universalistic structure encompassing the world and mankind – in other words, all nations (although it must not necessarily have this meaning, since several differently styled imperia can exist alongside one another), our *Deutsches Reich* is fundamentally determined on the basis of nation and is a fundamentally non-universalistic legal order built on the foundation of respect for every national identity. While "imperialism" has become a catchphrase often misused as a description for economic-capitalistic methods of colonization and expansion since the end of the nineteenth century,[240] the word "*Reich*" remains free of this stigma. The memories of the mix of nations in the declining Roman imperium, as well as the ideals of assimilation and melting pots of the imperia of Western democracies, draw the sharpest opposition between the concept of imperium and a nationally interpreted concept of *Reich* with respect for all national life. This is all the more true as the *Deutsches Reich*, in the middle of Europe between the universalism of the powers of the liberal-democratic, nation-assimilating West and the universalism of the Bolshevik, globally revolutionary East, has the holy honor of defending a non-universalistic, *völkisch* order of life with respect for the nation.

An examination from the perspective of international law must, however, perceive not only the unique nature but also the coexistence of the political eminencies that are the upholders and designers of the international legal order. It is necessary for both practical and theoretical reasons to keep in mind this fact of the existence of great powers next to, with, and against one another. Any other way of regarding the situation either denies international law by isolating every individual nation, or corrupts the right of nations into a universalistic global right, as was done by the jurisprudence of the Geneva League of Nations. The possibility and future of international law depend, in other words, on the great powers that actually determine and bear the responsibility of the coexistence of nations being properly recognized and being made into the point of departure for the discussion and the formation of concepts. These powers that determine order and bear responsibility are today no longer, as in the eighteenth and nineteenth centuries, empires, but rather *Reich*s.

The correct naming of these entities is of great significance. Words and names are never of secondary importance, not least in the case of political-historical eminencies that have been determined to uphold international law. The argument surrounding words like "state," "sovereignty," and "independence" was the mark of deep-seated political

---

* German: *sind von innen gesehen untereinander nicht vergleichbar.*

debates and confrontations, and the victor not only wrote the history but also determined the vocabulary and the terminology. The designation "*Reich*s" that is suggested here best characterizes the facts, in international law, of the connection of *Großraum*, nation, and political idea that represent our point of departure. The designation "*Reich*" in no way denies the unique nature of each and every one of these *Reich*s. It avoids the empty generality that endangers international law, as would be the risk in phrases like "great power sphere," "block," "space and power complex," "common entity," "commonwealth," etc., or in the totally meaningless spatial designation "zone." *Reich* is concrete and pregnant with respect for the reality of the contemporary global situation. It also provides the many substantial great eminencies without which every discussion and common understanding of international law must stop with a common name. It avoids the other error that endangers international law: that of turning a concretization into an isolation of the several political eminencies that neutralizes all context. The term *Reich*, finally, corresponds to the German practice that employs the word "*Reich*" in diverse contexts: *Reich* of good and evil, *Reich* of light and *Reich* of darkness, even in the "animal and plant *Reich*" – as an expression, be it a cosmos in the sense of a concrete order, in the sense of a historical power ready for war and struggle, grown to the challenge of its counter-*Reich*s; the great objects that make world history have always been called *Reich* – the *Reich* of the Babylonians,[241] of the Persians, of the Macedonians and the Romans, the *Reich*s of the German peoples just as the *Reich*s of their opponents – all of these were always called *Reich* in a specific sense. It would distract us from the pure meaning and goal of our task in international law and would conjure up the danger of endless petty chatter if we desired to delve further into all of the conceivable possibilities of interpreting the word *Reich* in the philosophy of history, theology, and in other such fields. Here, the point is only to oppose a simple concept usable in international law – but still a superior and eminent concept by virtue of its proximity to contemporary reality – to the previously central concept of international law, the state.

The international law developed in the eighteenth and nineteenth centuries and continued into the twentieth century to date was a pure law of states. In spite of some unique characteristics and renovations, it fundamentally only recognizes states as the subjects of international law. Nothing is said of *Reich*s, even though every attentive examiner has marveled at how much the political and economic vital interests of the English world empire have harmonized with the clauses of this international law. The English global empire, too, can only conceive of the textbooks of international law as a "connection of states." Here, the English empire's concept of *Reich* is of a thoroughly unique nature and cannot be comprehended as a "community of states."[242] It is, as was shown above (under III), already determined to be universalistic through its geographically incoherent condition. The title of emperor of the King of England that brings this kind of thought of global *Reich* to expression is linked to far removed, overseas, Far East Asian colonial properties – to India. The title of an "Empress of India," Benjamin Disraeli's invention, is not only a personal document of the "orientalism" of its inventor, but also corresponds to the fact that Disraeli himself formulated in the saying: "England is really more an Asiatic Power than a European [one]."

No international law belongs to such a world *Reich*, but rather a general law of the world and mankind. The systematic and conceptual world of international jurisprudence has, to this point, as already said, never recognized *Reich*s, but rather only states. In political and historical reality there have, of course, always been leading great powers; there was a "concert of the European powers" and, in the Versailles system, the "head Allied powers." The legal conceptual formation held firmly both to a general concept, "state," as well as to the legal equality of all independent and sovereign states.[243] A genuine order built on a ranking of the subjects of international law was fundamentally ignored by international jurisprudence. The objective and qualitative difference between states has found, in spite of several related discussions, no open and consistent conclusion in the jurisprudence of the League of Nations. This has continued even as the fiction of the equality of international law constantly and continually slaps all truth and reality in the face in light of the open and obvious hegemony of England and France in the Geneva League of Nations.

The fact that this obsolete concept of the state as the central concept of international law no longer corresponds to truth and reality has long come to awareness. A large part of the international jurisprudence of the Western democracies, especially that of the jurisprudence of the Geneva League of Nations, has tackled the dethroning of the concept of the state by assaulting the concept of sovereignty. This occurred via the tendency of giving the doubtlessly long due overcoming of the concept of the state in international law a turn in the pacifistic-humanitarian direction, in the direction of a universalistic global law whose hour seemed to have come with the defeat of Germany and the founding of the Geneva League of Nations. Even today, this pre-stabilized harmony of international law and the political interest of the English world *Reich* mentioned above remained preserved – indeed, it had reached its high point. Germany stood, as long as it was defenseless and weak, on the defensive against these tendencies and could have been content, as far as international law was concerned, if it succeeded in defending its stately independence, its mere quality as a state. Yet with the victory of the National Socialist movement, an assault to overturn the concept of the state in international law turned out successfully in Germany – with, granted, totally different points of departure and with totally different goals from that pacifistic-universalistic dethroning of the state. In light of the powerful dynamics of our foreign policy, the state of international law from now on shall be concisely discussed in the following section. Its position in international law shall be clarified through the introduction of our concept of *Reich* – a concept whose meaning for the state and constitution has been made clear through the presentations and expositions of *Reich* Minister Lammers* and State Secretary Stuckart.[244†]

The obsolete interstate international law found its order in the fact that it presupposed a certain concrete order with certain characteristics, namely a "state," which was the same for all members of the community of international law. If the rule of the concept of state in international law has been shaken in recent years through the concept of nation in Germany, then I have no intention of diminishing the service of this accomplishment in international jurisprudence. One should not, however, overlook the fact that the hitherto existing concept of state contained a minimal standard of inner, calculable organization and inner discipline. This organizational minimum formed the real foundation of all that one could see as the concrete order "*Volksgemeinschaft.*" War, which was always a recognized institution of this interstate order, had its justice and order fundamentally in the fact that it was a war between states – the fact, that is, that states conducted war against other states as a concrete order on the same level. This is similar to how a duel, if duels are legally recognized in a given system, finds its inner order and justice in the fact that two honorable men demanding satisfaction stand against one another, even if these two men are perhaps of very different physical strength and skill with weapons. War in this system of international law is a relationship of one order to another order, and not from order to disorder. This relationship of order to disorder is "civil war."

The non-partisan witnesses that belong to such a duel of a war between states can only be the neutrals in an interstate international law. Hitherto existing interstate international law found its real guarantee not in the content of some concept of justice or in any objective principle of division, not in an international legal consciousness that showed itself to be absent during the world war and at Versailles, but rather – again, in full harmony with the foreign policy interests of the British *Reich*[245] – in

---

* Hans Lammers (1879–1962) was a German lawyer and the head of the *Reich* Chancellery in Nazi Germany.

† Wilhelm Stuckart (1902–53) was a German lawyer and the co-author of the Nuremberg Laws.

the equal weight of states. The decisive conception is that the power relations of the numerous states, great and small, will continually balance one another out, and that a coalition of the weak will always automatically come about against those stronger powers that possess overwhelming force and, therefore, endanger international law. This wavering, continually shifting equal weight that manifests itself from case to case and is, therefore, extremely flexible, can occasionally actually amount to a guarantee of international law if enough strong neutral powers are found. The neutrals become in this way not only the non-partisan witnesses of the duel of war, but also the real guarantors and guardians of international law. In such a system of international law, there exists just as much real international law as there exists real neutrality. Not by coincidence does the Geneva League of Nations have its seat in Geneva. The International Permanent Court resides in The Hague for good reason.[246] But neither Switzerland nor the Netherlands is a strong neutral party that could defend international law with its own strength in a serious case. If there are no longer strong neutral parties, as was the case during the last world war from 1917–18, then there is, as we have experienced, no longer any international law.

International law as it existed until now rested, further, on the unarticulated, but still fundamental and centuries-long genuine presupposition that the equal weight that guaranteed international law hinged around a weak European middle. This international order could only truly function when many middling and smaller states could be played off against one another. The numerous German and Italian states of the eighteenth and nineteenth centuries became, as Clausewitz illustratively said, the smaller and medium weighing stones that were at one moment tossed into this, at the other moment that, tray on the weighing scale to balance out the great powers. A strong political power in the middle of Europe must destroy an international order so constructed. The jurists of such an international law could, therefore, claim and, in many cases, really believe that the world war directed against a strong Germany from 1914 to 1918 was a war of international law itself, and that the apparent annihilation of Germany's political power in 1918 was "the victory of international law over brutal violence." It is necessary and in no way unjuristic for not only historical-political but also legal analysis and research to reflect on this state of affairs if one wishes to correctly comprehend the contemporary turning point of the development of international law. After all, today, in light of a new and strong *Deutsches Reich*, that very same conceptual world directed against a strong *Deutsches Reich* will be newly mobilized in the Western democracies and in all of the countries influenced by them. Strictly "scholarly" journals of international law put themselves in the service of these politics and work towards the moral and juridical preparation of a "just war" against the *Deutsches Reich*. The essay by J.W. Garner,* "The Nazi proscription of German professors of international law," that appeared in the January 1939 issue of the *American Journal of International Law* is a particularly astonishing document in this regard.

German jurisprudence has, as I have said, undertaken a most meaningful push towards making a real law of nations out of the mere interstate order in recent years. Norbert Gürke's *Volk und Völkerrecht* (Tübingen, 1935), the first systematic draft of a new international law built upon the concept of *Volk*,[†] must be named above all as a positive scholarly achievement in this direction. But it is obviously not possible – nor is it Gürke's vision – to simply make an inter-*Volk* order out of the hitherto existing interstate order. Through doing so, the old interstate order would only be supplied with new substance and new life through the concept of nation. A substantial concept of nation would take the place of an internally neutral, abstract concept of state, but the systematic structure of the obsolete order of international law would be retained. This would, in the end, amount only to a blood transfusion into the same old veins; only an upgrade or replenishment of the old law of states into an international law. However correct and of however great service this new push may be, two points of view should not, I believe, go unregarded.

The first point of view concerns the elements of order of international law that lie behind the hitherto existing concept of state as an organizationally determined eminence. "State," in the sense of the order of international law, assumes in any event a minimal standard of organization, calculable functioning, and discipline. I do not want to go into the controversy led by Reinhard Höhn,[‡] who decisively and logically determines the state to be an "apparatus," while others use different conceptions, such as the state as a "form" or as a "figure." Let us content ourselves with Gottfried Neeße's[§] formulation that the state is fundamentally an organization, the nation fundamentally an organism. Apparatus and organization are, however, as Höhn undoubtedly knows, in no way "unspiritual" things. The modern coexistence of different nations, especially of great or even threatened nations, demands a strict and disciplined organization in the authentic sense of the word. This coexistence demands a minimal standard of inner consistency and secure calculability. High spiritual and moral qualities belong to this standard, and far from every nation measures up to this minimal standard of organization and discipline. The

---

* James Wilford Garner (1871–1938) was an American political scientist.

† In German: *Volksbegriff*. "*Volk*" is a German word meaning "people" in the collective sense that also retains strong connotations of biological and racial nationalism.

‡ Reinhard Höhn (1904–2000) was a German jurist.

§ Gottfried Neeße (1911–87) was a German jurist.

struggle in international law against the concept of state would miss its goal if it did not do justice to the achievement of organization that was fundamental to the hitherto existing concept of state. Even if this was problematic in reality, it was always demanded in principle. A nation incapable of being a state in this purely organizational sense cannot be the subject of international law. In early 1936, it became evident that Abyssinia was not a state. Not all nations are in the position to withstand the test of ability that is the creation of a good modern state apparatus, and very few nations are up to a modern war run on the basis of their own organizational, industrial, and technical powers of achievement. Central to the new order of the earth and, with it, the capability of being a subject of international law of the first order, belong not only "natural" characteristics (in the sense of those purely given by nature) but also conscious discipline, increased organization, and the ability to create the apparatus – an apparatus that can only be managed through a great outpouring of human mental power – of a modern polity from a nation's own power, and for this nation to hold this apparatus securely in its own hand.

The second point of view concerns the elements of order of international law that lie within the state as a spatial order. Every concept of an upholder or subject of an order of international law that is to be usable must contain, besides a personal determination (belonging to a state or nation), the possibility of territorial demarcation. Even the most extreme English pluralists recognize this side of the concept of state. G.D.H. Cole,* whose views in this regard are perhaps more authentic than those of the most cited author for English pluralism, the Jew Laski, says, for example that the state as "political body" is "an essentially geographical grouping."[247] In lieu of further remarks, I would like to draw the reader's attention here to a symptom of great import: the modern technical overcoming of space through the airplane and radio has not had the consequence in international law that airspace be treated according to the analogy of the free seas (as was first suspected, and as one should have expected following several other analogies, some of which were quite important). More than this, the concept of the territorial sovereignty of the state in atmospheric space has markedly become the foundation of all regulations of the international flight and radio system in existence to date. This is curious and practically grotesque from the technical point of view, especially with respect to territorially small states when one considers how many "sovereignties" a modern airplane would be subject to when it flies over many small states in a matter of a few hours. The situation becomes especially ridiculous when one considers what should become of the many state eminences through whose airspaces

---

* George Douglas Howard Cole (1899–1959) was an English historian and economist.

the electric waves that circle the earth's atmospheric space pass without interruption in a matter of seconds. As can be seen from these situations, the overcoming of the old, central concept of state in international jurisprudence is now long past. Some important positions have already been taken regarding this problem. In Germany, we have not paid sufficient attention to the extent to which a theory represented in England has used just this modern technical development to overcome the state and, in doing so, directly establish a universalistic world law, be it upheld by the Geneva League of Nations or by other organizations. In doing so, this theory makes the overcoming of the state in the universalistic sense plausible. J.M. Spaight in particular has used such considerations in many writings[248] to advance the idea that modern technical development, especially air forces, will supersede wars between states, that the air force will so suffice to maintain the world in tranquility and order that wars between states will stop by themselves, and that eventually only civil wars and wars of sanction shall remain as options. Such constructions, which often make a great impression, show that the problem of a new spatial order can no longer be disregarded by international jurisprudence. And yet a totally new element of spatial order has still not been articulated clearly enough in the concept of nation – a concept which overcomes the mere nation-state idea of the nineteenth century – to the extent necessary for the hitherto existing interstate order to be overturned.

The measures and standards of our conceptions of space have indeed fundamentally changed. This is of decisive significance for the development of international law. European international law of the nineteenth century, with its weak European middle and the Western global powers in the background, seems to us today a miniature world standing in the shadow of giants. Today, we think planetarily and in *Großräume*. We recognize the inevitability of the coming spatial planning schemes of which both Ministerial Director H. Wohlthat and *Reichsleiter* General Ritter von Epp* have already spoken.[249] In this situation, it is the task of German jurisprudence to escape from the false alternative of, on the one hand, the merely conservative maintenance of the interstate way of thinking that has prevailed until now and, on the other hand, a non-stately, non-national overreach into a universalistic global law as carried out by the Western democracies. It must find between these two the concept of a concrete great spatial order, one that corresponds to both the spatial dimensions of our picture of the earth as well as our new concepts of state and nation. For us, this can only be the juridical concept of the *Reich* – *Reich* as a *Großraum* order ruled by certain ideological ideas

---

* Franz Ritter von Epp (1868–1946) was a German military officer and spokesman for the recovery of German colonies.

and principles, a *Großraum* order that excludes the possibility of intervention on the part of spatially foreign powers and whose guarantor and guardian is a nation that shows itself to be up to this task.

With the introduction of the concepts *Reich* and *Großraum*, the relevant question of whether "international law" only concerns the relationships between these *Reich*s and *Großräume*, or whether international law is only the law of those free peoples living within a common *Großraum* immediately raises itself – assuming that developments really do tend towards the *Reich* and towards the *Großraum*. Obviously, *four* different kinds of conceivable legal relations emerge: first, between *Großräume* as wholes, since these *Großräume* should of course not be hermetically sealed blocks; rather, economic and other forms of exchange, and, in this sense "global commerce," should take place between them; second, inter-*Reich* relations between the leading *Reich*s of these *Großräume*; third, inter-popular relations inside of a *Großraum*; and finally – under the stipulation of the non-interference of spatially foreign powers – inter-popular relations between peoples of different *Großräume*. The designation "international" is applicable to all of these relations owing to that term's elasticity and multiplicity of meaning. Besides all of this, it should go without saying that the expressions and vocabulary relating to *Großräume* will be clarified, and that handier, more eloquent expressions will be found. The worst source of errors for the foreseeable future will lie in the simply transference of terms and concepts referring to states, from the purely inter*state* international law to the two relations between and inside *Großräume*. I would especially like to point out this danger, which may be hazardous to fruitful discussion.

Although scholarly work will still be necessary in order to secure our very specific concept of *Reich*, its foundational position for a new international order is as little debatable as its unique nature. This unique nature of the concept of *Reich*, standing as it does between the old state order of the nineteenth century and the universalistic goal of a global *Reich*, is recognizable and differentiable from these other legal orders. When I presented my report on "The Turn to the Discriminating Concept of War" to the Division for Legal Research of the Academy for German Law at their fourth Annual Conference, the political situation of the time was fundamentally different from that of today. Then, the concept of *Reich* could not, as is happening now, have been raised to the center point of the new international law. In a discussion that followed that report, the question was raised of what I had to replace the old state order that was really new, since I, at the time, neither wanted to remain with the old concepts, nor subject myself to the concepts of the Western democracies. Today, I can give the answer to that question. The new concept of the order of a new international law is our concept of the *Reich*, which proceeds from a *völkisch Großraum* order upheld by a nation. In it, we have the core of a new way of thinking about international law, one that proceeds from the concept of nation and thoroughly permits the elements of order in the concept of state to exist. It is, further, a way of thinking about international law that is capable of doing justice to the spatial conceptions of today and the real political vital forces in the world of today; a way of thinking that can be "planetary" – that is, that thinks in terms of the globe – without annihilating nations and states and without, as does the imperialistic international law of the Western democracies, steering the world out of the unavoidable overturning of the old concept of state into a universalistic-imperialistic world law.

The concept of a *Deutsches Reich* belonging to the upholders and designers of a new international law would earlier have been a utopian dream, an international law built upon the *Reich* but an empty legal fantasy. Today, however, a powerful German *Reich* has arisen. From what was only weak and impotent, there has emerged a strong center of Europe that is impossible to attack and ready to provide its great political idea, the respect of every nation as a reality of life determined through species and origin, blood and soil, with its radiation into the Middle and East European space, and to reject the interference of spatially alien and un*völkisch* powers. The action of the *Führer* has lent the concept of our *Reich* political reality, historical truth, and a great future in international law.

VI. Reich *and Space*

The concept of the *Großraum*, which was first established in the context of economic-industrial-organizational development,[250] took little time to gain acceptance in international legal thought and met little resistance. The changes in the spatial dimensions and standards of today are too conspicuous and above all too impactful for the pre-war conceptions to be maintained. In light of the current domination of the Baltic Sea through the German Navy and the *Luftwaffe*, who would seriously want to repeat again the helpless argumentation about permissibility or impermissibility with which many attempted to solve the problem of "naval blockage" during the world war of 1914–18? Who wants to measure the new zones and spatial delineations claimed by both the states conducting war (as danger zones of all kinds), as well as by states not conducting war (as security zones), with the measures and spatial conceptions of the pre-war era?[251] Everyone is familiar with the decisive, all-determining position that must be attached to the concept of "efficacy" in international law: the occupation of territories under no one's rule, military occupation, coastal blockages, naval blockage, recognition as a war-conducting party, government, and state. Should a typically situationally and technically bound concept like "efficacy" remain tied to a technology that has been made obsolete a hundred times over? However convulsively the hitherto existing positivism of international law has strived in the service of the status quo, this positivism has led itself into an *ad absurdum* through the development of effective mastery of space that has come to light in the current war. The spatially revolutionary effect of the *Luftwaffe* is especially strong in this regard. With respect to a practical problem hitherto unrecognized by international law, such as the darkening of neutral territories neighboring the area of operations of the *Luftwaffe*, one would be better served by developing a non-anachronistic right of neutrality than to apply the art of interpretation to pre-war treaties. Indeed, I would like to make another wide-reaching claim here: while one formerly sought to determine analogies for the wartime and peacetime law of airspace through analogies from the law of the sea and of the ocean,[252] future developments seem to me to trend in a direction where the norms and concepts deciding the law of the sea will come from the law of airspace. For the sea, after all, is today not, as the authors of international law of the eighteenth and nineteenth centuries still supposed, an "element" inaccessible to human mastery; it is on the contrary a "space" of the most comprehensive human mastery and effective projection of power.

When *Reich*s collapse and parties battle for new orders, the structure of the system of international law attached to those old *Reich*s appears with a clarity that is easy to grasp. When these *Reich*s collapse, those second and third coats of paint of a subaltern positivism that distracted from the core question – which is always also a spatial question – peel off. The basic concepts that rule and uphold every system of international law, *war* and *peace*, become visible in the concreteness of their era, and the specific conception of the globe, of a spatial division of the earth, that characterizes every system of international law becomes fully evident. The centuries-long tradition of a sort of geopolitical claustrophilia in the spatial concept of the German state, which was almost always like that of a small or medium-sized state, obstructed the horizon of international law for us until now. This timid approach is rendered obsolete today with the same speed with which the great military and political events take their course and bring about the victory of the realization that not states, but rather *Reich*s, are the real "creators" of international law.

The state centricity of the earlier continental-claustrophilic school of thought on international law expressed itself above all in the fact that the spatial picture of this international law was oriented towards the concept "state territory." State territory is that piece of the earth's surface (along with the airspace lying above it and the underground space beneath it, down to the middle of the earth) that is exclusively and uniformly subjugated to the "authority of the state." We hardly need to treat the various theories and constructions of the theory of state territory.[253] At any rate, this theory's image of the earth appears as follows: the globe is either solid land (and then either already an actual state territory or a territory without a ruler accessible to acquisition through the occupation of a state authority – potential state territory, in other words) or free sea, whereby the freedom of the seas fundamentally exists due to the fact that the sea, the open ocean, is neither actual nor potential state territory. The great spatial problems of geopolitical reality, spheres of interest, claims to intervention, bans on intervention for spatially foreign powers, zones of all kinds, spatial delineations on the high seas (administrative zones, danger zones, blockades, naval blockages, convoys), problems of the colonies (which are, indeed, "state territory" in a totally different sense and in a totally different form than the motherland), protectorates of international law, dependent countries – all of these categories fell victim to the non-discriminating either-or of "state territory or not state territory?" The border became a mere line. The possibility of actual (not only domestic) border zones and intermediary zones is excluded from this state-centric way of thinking about territory.[254] Even neutral buffer states whose entire *raison d'être* was as a border zone and those intermediary zones, which thank their existence to the agreements of *Reich*s, are treated as sovereign states on the same level as these very same *Reich*s that permitted them to exist. The fact that there are in reality many unique, neither intra-state nor purely extra-state formations between the closed state territory and the – if I can call it thus – non-state nothing in international law, the fact that not only the territorial eminence of the state but also *spatial eminence* of various kinds belongs to the reality of international law – all of this was falsely construed by the simple either-or of interstate and intra-state, similarly to how the dualism of interstate and intra-state law failed to construct any kind of overarching coherence.[255] But as soon as *Reich*s rather than states are recognized as the bearers of the development of international law and the formation of law, state territory ceases to be the only spatial conception of international law. The state territory then appears as what it in reality is – as only a case of a possible spatial conception of international law – and indeed, a case formerly assigned to the once absolute concept of state, which has since been relativized through the concept of *Reich*. Other spatial concepts that are today indispensable include, above all, soil, which is to be ordered first to the nation in a specific way, and then to the *Großraum* of cultural and economic-industrial-organizational radiation that reaches out over the *national soil* and the *state territory*. To reiterate this following the recent misunderstandings of a further exposition on this topic:[256]

the *Reich* is not simply an expanded state, just as the *Großraum* is not an expanded minor space. Nor is the *Reich* identical with the *Großraum*, although every *Reich* has a *Großraum*. The *Reich* stands both over the state as characterized through the exclusivity of its spatially characterized state territory as well as over the national soil of an individual nation. A construction of power without this *Großraum* arching over state territory and national soil is not a *Reich*. In the hitherto existing history of international law, which in reality is a history of *Reich*s, there was never such a *Reich* without a *Großraum*, even when the content, structure, and consistency of *Großräume* were different in different eras.

The international law of the previous century was an intermediary and transitory construction between the old Christian-European international law that arose in the sixteenth century and a new order of space and nation that is gradually emerging today. The Congress of Vienna of 1814–15 still thought Europe-centrically.[257] After 1856 (the date of the admission of Turkey to the family of nations), international law formally ceased to be a European-Christian international law. Since 1890, the Europe-centric image of the earth has dissolved into a non-differentiating "international law."[258] This Europe-centric vision of the world took its first blow through the Monroe Dispatch of 1823. The Paris *Diktat*s of 1919 amounted to its ultimate collapse. In our time, 1940, however, an order of space and nations begins to emerge. In the intermediary time, the leading *Reich*s of hitherto existing international law, England and France, attempted to lead the old Europe-centric system further without being up to the task of a European order. The old Europe-centric system of international law rested upon the differentiation in international law of a *European* space of states of fully valid state order and implemented peace from a *non-European* space of free European expansion. The non-European space was without a master, uncivilized or half-civilized, an area of colonization, an object of the seizure of holdings through European powers that became *Reich*s through the fact that they owned such overseas colonies. *The colony is the basic spatial fact of hitherto existing European international law.* All *Reich*s of this system of international law had a *Großraum* available for expansion: Portugal, Spain, England, France, and Holland in their overseas colonies,[259] the Habsburg monarchy in the Balkans with respect to the holdings of the Ottoman *Reich* (which did not belong to the community of international law), the Russian *Reich* both with respect to Ottoman holdings as well as territories in Siberia, East and Middle Asia. Prussia was the only great power that was only a state, and the only great power that, if it became spatially larger, could only do so at the cost of neighbors who already belonged to the European community of international law. Because of this, it was easy to attach the reputation of peace breaker and brutal state concerned only with power to Prussia, even though its space was small and modest in comparison with that of the other *Reich*s.

The Western powers England and France were the leaders of this system of European international law. The concept of *Reich* hung, insofar as it was not a continuation and *translatio* of the Roman or *Deutsches Reich*, on overseas holdings. The first person to discover a concept of *Reich* determined by overseas wealth was not, as is commonly supposed, Disraeli, when he combined the crown of the King of England with the title of the Emperor of India in 1876 (to which Fascist Italy responded by combining not the title of the Emperor of Rome but that of the Emperor of Ethiopia with the Italian royal throne.)[260] Rather, already at the beginning of the new division of the earth in the early sixteenth century, after the conquest of Mexico, the Spanish conquistador Hernán Cortés suggested to the German Emperor Charles V that he name himself Emperor of his new Indian holdings because this title was better justified than that of Emperor of Germany.[261] This title of Emperor as connected to overseas colonial holdings may only be a symptom, but if so, it is an important and powerfully demonstrative symptom both for the image of space and for the concept of *Reich* of hitherto existing European international law as led by France and England.

The decisive meaning of the overseas colony for international law lies in the fact that the concrete reality of the concepts *war* and *peace* of hitherto existing international law could only be understood on the basis of this image of space. One must always be reminded of the fact that international law is a law of war and peace, *jus belli ac pacis*. The time-specific, spatially specific, concrete and specific reality of war and peace, vary though it may throughout different historical epochs, as well as the just as concrete and specific mutual relation of these two conditions, forms the core of every order of international law and every coexistence of organized nations in spaces, divided up as they may be. What was the peace of the European international law as apparently upheld by states from 1648 to 1914? How is a peace and, with it, an international law, possible between sovereign states, each of whom claims a free right to war left to its own sovereign decision? It goes without saying that the coexistence of such sovereign institutions of power proceeds not from a substantially given actual peace, but rather from the continual permissibility of war. This means that the peace here is only "not war."[262] But such a peace is possible for only so long, such a situation built upon a mere construction like "not war" is bearable only so long as war is not total. War as presupposed in the earlier system of European international law was, in reality, only a partial war, be it a cabinet war of the eighteenth century, be it a war of combatants – a tradition that held fast in the following era until 1914. This is the core of this international law. The important and unique fact (often mentioned in recent years) that the concept of war of this hitherto existing international law had to leave the question of the justice of a war alone, the fact that it was a "'non-discriminating' concept of war" belonged to the partial, non-total war.

The significance of the turn to the discriminating concept of war and towards total war has since been recognized.[263] The degree to which the earlier parceling up and relativization of war was achieved in international law through spatial methods has, however, not yet been made sufficiently clear. The method of a policy of equal weight belongs to these methods. This was a policy that, while it has often been debated and treated in monographs,[264] has not yet had its connection with the partial concept of war recognized, since international jurisprudence had lost all sense of spatial thinking. In connection with the fact that the colony was the foundation of hitherto existing European international law, an entire series of special formations of international law still have to be considered with great attention, even if they have remained disregarded by most Continental thinkers owing to the state-centric microspatiality of their thinking. One of these is an interesting – not only historically but rather generally interesting – fact: the express or tacit union of "*amity lines.*" Such lines delineate, to take the example of the sixteenth century, a not yet pacified space for the reckless struggle for power regulated in such a way that the mutual violations of law and inflicting of damages on both sides that play out inside the delineated space ("beyond the line") do not amount to a basis for war for the European relations of the colonial powers. Nor should they disturb European treaties and the European peace.[265] "Amity lines" lie, if in different spatial forms and in a carried-over way, at the foundation of every system of international law. As early as the eighteenth century, one can find numerous reversed examples of this fact: European wars were to have no effect in the colonies. In other words, the colony should be the pacified space and Europe the battle arena. The well-known and, in recent years, often cited determination of Article 11 of the Berlin Congo File from February 26, 1885, according to which the areas named in the Congo File should be regarded as neutral and as belonging to a non-war-conducting state, is one of the later examples of this development and the shifting of "amity lines." Numerous declarations of neutrality (Switzerland, Belgium, Luxembourg) and "independence" declarations of the nineteenth and twentieth centuries had the meaning of spatial delineations and bracketings, most often in the service of a policy of equal weight corresponding to the interests of the British world *Reich* – a policy whose primary foundation was a certain division of colonial world holdings.

The France that was totally defeated twice – after the coalition wars lasting more than 20 years from 1792 to 1815 and after the terrible defeat

of 1870–1 – could continue to exist as a European great power in such
a system. Even the bloody wars of this era were not total in the sense of
a struggle for final existence, since the upholders of this international
law had available sufficient free space in the colonies in order to rob
their mutual confrontations in Europe of a genuine existential severity.
Bismarck left the possibility of colonial expansion in Africa and East
Asia open to defeated France in 1871 out of a sense of European responsibility. But during the nineteenth century this free space gradually
closed. The significance of the Monroe Dispatch from 1823 lies mainly
in its creation of a *Großraum* with a ban on intervention. However, it is
also very important because it represented the first closing-off of a large
area from European colonialization. With the Monroe Doctrine there
appeared the first non-European *Reich*. The admission of Turkey to the
European community of nations as carried out by England amounted to
a further restriction, with which the English policy of the support of "sick
men" first outside and after 1919 also inside Europe began. In 1905, the
second non-European *Reich* appeared with Japan. At the same time, the
new European great powers, the *Deutsches Reich* and Italy, were held at
bay from the division of extra-European colonial ownership or fed with
colonial scraps while England and France divided North Africa, a land
without a ruler, between themselves (1882–1912), whereby Egypt was
allocated to England and Morocco to France. In doing so, the powers
of the old European international law unified themselves at the cost of
a third in the style of times past and on the foundation of the splitting-
up of overseas holdings. The further development as was determined
through the Paris *Diktat*s of 1919 and their legitimation through the
Geneva League of Nations is well known. The defeated European
power, Germany, was robbed of her colonies. Here, it becomes clear
once again that the colony was the basis of hitherto existing European
international law. Germany's exclusion from extra-European colonial
possessions was her real defamation and disqualification as a European
power. During the League of Nations' operations against Italy (1935–6)
and during the Spanish Civil War (1936–9), the total helplessness of
England and France was revealed in Geneva and in the London non-
intervention committee. One could no longer find sensible and effective
"amity lines" and delineations of enmity. Today, the Western powers of
England and France are paying the price of their inability to integrate
Europe's new and growing nations into the system of international law
they led and to realize a just "peaceful change" with genuine lines of
friendship. They are atoning for their guilt not only with the collapse
of their former global power, but also with the collapse of a system of
international law that rested upon them as the leading *Reich*s and a
spatial division of the earth created by them; a system that they, blinded

by victory and a lust for ever more possessions in 1919, have themselves destroyed.

VII. The Concept of Space in Jurisprudence

Ten years ago, the talented economic historian and professor at the Sorbonne, Henri Hauser,* published several lectures that he had given in England under the title: *Modernité du XVI siècle.*[266] He saw the "modernity" of the sixteenth century, a phenomenon that he even called a "*préfiguration*" of the twentieth century, in the fact that a political, moral, intellectual, and economic revolution had then already introduced the democracy of the nineteenth and twentieth centuries. For Hauser, meanwhile, the Counter-Reformation of the seventeenth century amounted to a step backwards. Hauser's treatise thus became an apology for the political system of the liberal democratic Western powers and for the status quo of Versailles. This learned author did not remark in 1930 that the modernity of the sixteenth century was totally different from both his interpretation and the meaning of "modernity" in the sense of the political system of the Western democracies. The genuine modernity of that past era lay namely in the fact that the spatially revolutionary shift of the medieval picture of the world as introduced in the sixteenth century and scientifically perfected in the seventeenth century offers us today the possibility of comparison in order to better and more thoroughly analyze today's change in the image of space and spatial conceptions. The change in the concept of space is underway today in all areas of human inquiry and activity with powerful depth and breadth. The great geopolitical events of the present, too, contain at their core such a change in hitherto existing conceptions of space and presuppositions of space that the only useful historical comparison we have for them is that shift in the planetary picture of space that took place 400 years ago.

The word "*Großraum*" should serve the end of bringing this change to scholarly awareness. This word stands, in spite of its current popularity, above all mere everyday political and journalistic trends, above the shifts in mere fashion that otherwise determine the fate of slogans and catchphrases. That said, a precise scholarly clarification is necessary in order to hinder misunderstandings and misuses, and to clear the way for a fruitful and consistent use of the term in theory and praxis.

One may not hold against the term "*Großraum*" the objection that it only combines the spatial conception "great" with the concept "space" and, therefore, only constitutes a spatial characterization of an expanded space with the help of a purely superficial comparative determination of

---

* Henri Hauser (1866–1946) was a French historian and economist.

scope and size. "*Groß*" here contains a meaning that is more than merely quantitative and mathematical-physical. From a linguistic point of view, this is totally permissible and indeed common practice. In many phrases involving the word "great" – "great power," "great king," the "great" revolution, the "great" army, etc., for example – the word amounts to a qualitative escalation and not an increase in the sense of mere expansion. Still, the conceptual formation, the term "*Großraum*," also contains a transitory character insofar as it proceeds from "space" and seeks to change and to overcome that word's hitherto fundamental essence. A general and indeterminate conception of space open to any character-lending determination is maintained, and yet at the same time conceptually taken to another level. One cannot, therefore, avoid the fact that "*Großraum*" is often interpreted as a mere negation of "minor space."* "*Großraum*" in that case becomes a merely negative, a merely comparative determination. It remains in that case in a conceptual and objective dependence on the concept of space that it itself seeks to negate and overcome. Such misunderstandings are unavoidable concomitants of every transition period. I mention these only to avert the danger of chatter and drivel that is especially great here. As soon as the earth has found its secure and just division into *Großräume*, and as soon as the various *Großräume* stand before us in their inner and outer order as solid eminencies and forms, other, more eloquent designations will be found for these new things and find acceptance. Until then, however, the word and concept of the *Großraum* remains an indispensable bridge from the obsolete to the future conceptions of space; from the old to the new concept of space.

Großraum is, therefore, not a space that is only greater compared to a relatively smaller space; it is not an expanded minor space. The merely mathematical-physical-natural scientific neutrality of the hitherto existing concept of space should now be overturned. "There is," as Ratzel† says, "already something greater – I would almost say creative and inspirational – in the wide space."[267] The addition of the word "great" should and can *change the conceptual field*. This is of decisive significance for jurisprudence, especially for conceptual formation in international and state law, since all linguistic and, therefore, all juridical concepts are determined through the conceptual field and coexist and grow in turn with their conceptual neighbors. Every juridical concept is subservient to what Ihering‡ has named the "pre-demand of its conceptual neighbors." The degree to which a word is determined in its conceptual meaning

---

* In German: *Kleinraum*.

† Rudolf von Ihering (Jhering) (1818–92) was a German professor of law.

‡ Friedrich Ratzel (1844–1904) was a German geographer who coined the term "*Lebensraum*."

through such a field of meaning is already long known in the linguistic sciences.[268] The mutual determination of concepts through their systematic conceptual connection is most illuminating. Words like: space, soil, land, field, areal, grounds, area, and district are not more or less arbitrarily exchangeable and only "terminological" nuances. Every concept can be most securely understood and, in case of need, refuted, on the basis of its own standpoint,[269] and "topography" is, unfortunately, a terribly neglected branch of jurisprudence. The shift in the field of meaning that the word "*Großraum*" effects as opposed to the word "space" lies above all in the fact that the mathematical-natural scientific and neutral field of meaning hitherto understood by the concept "space" is abandoned. Instead of an empty dimension of area or depth in which corporeal objects move, there appears the connected *achievement space* belonging to a historically fulfilled and historically appropriate *Reich* that brings and bears in itself its own space, inner measures, and borders.

The interpretation of space as an empty dimension of area and depth corresponded to the so-called "spatial theory" dominant until now in jurisprudence. This theory indiscriminately interpreted land, soil, territory, and state territory as a "space" of state activity in the sense of an empty space with linear borders. The theory transforms house and court from a concrete order into a mere entry on the land register's sheet. It turns the state territory into a mere *district* of administration or rule, an area of competence, an administrative parish, a sphere of competence, or whatever the various formulations are called. "The state is nothing more than a nation organized onto a certain areal for law": this is the definition that Fricker,* the founder of this spatial theory, has erected, one which has become dominant through Rosin,† Laband,‡ Jellinek,§ Otto Meyer,¶ and Anschütz.[270]**

Four factors accounting for the rise of this hitherto dominant spatial theory must be examined. First, its political-polemical direction: it wanted to reject certain earlier interpretations of the ground, namely all patrimonial and feudal conceptions of objects that turned the ground into a sort of private property, be it of the prince, be it of the state conceived of as a juridical person. This spatial theory thus represents an expression of the political development towards the constitutional state based on the

---

* Carl (Karl) Victor Fricker (1830–1907) was a German jurist and professor. Schmitt is referring to his *Gebiet und Gebietshoheit: mit einem Anhang: vom Staatsgebiet* (Tübingen: Laupp, 1901).

† Heinrich Rosin (1855–1927) was a German-Jewish jurist and professor.

‡ Paul Laband (1838–1918) was a German-Jewish jurist and professor.

§ Georg Jellinek (1851–1911) was a German-Jewish legal philosopher and a professor.

¶ Otto Meyer (1846–1924) was a German scholar of administrative law and French civil law.

** Gerhard Anschütz (1867–1948) was a German scholar of constitutional law.

foundation of the separation of public and private law, of imperium and dominium. In private law, the concrete conception of space is abolished through the fact that all landed property becomes property attached to a "plot of land." In public law, the state territory becomes a mere "stage of the imperium." Zitelmann's* famous formulation had its great success at the end of the nineteenth century. Today, it is easy to recognize that this still complete formulation stands under the influence of Baroque and representative concepts that thought of the soil of a nation as a sort of theater stage on which the play of public, state, exercise of power was performed. Alongside that inner political-polemical and this Baroque conception of the stage there takes effect, as the third factor, the positivistic-natural scientific conception of the empty space as a completely universal – in other words, not specifically juridical – category. All that is perceivable as an object and, therefore, every legally meaningful circumstance becomes a mere "appearance" in the categorical forms of space and time. The objective core of such theories of space and their presentation of evidence is always the same: law is the legal command. Commands and orders can only be directed towards humans. Rule is exercised not over things but only over men. State rule can therefore only be personally determined, and all spatial determinations are of legal significance only because those facts of a case regulated by the norm are, like every perceivable occurrence, determined spatially and temporally. That which is specifically legal, the concrete order, is thus turned into a universal form of knowledge and perception without any content.

It is precisely here that the Jewish influence comes forward as a fourth factor alongside these three factors – partly constitutionally determined and partly determined through the natural sciences – that determine the development of juridical spatial theories. The degree to which Jewish authors, whose opinions are otherwise associated with diverse and often opposed theories and scholarly directions, suddenly and unanimously drive forwards towards the empty conception of space is obvious to anyone who immerses himself in the study of the last phase of development of these theories of state territory. Among the jurists I will name only Rosin, Laband, Jellinek, Nawiasky,† Kelsen and his students; among the philosophers and sociologists, Georg Simmel, who declares every other conception of rule and territory besides that of one determined on the basis of ruled *men* as "nonsense." The real misunderstanding of the Jewish people with respect to everything that concerns soil, land, and territory, is grounded in its style of political existence. The relation of a nation to a soil arranged through its own work of colonization

---

* Ernst Zitelmann (1852–1923) was a German jurist and law professor.
† Hans Nawiasky (1860–1961) was a jurist of Austrian and Lithuanian-Jewish provenance.

and culture and to the concrete forms of power that arise from this arrangement is incomprehensible to the spirit of the Jew. He does not, moreover, even wish to understand this, but rather only to conceptually seize these relations in order to set his own concepts in their place. "*Comprendre c'est détruire*," as a French Jew once betrayed of himself.* These Jewish authors have of course as little made the hitherto existing spatial theories as little as they have made anything else. But they were here an important fermenting agent in the dissolution of concrete, spatially determined orders.

Considerable attempts towards overcoming this empty space can be found in the writings of German jurisprudence.[271] The founder of a new science of space, Fr. Ratzel, has already recognized that "*coming to terms with space*" is "the defining trait of all life."[272] But the comprehensive effect and the genuine depth of new conceptions of space appear even more convincing when we become aware of the overcoming of the hitherto existing natural scientific, so-called classical conceptions of space, especially in areas of work in the natural sciences. For it is in these areas that the degree to which the seemingly eternal "classical" categories were just a reflection of their time can be seen in its proper light. The empty, neutral, mathematical-natural scientific conception of space gained acceptance at the beginning of the contemporary political-historical epoch (which is also the contemporary epoch in terms of state and constitutional law) – in other words, in the sixteenth and seventeenth centuries. All the intellectual streams of this era have made their contribution in different ways: Renaissance, Reformation, Humanism, and Baroque; the changes in the planetary picture of the earth and world through the discovery of America and the circumnavigation of the world; the changes in the astronomical picture of the world as well as the great mathematical, mechanistic, and physical discoveries – in a word, everything that Max Weber designated as "Occidental rationalism" and whose legendary era was the seventeenth century. It was here that – to the same degree that the concept of the state became the all-ruling concept for the order of the European continent – the conception of the empty space gained acceptance; an empty space, that is, filled with corporeal objects (and through the objects, sensory perception.) The perceiving subject in this empty space registers the objects of its perception in order to "localize" them. "Movement" occurs before the subject through a change in the subject's standpoint. This conception of space reached its philosophical highpoint in the aprioriality of Kantian philosophy, where space is an *a priori* form of knowledge.

The scientific changes to this conception of space also deserve our special consideration. Max Planck's quantum physics abolishes space

---

* It is unclear whom Schmitt is citing here.

by reducing every event of movement into individual, periodic material waves and therefore leads into wave mechanics. According to these new mechanics, every individual material point of the system is, in a certain sense, at every position of the entire space available to the system.[273] Even more meaningful for our new concrete concept of space are the biological investigations in which, going beyond the space-abolishing problematization of the concept of space, another concept of space has found acceptance. According to this theory, "movement" for biological knowledge does not proceed in the hitherto existing space of natural science; rather, movement *produces* the spatial and temporal arrangement. The spatial as such is produced only along with and in objects, and the spatial and temporal orders are no longer mere entries in the given empty space; they correspond, rather, to an actual situation, an event. It is now that the conceptions of an empty dimension of depth and a merely formal category of space are conclusively overcome. Space becomes an achievement space.

These formulations, for which I have the important work of the Heidelberg biologist Viktor von Weiszäcker to thank,[274] can also be fruitful for our spatial problem in jurisprudence. A universal designation such as "space" remains a common comprehensive concept for the various conceptions of space of different eras and nations for reasons of practical understanding. And yet all of today's efforts towards the overcoming of the "classical" – that is, empty and neutral – concept of space lead us towards a connection fundamental for jurisprudence, one that was very much alive at great points in German legal history, and that the dissolution of law dissolved into a state-referential legal positivism: namely, the connection of concrete *order* and *positioning*. Space as such is, of course, not a concrete order. Still, every concrete order and community has specific contents for place and space. In this sense it may be said that every legal institution, that every institution contains its own concepts of space within itself and therefore brings its inner measure and inner border with it. House and court belong in this way to clan* and family. The word "peasant" (*Bauer*) comes, from the perspective of legal history, not from the action of agriculture but rather from construction (*Bau*), building (*Gebäude*), just as "*dominus*" comes from "*domus*." "City" (*Stadt*) means "site" (*Stätte*). A "*Mark*" is not a linear border, but rather a spatially determinate border zone. "Property" (*Gut*) is the upholder of a rule on property (*Gutherrschaft*), just as the "court" (*Hof*) is the upholder of court law (*Hofrecht*). "Country" (*Land*) is (in distinction from, for

---

* In German: "*Sippe*," a word meaning "family" or "clan," depending on the context. It originally referred to Germanic clans or confederations that were bound not by blood but by oath or treaty, but was later picked up rhetorically during the 1930s and 1940s as a *völkisch* term for family.

example, forest or city or sea) the legal organization of those people building on the country and those ruling the country with their spatially concrete order of peace.[275] Otto von Gierke has shown in his history of the German concept of the corporation[276] the degree to which the legal conceptions of the German Middle Ages were primarily spatial conceptions, or, as he expresses himself, "juridical-qualified, spatial-tangible units." This is above all true for the "city." While *"civitas"* in Roman law meant the compiled collection of persons, of *"cives,"* of citizens, in other words, the medieval word *"civitas"* proceeds from locational meaning as a translation of city, castle, or settlement (*Wiek*), and the Latin word for citizen is therefore sometimes even *civitatensis* instead of *civis.* A word like "peace," which since the nineteenth century has become in part an emotionally vague, in part an intellectually abstract term, always resides in the concept of order of the German Middle Ages as a locational and therefore concrete concept: as peace of the house, peace of the market, peace of the castle, peace of the thing, peace of the church, peace of the land. A concrete localization is always bound to the concrete order.

Of course, these considerations should not be taken as a recommendation to return to medieval conditions. Today, a different way of thinking must be overcome and abolished: the spatially shy way of thinking and imagining that came to rule in the nineteenth century, that today still generally determines the formation of juridical concepts. This way of thinking was oriented towards (from the point of view of geopolitics) the terrestrially foreign, and therefore shoreless universalism of the Anglo-Saxon rule of the seas. The sea is free in the sense of being free of states – free, in other words, from the singular conception of the spatial order of legal thinking, which is oriented towards the state.[277] On land, however, the tendency of positivistic thinking about laws to refer exclusively to the state has juridically smoothed over a wonderful gap of lively spatial arrangements into a true *tabula rasa.* That which called itself a "spatial theory" in the course of the past century is the complete opposite of that which we today understand under the same term. The concept of the *Großraum* serves us well to overcome the monopolistic position of an empty concept of state territory and to raise the *Reich* to the decisive concept of our legal thinking in both the spheres of constitutional and international law. This development is bound up with a renewal of legal thinking, one which may again interpret the old and ancient connection of order and positioning for institutions; a renewal of legal thinking that can restore to the word "peace" its content, to the word "homeland" the character of a species-determining fundamental distinguishing characteristic.*

* In German: *eines artbestimmenden Wesensmerkmals.*

The International Crime of the War of Aggression and the Principle "Nullum crimen, nulla poena sine lege" (1945)

Notes on the Text

The following text was originally dictated by Schmitt to his secretary Anni Stand at Schmitt's residence in the Schlachtensee neighborhood of Berlin in the summer of 1945. The text was intended as a legal memorandum for Friedrich Flick (1883–1972), a leading German industrialist. As far as can be established, Flick, who was arrested in the south of Germany by American officers on June 13, 1945, had read while in American custody an article in the July 15, 1945 issue of *The Stars and Stripes Magazine* to the effect that Justice Robert Jackson intended to try "leaders of industry and finance" at the upcoming war crimes trials to take place that fall. At the same time, the June 6, 1945 Jackson Report, which included plans to try "persons from financial, economics, and industrial circles" as well as "industrialists" was widely reported in the German press. Konrad Kaletsch (1898–1978), a colleague and representative of Flick, accompanied by the jurist Karl Tillman, contacted Schmitt at some time in late June to prepare a legal memorandum for Flick's defense against the charge of "conspiracy to commit aggressive war" before the International Military Tribunal. Schmitt did so and attached to his memorandum an English-language "note," presumably directed at the American judges; I have made minor corrections of punctuation and orthography to this note. Kaletsch paid Schmitt approximately 10,000 *Reichmark*s in the summer of 1945 for his services and later reimbursed Schmitt for an additional 1,000 *Deutschmarks* in 1951. However, Schmitt's memorandum was never used in the trial: Flick was ultimately tried not before the IMT for conspiracy to commit aggressive war but rather in the so-called "Flick Trial" for war crimes and crimes against humanity and sentenced to seven years in prison before being released in 1950.

The basis for this translation is the 1994 edition of *Das*

internationalrechtliche Verbrechen des Angriffskrieges und der Grundsatz "Nullum crimen, nulla poena sine lege," published in Berlin by Duncker and Humblot and edited by Helmut Quaritsch. That text is based on Schmitt's final draft of the memorandum, located in the Nordrhein-Westphalian State Archive in File 265–124, Number 18. Quaritsch provides an extensively researched and exhaustive back history to the memorandum in his edition of *The International Crime of the War of Aggression* on pages 125–47.

Introduction: The International Crime of War in its Particularity As Opposed to War Crimes (Violations of the Rules of the Laws of War and Crimes Against Humanity, Atrocities)

A great number of circumstances different from one another not only externally and in the details, but also in a fundamental way, in their legal structure, are designated by the term "war crime." The difference between them is not merely theoretical. It immediately assumes the greatest practical significance when it concerns the juridical execution and the character of a trial. Then the legal difference of the circumstances becomes relevant in all relevant points, as well as in the questions of material justice: what are the elements of the crime? Who is the perpetrator? Who is the accomplice, accessory, and abettor? The same is true for questions concerning the process: who is the plaintiff? Who the defendant? Who is a party? Who is the judge and the court, and in whose name is the judgment issued?

All of these questions have a specifically different meaning in the different circumstances. The meaning and the success of the trial depend on the correct answering of these questions. Not the law and justice, but rather only the criminal stands to gain from their obfuscation. Here, two kinds of war crimes should first be excluded from the discussion:

1) Violations of the rules and customs of war, which are primarily committed by members of the armed forces of a state conducting war. This concerns breaches against the so-called law *in* war, the *jus in bello* – for example, violations of the Hague Conventions, of the norms of the naval laws of war, of the rights of wartime prisoners, etc. Such laws presuppose war to be permitted and legal. They must fundamentally change if war itself is banned or even becomes a crime. But the exclusion of these kinds of war crimes causes no fundamental difficulties because their unique nature is recognizable without further explanation. When "war crimes" were spoken of before 1914, in general only this kind of delict was meant. This kind of delict has long been known and discussed in the realm of penal laws and military instruction of the states conducting war

and in the literature of international law, and indeed, both as concerns the assumptions as well as the legal consequences (reprisals, liability for damages, legal responsibility of the perpetrator towards his own and the opposing state). Moreover, the meaning of the military order as a ground for justification or exculpation has often been discussed for these delicts.*

Articles 228–30 of the Treaty of Versailles (Article 173 of the Treaty of Saint Germain, respectively, the other Paris Peace Treaties) are concerned with this kind of war crime in the sense of violations of the *jus in bello*. The settlement of these peace treaties contains, only in a certain regard, an innovation with regard to recognized international law as valid before 1914 – namely, insofar as the defeated state obligated itself to deliver its own subjects who were war criminals to the adversarial state. One should incidentally notice here that in spite of this distinctive feature in Articles 228–30, the contractual basis for the delivery of one's own national subjects is retained. Moreover, the principle "*nullum crimen sine lege*" remains guaranteed, even with respect to the assumptions of these delicts (acts of violation of the laws and customs of war) as well as with respect to the punishment and the degree of punishment (punishments laid down by law).

The further course of the punishment of the war criminals of the First World War, especially the later proceedings before the German *Reichsgericht* in Leipzig, can be presupposed as known.[†]

2) The second kind of war crimes that must be distinguished here are of a fundamentally different nature. These are atrocities in a specific sense, planned killings and inhuman atrocities whose victims were defenseless humans. They are not military actions, although they stand in a certain connection with the war of 1939, because they were committed either in preparation for or during this war, and because they are characteristic expressions of a certain inhuman mentality, expressions that finally

---

* For a textbook treatment with bibliographical references, one finds the typical treatment of these questions in Josef L. Kunz' book, "*Kriegsrecht und Neutralitätsrecht*," Vienna, 1935, 35ff.; Alfred Verdroß' "*Die völkerrechtswidrige Kriegshandlung und der Strafanspruch der Staaten*," Berlin, 2920, contains an especially solid monographic analysis and deepening of this question.

† Following the First World War, the Western Allies presented the leadership of the Weimar Republic with a list of 854 suspected German war criminals, among them many prominent army officers, who were to be extradited and tried outside Germany. Due to immense public outrage in Germany and an unwillingness on the part of the Allies to risk war again in order to extradite these Germans, the Western Allies agreed to task the German *Reichsgericht* (the highest court of the German *Reich*) with the trial and sentencing of these individuals. Only nine of the original named suspects were ever actually tried, and all of these individuals were either released as innocent or sentenced to probation. One major reason for the failure of the trials was an insufficient pool of evidence to successfully convict the suspects, which the Allies themselves seemed to have recognized: they eventually narrowed their list of suspects down to 45 names.

culminated in the world war of 1939. The rawness and bestiality of these crimes transcends normal human comprehension. They are parts of and manifestations of an iniquitous "*scelus infandum*" in the full sense of this word. They explode the framework of all the usual and familiar dimensions of international law and penal law. Such crimes proscribe the perpetrator in his or her entirety by placing him outside the law and making him or her into an outlaw. The order of a superior cannot justify or excuse such crimes; it can, at the most and under certain circumstances, give occasion to raise the question of whether the perpetrator found him or herself in an emergency in light of this order and whether the emergency excuses him or her. By no means can the fact of the abnormality of the crimes become an object of a discussion that turns away from the monstrosity of these crimes and that diminishes any consciousness of their abnormality. I will point to the singularity of this kind of war crimes, the real "atrocities" and the "*scelus infandum*" quite often in the course of my analysis, and in a note in the conclusion I will refer to a point of view whose heeding seems to me necessary for the clarification of the legal situation.

Many further differentiations are conceivable within both kinds of war crimes mentioned above – violations of the *jus in bello* and the real atrocities. These, however, do not yet need to be developed and worked through. Due to the fact that the unique nature of both of these categories has been succinctly foreshadowed, now the legal specificity of the third, and here most interesting, kind of war crime should emerge clearly enough.

3) War crime in the third sense of the word is the war of aggression, which is interpreted as a crime as such, and moreover as a crime against international law. Here, war itself is a crime, and here one is really concerned not with a war crime but rather, more exactly, with "the crime of war." The interpretation of war as an international crime represents, both in respect of international law as well as penal law, not only something new compared to the previous legal status, but something novel. Without a doubt, every sovereign state prior to this point had a *jus ad bellum* according to hitherto existing, recognized international law, without there being a distinction between a war of aggression and a war of defense. The criminalization of the war of aggression in international law held – if one looks past earlier statements of interest only to intellectual history – practical interest only since the First World War and the Paris Peace Treaties. In the period from 1920 to 1939, the efforts towards the strengthening and activation of the Geneva League,* the

---

* Schmitt is referring here to the League of Nations.

discussions on the so-called Geneva Protocol of October 2, 1924, and, finally, certain interpretations of the Kellogg Pact from August 27, 1928 fundamentally contributed to the unusual intensification of the idea of treating the war of aggression as an international crime. As a result of this, the question naturally arises: whether at the time of the outbreak of the Second World War, in the summer of 1939, the criminalization of the war of aggression as such in international law had already so prospered that the war of aggression as such was to be seen not only as a postulate and a program – in other words, not only, in a universal sense, *de jure condendo* – but also as an international crime established by recognized law. This meaning under consideration is of the viewpoint "*nullum crimen, nulla poena sine lege.*"* Therefore, a short analysis of the practical meaning of this principle is necessary.

I. The Practical Meaning of the Principle "Nullum crimen, nulla poena sine lege"

Neither in previously existing international law nor in previously existing penal law was the war of aggression as such an act threatened with criminal punishment. It is, at the least, doubtful whether the international criminalization of the war of aggression, as claimed by the American side, had already been implemented by the summer of 1939. The war of aggression as an international crime is, therefore – unlike other kinds of war crimes – in any event a new crime. As a result, the first criminal convictions issued on account of this crime will have to confront the clause: "*nullum crimen, nulla poena sine lege.*" This universally and internationally recognized clause contains the clear prohibition of recognizing a criminal punishment if the act was not threatened with punishment at the time of its perpetration.

Every jurist remembers the great indignation that arose throughout the world, inside and outside Germany, when the National Socialist regime, through the *Lex van der Lubbe* of March 29, 1933, introduced the possibility of an execution of the death penalty through hanging for van der Lubbe, even though his alleged or actual crime was threatened with another form of death penalty at the time of its perpetration.† Article 13 of the *Strafgesetzbuch* determined that the death penalty was to be carried out through beheading. The prohibition of retroactive

---

* No crime, no punishment without law.

† A 1933 law applying post facto punishments to German penal law. It made execution rather than imprisonment, and execution via hanging instead of the guillotine, possible for certain crimes, and expanded the range of prison terms. The law had a retroactive effect of almost two months.

penalties was referenced here not to the penalization itself but rather to the way the punishment was to be executed. The indignation of international public opinion on this occasion was so strong that van der Lubbe was, on Hitler's orders in the summer of 1933, not hung but rather executed with an axe. I can further recall the great international discussions that arose on the occasion of the introduction of the new Article 2 to the *German Penal Law Book*, when through the law passed on June 28, 1935, the analogy in penal law was declared permissible and a creation of justice according to law *and* popular sentiment was permitted for penal decisions. Here, the point is not to recognize these legal alterations of the National Socialist regime as concerns their objective content. The uproar they created in public opinion still remains in memory and shows that the clause *"nullum crimen sine lege"* is universally recognized. Later, in the case of the speed trap law of June 22, 1938, when a street robbery committed by means of a speed trap at any date after January 1, 1936 was threatened with the death penalty,* the same sense of outrage was repeated, although perhaps not to quite the same degree. This, however, was due to the fact that one had, by 1938, become used to viewing Hitler's regime as an abnormality outside all conceptions of justice in the civilized world.

Considering this universal conviction and these historical facts, it is at first remarkable that today's circumstances, for which there have to this point existed no positive threat of punishment, should be treated as a crime, even as a crime worthy of death, according to the very same side that brought the clause *"nullum crimen sine lege"* into the debate with such decisiveness. I speak here, as I said before, not of the other kinds of war crimes, but rather exclusively of the new international crime of the war of aggression as an "international crime." In light of the controversial character of such a new crime, some jurists may tend towards seeing in the mere mention of the clause *"nullum crimen sine lege"* a solution to the problem and an argument for the legal impermissibility of a penalty. Jurists of Continental European penal law oriented towards positive penal law will tend especially towards this conclusion. In contrast to this, one nonetheless has to observe that while the principle *"nullum crimen"* is universally recognized, it is represented through its application in extraordinarily different ways by Continental European, English, and American praxis.

---

* A law targeted at a pair of notorious Berlin criminals, Max and Walter Götze, who had repeatedly robbed couples in parked cars and had robbed several motorists by posing as policemen running a speed trap. The law specified the death penalty with a retroactive effect of two and a half years.

1) The distinctive feature of the *Contintental European* way of thinking is characterized by the fact that it interprets the word "*lex*" in the phrase "*sine lege*" in the positive sense of a written, formally promulgated, penal law issued by the state. This interpretation has become so self-evident to the average jurist of the European Continent over the course of the past two centuries that he is, to a man, hardly aware of the possibility of other interpretations. As law on the European Continent became a written, positive, state law with legal codifications as the typical form of appearance of all law, the requirements that were tied to the principle of "*nullum crimen*" became more acute in connection with the development of the *Rechtsstaat*.* The development of French law became here the example for most of the remaining Continental countries. This development begins with Articles 7 and 8 of the Declaration of Rights of Man and Citizen of 1789, where it is declared:

> 7. *Nul homme ne peut être accusé, arrêté, ni détenu que dans les cas déterminés par la loi, et selon les formes qu'elle a prescrites.*
> 8. *et nul ne peut être puni qu'en vertu d'une loi établie et promulguée antérieurement au délit et légalement appliquée.*†

In the German states, this interpretation became dominant first and foremost through Anselm von Feuerbach, the founder of modern German penal jurisprudence. I mention his name because the formulation of the clause "*nullum crimen*," common around the world today, is not of ancient Roman legal origin, nor of English heritage, but rather comes in this version from Feuerbach, and first appeared in his textbook (1801). Numerous written constitutions and legal determinations, among them Article 2 of the German *Strafgesetzbuch* of 1871 and Article 116 of the Weimar Constitution, articulate the same thought in the same legal positivist interpretation. The positivization of the concept "justice" to a state law goes here so far that only a written law can penalize an act. Every instance of common law attempting to found or intensify a penalty, and even every analogous application of determinations of penal law attempting to found a penalty, is forbidden. The positive law that founds a punishment must therefore threaten discrete punishments if it is to be correct in the sense of the legal state. In this way, the clause "*nullum crimen*" contains, according to the Continental European

---

* Legal state, constitutional state, as opposed to a state with arbitrary rule.
† 7. No person shall be accused, arrested, or imprisoned except in cases and according to the forms prescribed by law.
  8. . . . and no one shall suffer punishment unless it be legally inflicted in virtue of a law passed and promulgated before the commission of the offense.

interpretation, a triple prohibition: it bars not only the retroactive application of penal laws, but also any common law attempting to found or intensify a punishment as well as any analogous application from existing penal law.

2) Under the *English* interpretation, the ban on the retroactive enforcement of penal laws fundamentally goes without saying. It has often even been claimed in respected textbooks and commentaries that the clause "*nullum crimen*" is of English origin and is a result of a specifically English way of legal thinking. The clause is most often traced back to the Magna Carta of 1215, although here it is irrelevant for most people as to whether this traditional opinion stands up to a legal-historical critique. I dare to bring the wording of the Magna Carta back into memory:

> *Nullus liber homo capiatur vel imprisonetur aut discceisiatur aut utlegatur aut exuletur aut aliquo modo destruatur nec super eum ibimus nec super eum mittemus nisi per legale judicum parium [suorum] vel per legem terrae**

The "*lex terrae*" is the Law of the Land, the English common law. In the Institutes of Coke, an influential work of 1628 typical for the English legal conviction, the "*lex terrae*" (the Law of the Land) is translated as "due process of law." The clause "*nullum crimen*" thereby becomes a component of the sweeping formulation of the "due process of law," from which, besides the prohibition of the retroactive application of penal laws, still further assurances for the defendant can be derived. Locke, who is important for the further development of thinking for the legal state, emphasizes that a judge's judgment may rest only on closed rules (settled standing rules), and that a punishment is only permissible "with such Penalties as the Law has established." Locke's influence in England, on the European Continent, and in the United States of America was unusually large. He also conveyed the fundamental prohibition of ex post facto laws into the consciousness of all modern jurists.

In this way, there has arisen an accordance of numerous concepts and formulae between English and Continental European law with respect to the phrase "*nullum crimen sine lege*" that could easily lead one to the conclusion that the distinctiveness of the English way of thinking has been disregarded. But it is precisely here that the difference between Continental and English legal thinking is especially important. I will return to the central meaning of the clause "*nullum crimen sine lege*,"

---

* No free man shall be arrested or imprisoned or disseized or outlawed or exiled or in any way victimized, neither will we attack him or send anyone to attack him, except by the lawful judgment of his peers or by the law of the land.

with a few additions. While legal practice and jurisprudence on the Continent consider the written, exactly formulated, state law to be the normal form of appearance of the law, English law, especially English penal law, has fundamentally and overwhelmingly remained common law – customary law, in other words. There may be numerous individual statutes, but there are no penal legal codifications that bar common law. Common law is by its very nature customary law and is carried out and developed through precedent-setting cases decided by judges. The conception lying at the bottom of it all is, in principle, still medieval: law is fundamentally not made but rather found in the judicial decision of a case. The precedent does not, therefore, create new law; rather, it only brings a somehow already present law to light. There is, indeed, in this sense, no new law. The new and creative essence of a precedent lies in the unveiling of that which, veiled though it may have been before, was already in existence.

The customary and legal character of the common law reveals its entire difference from the positive law-centric legal thinking of Continental European jurisprudence through the case of penal law. While Continental European jurisprudence rejects any customary law that creates a new punishment and declares impermissible penalizations through customary law, English penal law is, in its entirety, fundamentally common law. With this, it is stated that the precedent that establishes legal punishment constitutes punishability not in the sense of a "penalizing" penal law that creates a punishment; rather, the precedent unveils and establishes punishability. But how can new penalizations of new circumstances be possible with this approach? The answer is through a "constructive" approach with the help of argumentation – one that the jurist of Continental European law would perceive not as "positive penal law," but rather as natural law. Mention of "natural justice," "practical expediency," and "common sense," serve such argumentation. The possibility for "constructive" case law and so-called "creative precedents" rests on such a *rationes decidendi*.

According to an old formulation that also comes up in traditional English jurisprudence, all punishable acts are either "*mala in se*" or "*mala prohibita*." Hascal R. Brill's Encyclopedia of Criminal Law (Chicago, 1922, p. 852) states the following:

> Crimes *mala in se* include all breaches of the public peace or order, injuries to person or property, outrages upon public decency or good morals and willful and corrupt breaches of official duty.

In the case of a "*malum in se*" the purely unveiling character of the precedent is clear without further discussion. No new crime is established here; rather only something which was a crime for every healthy, human sense of justice always and at all times is designated as such, even if the circumstances appear to be new and unheard of. In contrast to this, the "*mala prohibita*" are made into punishable acts first through positive legal regulations, through statutes and are "not otherwise wrong." Such statutes are therefore very carefully designed. For these statutes, the clause "*nullum crimen sine lege*" may occasionally apply in such a strict interpretation that the legal positivist of Continental penal law would perceive it as artificial and sophistic. The interpretation of the words "stealing horses" in the statute Edw. VI c. 12,38 is a classic example of this.[278] This is totally different from the "*mala in se.*" For a traditionally common law-oriented way of thinking, the problem of "*nullum crimen*" is here not present and is in principle incomprehensible. The legal positivistic interpretation of Continental European jurists depicted above means, in the eyes of a jurist working with "natural justice," nothing else than the transformation of all crimes into mere "*mala prohibita.*"

3) The *American* interpretation is overwhelmingly determined by the English common law, but is not simply identical to it. The influence of Continental European ideas is immediately apparent. The United States has a written constitution. It recognizes written law as well as written penal law to a totally different extent from English praxis. The influence of Locke's and Montesqiueu's thoughts is extraordinarily strong and has its effect in a Continental European way. In numerous declarations of human rights of American states – Maryland, North Carolina, Massachusetts, New Hampshire – the ban on the retroactive power of laws, especially penal laws, is solemnly declared, and, in this way, has even become an exemplary model of the aforementioned French declarations from 1789:

> That retrospective laws, punishing facts committed before the existence of such laws, and by then only declared criminal, are oppressive, unjust, and incompatible with liberty, wherefore no ex post facto law ought to be made. (Maryland XV)

Even in the light of such formulations, one cannot disregard the fundamental difference of the positive concept of law and Anglo-Saxon common law. Nonetheless, a pronounced sense of the opposition between positive legality on the one hand and moral legality, one based on natural law and its forms of convictions on the other hand, can be seen in the thought of American jurists. The intellectual landscape of the United States is, on this point, an indecisive mirror image of the European set of problems and especially of the great antithesis that separates Continental and English thought. The ban on the retroactive power of penal laws is completely self-evident as a principle for the American sense of justice and American legal thinking.

But here, perhaps still more sharply than for English legal thought, there arises even in the American interpretation the question of what constitutes a novel crime. Such questions often consequently lead to a connection and blending of moral and juristic points of view. To the thinking of the Continental jurist schooled in positivist thought, the separation of moral and juristic points of view is, even in the question of punishment under new circumstances, familiar. In the United States of America, the connection between the two viewpoints could effect such a situation that the restraints arising from the principle "*nullum crimen sine lege*" would be even less effective than for a jurist of the purely English tradition.

4) It is apparently Mr. Jackson's intention to use the current war criminal trials as an especially effective creative precedent for the new international crime of the war of aggression.* One cannot refute this plan with a general reference to the principle "*nullum crimen.*" It is, rather, necessary to develop the inner problematic of the new crime and to show that while the points of view of a creative precedent and a "*malum in se*" may well apply to crimes against humanity – in other words, for the real atrocities – they do not apply for the new international crime of the war of aggression. The atrocities in the special sense that were committed before the last world war and during this war must indeed be regarded as "*mala in se.*" Their inhumanity is so great and so evident that it suffices to establish the facts and their perpetrators in order to ground criminal liability without any regard for hitherto existing positive penal laws. Here, all arguments of natural sensation, of human feeling, of reason, and of justice concur in a practically elemental way to justify a conviction that requires no positivistic norm in any formal sense. Nor must one enquire here as to the extent to which the perpetrators had a criminal intent. All of this goes without saying. Whoever raises the objection of "*nullum crimen*" in the face of such crimes, whoever would want to refer to the hitherto existing positivistic penal legal determinations would put himself in a suspicious light. If the particular inhumanity of such atrocities were not covered in the hitherto existing circumstances prescribed by positive laws, this can be explained by way of the answer that an ancient lawmaker gave when someone asked him why he had not included patricide as a particular delict in his penal law. The celebrated lawmaker

---

* Robert Jackson (1892–1954) was an American Supreme Court Justice and prosecutor at the Nuremberg Trials.

responded that one cannot even name such abominable crimes and may not articulate their mere possibility.

All of this refers, however, only to the kind of war crimes that have been designated above as atrocities, and it cannot be repeated often enough that our task here is not to strip these atrocities of their justified punishment, or to discuss their punishability. For another kind of war crimes, the "war crimes" in the old sense, the clause "*nullum crimen*" has already been expressly stressed by the American delegates in the Commission of *responsabilités* at the Paris Peace Conference of 1919. I will cite these arresting statements below (p. 139). But the case is completely different in the case of the third kind of war crime, the new crime of the war of aggression as an "international crime," which is in question here. Here, both the elements of the offense (act of aggression and war of aggression) as well as the connection of international and criminal character are indeed a novelty whose unique character must be brought to awareness in order to show that the principle "*nullum crimen*" must amount here to a restriction on punishment, especially if the viewpoint of equity, of common law, and of a penal justice based on precedents is to be maintained. This will become clear as a result of the following detailed presentation.

II. War Crimes and War Guilt in the Treaty of Versailles

The most important approaches to a new concept of war tending away from previous international law are to be found in two articles of the Treaty of Versailles: in Article 227, which charges the former *Kaiser* Wilhelm II, and in Article 231, the so-called War Guilt Article. Both refer, in their positivistic, contractual formulation, only to the First World War from 1914 to 1918. Yet they must be regarded as symptoms of a change, if not a precedent, in the interpretation of war in international law. Along with Article 227, Article 228 should be included for reasons of the history of the origin of these articles, although this article, as already mentioned, speaks exclusively of war crimes in the old sense of the word, while Article 227 contains this new kind of war as a crime.

1) *Article 227*, directed against the former *Kaiser* Wilhelm II, stands under the heading "Penalties" in Part VII of the Treaty of Versailles. Here, the qualification of a punishable act is already consciously articulated through the heading.

Acting as the *plaintiffs* are "the allied and associated powers," not only the five major powers. Whether every individual power or rather several powers or all powers together are the plaintiffs is not said. They publicly charge the *Kaiser* through the peace treaty itself. The *Kaiser* is *the only* *defendant* and is named personally ("Wilhelm II of Hohenzollern, former *Kaiser*"). The *Kaiser* remained, then, the only defendant to this new kind of international crime, even though the *Reich* Chancellor, Bethmann-Hollweg, publicly declared in 1919 that he assumed full responsibility for all of the *Kaiser's* acts of office undertaken during his Chancellorship (1914 until 1917).* None of the plaintiffs responded to this explanation of the constitutionally responsible *Reich* Chancellor. The charge remained personally limited to the head of state because of the new war crime.

The "supreme offense against international morality and sanctity of treaties" is given as the *facts of the case* of the crime on the basis of which the charge is raised. Moreover, the court receives guidelines in Article 227, Paragraph 3: the court should be led by the highest motives of international policy, and here "international policy" and not "international law" is stated in consciousness of the fact that hitherto existing law does not recognize this crime. Further, the court should show respect for the solemn commitments of international undertakings. Five judges should serve as the *court*: each of the allied and associated main powers, which are, however, not noted here as main powers, names one judge.

With respect to the *procedure*, it is said that the defendant will be accorded the fundamental guarantees of the right to a defense ("assuring him the guarantees essential to the right of defense"). With respect to the *punishment*, it is stated that the court shall determine the punishment that it holds to be appropriate ("the punishment which it considers should be imposed.")

It was no hard task at the time to criticize and refute Article 227, both according to previously existing international law as well as with respect to principles of penal law. Existing international law did not recognize an international jurisdiction of one state over another state or over the head of state of another sovereign state. *Par in parem non habet jursdictionem.*† The lone legal subject of international law, even with respect to a delict of international law, was according to the dominant view, the state as such. A delict of international law therefore in no way amounts to a crime in the criminal sense as occurs in domestic penal law. War in all its severity was interpreted as a relation of state to state, not one of individuals to individuals or of groups to groups. War was, as far as international law was concerned, led not by individual men, or personally by the head of state, but rather by the state as such. As regards the facts of the case of the new crime, this was specified most indeterminately in Article 227. The guidelines for the judge referred to morality and politics rather than

---

* Theobald von Bethmann Hollweg (1856–1921) was the *Reich* Chancellor from 1909–17.
† An equal has no jurisdiction over an equal.

exclusively to law. The punishment was uncertain and left entirely to the discretion of the judge. It was seemingly assumed that the court in any case would impose a punishment, so the decision of the judge was already anticipated through the accusation itself. The principle *"nullum crimen, nulla poena sine lege"* was clearly violated. Through the naming of a specific individual person, Wilhelm II, as well as through the uncertain facts of the case and an indefinite threat of punishment, Article 227 received the odium of an all too personal exceptional justice.

It is, therefore, easy to explain the fact that this approach to an international criminalization of the war of aggression in Europe left no lasting effect on the legal consciousness of the European peoples and governments. The entire occasion of this attempt to bring Wilhelm II, the former *Kaiser*, before an international court on account of an international crime was quickly forgotten by the public opinion of European nations. Already in 1920 the English and French governments had practically abandoned the realization of this attempt.

Wilhelm II remained in a neutral state, in Holland, from November 1918 onwards. The Dutch government rejected the demands for extradition that the English and French governments had made as impermissible according to international law. Both of the named governments did not insist further on extradition.* The conviction must have spread, at least in Europe, that the approach contained in Article 227 creating a new kind of war crime had not only remained unsuccessful but also had become a sort of precedent for the opposing view.

But what about the United States of America? In the consultations of the Paris Peace Conference, it was indeed American delegates who with great insistence described the war of aggression as a great injustice. Admittedly, such statements stand decisively in contrast to other statements that stress the fact that war as such was, according to hitherto existing international law, not an illegal act. The confusion became even greater because the different legal aspects of the case – the punishment of Wilhelm II, the punishment of violations of the law of war, and the problem of reparations – could give occasion to speak of war crimes in a universal sense. I will make a few remarks on the war guilt article, Article 231, in the following text (under 2).

First, the statements in the *"Commission des responsabilités des auteurs de la guerre"* are of interest here.† This commission dealt both with what

---

* Both of these Allied notes to the Netherlands from January 15 and February 14, 1920 as well as the answer notes of the Netherlands rejecting these notes of January 21 and March 2, 1920 are published in *Das Diktat von Versailles*, ed. Fritz Berber (Essen: Veröffentlichungen des Deutschen Instituts für außenpolitische Forschung, 1939), 1195–202.

† *La documenation internationale. La Paix de Versailles*, Vol. III: *Responsabilités des auteurs de la guerre et sanctions* (Paris, 1930).

was to become Article 227, the punishment of Wilhelm II, as well as
with Article 228, the punishment of the earlier discussed war crimes
in the old sense. With reference to the latter, the American delegates,
under Lansing's leadership,* declared with all due severity against the
English and French representatives that it was impermissible to speak of
a punishment of the violation of the laws of war next to a punishment
of the violation of laws of humanity. They referred to the precedent of
Henri Wirz from 1865. The case concerns the proceedings of a military
tribunal carried out by a military tribunal commission in Washington
against a prison commander from the southern states after the ending of
the war of secession, proceedings that ended in November 1865 with a
death sentence against this officer and his execution. The American delegates emphasized that for such war crimes – that is to say, for violations
of the *jus in bello* and for their punishment – the principle "*nullum crimen
sine lege*" must be steadfastly valid. They also mentioned the precedent
of *USA v. Hudson* (7 Cranch 32) from 1812, which stipulated that an act
is designated as a crime and threatened with punishment through the
legislative power of the union, and that further, this legislative power
must have designated the responsible court if a court sentencing is to be
deemed permissible. Insofar as this concerns war crimes in the old sense,
the American delegates rejected the concept of a new crime against
humanity. "The American delegates," so it says in an explanation of this
consultation, "recognize no written international law and no state treaty
that makes an international crime designable and punishable by the
competent court out of a violation of the laws and customs of war." The
explanation continues:

> As the American delegates have remarked more than once, war has always
> been and is still inhuman by virtue of its very nature. But the acts that cor-
> respond to the laws and customs of war are not subject to any court in spite
> of their inhumanity. A court concerns itself only with valid existing law,
> it applies only this law in its findings, and turns over to a higher judge the
> misdeeds against morality and acts that run contrary to the principles of
> humanity. The American delegates have the very certain feeling that the plan
> towards the creation of an international penal court is worthy of no further
> attention: there is no precedent for it, and it does not correspond to the
> customs of nations.

Such explanations are clear and decisive. But they refer *in concreto* not
to Article 227, but to Article 228, and are therefore not directly useable
for the question of the war of aggression as such, but rather only for war

---

* Robert Lansing (1864–1928) was the American Secretary of State from 1915–20.

crimes in the old sense. In light of Article 227, indeed, it was precisely the American delegates who demanded a punishment for the heads of states as well as a punishment of the war of aggression as a moral crime against mankind. The typically American interpretation to be found in the *Commission des responsabilités des auteurs de la guerre* is to be found in the following, a draft from March 12, 1919:

> *Le droit moral de faire la guerre existe seulement lorsqu'il y a nécessité impérieuse d'employer la force pour la protection de la vie nationale, le maintien du droit national ou la défense de la liberté et de l'humanité.*
>
> *La guerre inspirée par tout autre motif est arbitraire, inutile, et s'accomplie en violation de la morale et de la justice internationale. Elle ne peut être justifiée.*
>
> *Jugée d'après ce critérium, la guerre commencée en 1914 était injuste et inadmissible. Ce fut une guerre d'agression.*

A longer explanation on the responsibility of heads of state connects to this:

> The heads of the Central Powers [this is in the original text], animated by the wish to obtain the possession of land and the sovereign rights of other powers, have allowed themselves into a war of conquest, a war that exceeds all other wars of modern times in its scope, its unnecessary destruction of human lives and property, its grim horrors and its unbearable suffering. The evidence for this moral crime against mankind is convincing and conclusive. Held back by an esteem for the law that is inseparable from the feeling of justice, the nations that had so gruesomely suffered could not have the power to appropriately punish the guilty through the means of the law. But the instigators of this shameful war should not go into history without having been branded. They should be cited before the bounds of world opinion in order to suffer the judgment that humanity articulates against the instigators of the greatest crime ever committed against the world.

A conscious deviation from the hitherto existing interpretation of war is clearly articulated in such explanations. However, here one speaks not of a universal criminalization of the war of aggression but rather of a moral crime against humanity, a crime that only the heads of state and no one else have committed. For an appreciation of the effect of precedent here, one should also observe that the explanations of James Brown Scott* and Lansing concern "internal" statements in a consultation not intended for the public, and that such statements stand in opposition to the posi-

---

* James Brown Scott (1866–1943) was the consultant to the American delegation at the Paris Peace Conferences.

tions of other American delegates, for example, that of the later cited (p. 142) statement of John Foster Dulles on the problem of war guilt, a statement that expressly clings to the old concept of war. However, as concerns precedence, only that which has come into effect in the final treaty is relevant. In this regard, however, it is the case that the United States did not carry over this Section VII about penalties into their final decision.

As is generally well known, the United States did not ratify the Treaty of Versailles and instead signed a special peace treaty on August 25, 1921 with Germany. In Article II of this treaty are enumerated those sections of the Treaty of Versailles whose rights and advantages the United States did claim for itself: among them, Section V, VI, IX, etc. But Section VII, which contains Articles 227 and 228, in other words, war crimes, is lacking. This section was, with deliberate intention, not made an object of international relations between the United States and Germany. Any effect of precedent that might have been accorded to those statements of the American delegates in the *Commission des responsabilités des auteurs de la guerre* thus became inapplicable to Germany.

Of course, one cannot disregard here the prevalent American opinion of the time, which tended strongly in another direction. The esteemed American weekly magazine *The Literary Digest*, in the middle of 1920, posed a survey to American judges in order to ascertain their opinion on the criminal proceedings against Wilhelm II. Out of 328 responses, approximately 106 demanded the death sentence, 137 exile, 58 imprisonment and other punishments, and only 27 were against a criminal conviction. This polarity of official behavior on the one hand and public opinion on the other should not be disregarded. Just what such an opposition was to mean for the crime against international law that was the Second World War with respect to the question of *"nullum crimen sine lege"* is to be discussed later, as soon as further and important cases of this opposition have been established. In Europe, it is not possible, in any event, to observe any effect of precedent this case had, based on the behavior of the European governments.

2) The *War Guilt Article 231* of the Treaty of Versailles stands not under the heading "Penalties," but rather "Reparations" and is therefore positioned more under economic points of view than any pertaining to criminal law. It concerns financial and economic demands of the victor, which are not war reparations in the old style but rather claims for damages: in other words, legal demands that can be derived from the legal responsibility of the defeated. We need not here go into the problem of war guilt in its entirety, which, as is well known, has already been treated in an entire mass of publications of every kind. The discussions concern above

all the question of whether the Central Powers – as the Entente had already claimed in its note of January 10, 1917 – had led an unjust war of aggression and could therefore be held liable for all damages without restriction, or whether the legal foundations of the claim for reparations lie in the fact that Germany in fall 1918 had accepted Wilson's program, in particular the Lansing Note dated November 5, 1918, and that reparations were necessary only to the extent prescribed by the Note. The French delegation acted on the assumption of civil legal constructions, mentioning, for example, Article 823 of the German civil code, which cites a liability for damages caused by unpermitted acts. An Italian cited Germany's liability with reference to Article 830 of the civil code as a liability from a *societas sclericis*. These are examples of constructions based on, at the core, the idea that Germany's war was an unjust war and a war of aggression. But one cannot say here that the transformation of the war of aggression into an international crime in the full criminal-legal sense was fully intended. The allegation that the Central Powers, united together, led a war of aggression, served to expand the scope of liabilities for reparations and to reject all limitations (for example, compensation for violation of Belgian neutrality, compensation for damages to the civil population).

It is of interest to the question of the interpretation of the concept of war that in the consultations resulting in Article 231, even the American representative, John Foster Dulles, proceeded from the assumption that war as such and in its entirety is not, according to existing international law, an illegal act:

> Reparation would not be due for all damage caused by the war unless the war in its totality were an illegal act. This is by no means a conclusion which can be assumed in view of the fact that international law (see in particular the Hague Conventions) recognized the right of a nation, in the absence of a treaty engagement to the contrary, to declare and prosecute, in certain defined ways, war against another nation.

President Wilson himself was an adherent of the theory of the just war. But the legal implications that he drew from this cannot be unambiguously recognized. Even regarding the question of moral guilt for war, his standpoint is not simply one of criminal law. In his speech from October 26, 1919, he said, for example,

> that not a single fact called forth the war, but rather in the final analysis the entire European system carries guilt for the war, its entanglement of alliances and agreements, a convoluted web of intrigues and espionage that, it is safe to say, captured the entire family of nations in its meshes.

The connection of the war of aggression and the obligation of reparations was finally handled not only in the consultations of the commissions, but also, in May 1919, in a written correspondence between the German delegation at Versailles and the Allied governments. In its note, the German delegation protested against the allegation that it had been the sole initiator of the war and referred to the fact that the German obligation of reparations was based on the Lansing Note dated November 5, 1918. In response to this, the Allies emphasized that the Lansing Note contained the word "aggression" and that Germany, through its acceptance of the Note, had also recognized its *responsabilité* for the world war. In fact, the word "aggression" appears in the Lansing Note in the following context:

> Further in the conditions of peace laid down in his address to Congress of January the eight 1918 the President declared that the invaded territories must be restored as well as evacuated and freed. The Allied Governments feel that no doubt ought to be allowed to exist as to what this provision implies. By it they understand that compensation will be made by Germany for all damage done to the civilian population of the Allied and their property by the *aggression of Germany* by land, by sea, and from the air.*

Both here and also in numerous allegations of guilt in the discussion of the obligation of reparations, the question is raised: can the word "aggression" be seen in this context as a precedent for the international criminalization of the war of aggression? If one speaks of a guilt on the part of Germany and finds this guilt in the war of aggression, then it is, generally speaking, entirely possible that with this a penal guilt is meant, the pertinent facts of which represent a crime in the full criminal sense. But in the concrete case, only reparations – only economic and financial payments on the part of Germany, in other words – were up for discussion, not punishments, as in Section VII of the Treaty of Versailles. There existed in no way at Versailles a common intent to create a new crime of international law. There was no intention of abolishing a concept of war that had been recognized for 200 years, one that had determined the legal structure of all hitherto existing European international law, one with all its effects on war-conducting states and neutrals. Had that been intended, then more precise explanations would have been needed, explanations that would unambiguously express a criminalization and not merely a universal declaration of injustice. The relevant passage of

---

* The Lansing Note was Woodrow Wilson's fourth note directed to the *Reich* Chancellor Prince Max von Baden on November 5, 1918. See *Foreign Relations of the United States, 1918*, Supplement 1: *The World War*, Volume 1, 468–9.

the Lansing Note refers only to the German invasion of neutralized Belgium and to the question of the scope of reparations for the damages of the civil population. An intention to go beyond the declaration of the injustice of these proceedings and to create both a new concept of war and a new type of international crime cannot be recognized in the note.

The entire question of war guilt has been discussed since 1919 only in connection with the question of reparations. The consciousness of the discrepancy between the criminal guilt of a specific person and the responsibility of a state, which is based on only financial and economic legal consequences, had already become too widespread in the domestic law of all European countries for the discovery of a legally impermissible act that still led to the payment of damages, or for a completely new species of international crime to be introduced into European law.

Had one intended such an effect at Versailles, then the League of Nations Pact would, at the very least, have had to formally declare the war of aggression as such a criminal felony. That did not happen. As a result, the approximate precedent that could have been achieved through the determination of Germany's war guilt was immediately paralyzed. Insofar as doubts were still possible in this regard, they were decided for the European legal consciousness when the United States, in spite of the signature of President Woodrow Wilson, pulled back from Versailles after 1919 and isolated itself from Europe's political questions. In the separate peace with Germany of August 25, 1921, any reference to the question of criminal guilt was, as we have already said, deliberately avoided.

III. Development of the Penalization of the War of Aggression in International Law, 1919–1939

The two decades from 1919 to 1939 were a time of attempts towards a new order of international law. The president of the United States of America, W. Wilson, made the most important attempt at such a new order at the Paris Peace Conference in 1919, but the United States of America then withdrew from Europe and left the European nations to their own political fate. The following overview should not give an exhaustive picture of the chaotic transitional period of 1919 to 1939, but rather only answer the question of whether the attempts towards the abolishment and outlawry of war that occurred during this time would really lead to the genuine penalization of the ordinary state citizen of a European state. In other words: did these suggestions and attempts in the period from 1919 to 1939 towards an outlawry of war convince the state citizen, who did not belong to the political ruling class, of a

new order of international law? Would the ordinary businessman of any
European state have reached the conviction that the war of aggression
– as opposed to the hitherto existing, secular tradition – had been made
into a real criminal act not only in controversial projects and compromise
formulations, but also in an international "norm-ification" backed by
law? Only if the individual state citizen had come to this conclusion can
one make him responsible today as the perpetrator of or participant in
the new international crime of war.

Every state citizen, especially every businessman, knew that the question of the abolition of war was really a question of disarmament and
security. He could only judge the juridical formulations of the abolition
of war on their practical effect. The numerous controversial projects,
with their subtle distinctions, must have appeared to him as the spawn
of the lack of sovereignty among the many European states. In the difficult juristic compromise formulations he could only behold the political maneuvers of governments fighting for or against a revision of the
Treaty of Versailles. The great impression that the strong participation
of American citizens – I think here of names such as James Brown Scott,
James T. Shotwell,[*] and Hunter Miller,[†] among others – could have
made on him was stymied by the fact that the government of the United
States pursued a strict policy of neutrality and even isolation. The opposition between public opinion and the official policy of the United States
was most striking. The state citizen of a European state could only orient
himself according to official policy.

Indeed, the great attempt towards a penalization of war by international law at that time fell into a series of difficult antitheses that were
incomprehensible to the sense of justice of the ordinary citizen: in the
opposition of juristic and political ways of thinking, but also in the difference between moral and legal obligation and in the opposition between
political and economic problems. Finally, the opposition between private
presence and official absence must also not be allowed to pass unobserved
– an opposition that was characteristic for the relations of the United
States of America with Europe at this time. The following discussion
aims to keep in view the particular difficulties for the state citizen as a
European participant that arose out of this development.

1) *The Geneva Protocol of October 2, 1924.* The pact of the Geneva
League of 1919 contained prescriptions towards the prevention of war

---

[*] James Thomson Shotwell (1874–1965) was a historian, diplomat, and member of the
American delegation to the Paris Peace Conferences.
[†] David Hunter Miller (1875–1961) was an American scholar and a consultant to the
American delegation at the Paris Peace Conferences.

(Articles 10–17). The breaker of peace was the state that "resorted to war" without having observed a certain process. Financial, economic, and military measures were foreseen as sanctions against this breach of the peace (Article 16). A penalization of war as such was not mentioned. The idea of the equality of all states on the basis of equal sovereignty was still too strong in 1919 for the pact of the League of Nations to contain, even implicitly, a ban on war based on criminal law. There were, perhaps, a few attempts that could have been used towards a practical interpretation of the criminal ban on war. But the United States of America, whose influence over the Paris Conference of 1919 had triumphed, remained, as already stated, officially removed from the League.

In the years from 1920 to 1924, many attempts and suggestions were made in order to strengthen the war prevention system of the Geneva League. It did not, however, come to the arrangement that war, or certain kinds of war, should be a punishable international crime committed by certain men. For a jurist of the Continental European way of thinking, it was self-explanatory that the mere usage of the word "crime" did not amount to a penalization in the sense of the principle "*nullum crimen, nulla poena sine lege*" in international law so long as the facts of the case, the perpetrators, the punishment, and the court were not determined and circumscribed by clear wording.

In the so-called Geneva Protocol of October 2, 1924 "on the peaceful regulation of international issues," one finds the principle that the war of aggression is an international crime. In this, the concept of war as a crime found its first widely visible expression for Europe. Previously, drafts of a guarantee pact and a contract for mutual assistance had been arranged in which aggression, or the war of aggression, had been spoken of as an international crime. Still, none of these drafts was consummated as an international agreement. But neither did the Geneva Protocol come into effect. It was, to be certain, taken up as a suggestion by the 5th Meeting of the League of Nations on October 2, 1924. The following states signed it: Albania, Belgium, Brazil, Bulgaria, Chile, Czechoslovakia, Estonia, Finland, France, Greece, Haiti, Latvia, Liberia, Paraguay, Poland, Portugal, Spain, Uruguay, Yugoslavia. Only Czechoslovakia ratified (on October 28, 1924) the Protocol. It failed primarily as a result of English resistance. The declaration of the English government that was delivered by Sir Austen Chamberlain before the Council of the Geneva League on March 12, 1925, is an especially important document that should be cited below.

The Geneva Protocol of 1924 came from the initiative of a group of American citizens. Dr. James T. Shotwell, Professor of History at Columbia University, member of the American peace delegation at the Paris Peace Conference, was the speaker for this group. At its meeting in

June 1924, the Council of the Geneva League resolved to take an "action of unprecedented nature" by giving a report of this group, the so-called Shotwell Draft, to the League as an official document, the result being that a group of private "distinguished Americans" had direct influence on a resolution of the League of Nations, even though the United States itself was not a member of the League of Nations and distanced itself from all of Europe's political questions in a fundamental isolationism. This Shotwell Draft contained under the heading "Outlawry of Aggressive War" the sentences:

> Art. 1 The High Contracting Parties solemnly declare that aggressive war is an international crime. They severally undertake not to be guilty of its commission.
> Art. 2 A *State* engaging in war for other than purposes of defense commits the international crime described in Article 1.
> Art. 3 The Permanent Court of International Justice shall have jurisdiction, on the complaint of any signatory, to make a judgment to the effect that the international crime described in Article 1 has or has not in any given case been committed.

There then followed a more precise definition of the Acts of Aggression and sanctions. These were oriented primarily not towards criminal law but towards economics. Indeed, every signatory power could take steps towards sanctioning measures against the aggressor state. The guilty state was, further, to compensate the costs of other states that its aggression had caused.

The Geneva Protocol also declared the war of aggression a crime. It speaks, likewise, only of the "state" as aggressor and perpetrator of the new, international crime and respects state sovereignty – the real hindrance, to be clear, of a penalization of war in a truly criminal-legal sense. The threatened "sanctions" are economic, financial, and military, and they are directed only against the state as such. They contain nothing concerning specific initiators of the war – for example, the head of state, members of the government or further responsible persons as perpetrators of the new crime. In fact, they do the opposite. In Article 15, Paragraph 2 of the Geneva Protocol it is spelled out that the aggressor state against which such sanctions are to be carried out is on the one hand to carry all the costs of the sanctions to the fullest extent that it can do so, but on the other hand (because of the territorial guarantee given to all members of the League in Article 10 of the Geneva Pact) neither its territorial integrity nor its political independence is allowed to be impaired. According to Article 15, Paragraph 2:

Toutefois, vu l'article 10 du Pacte, il ne pourra, comme suite à l'application des sanctions visées au présent Protocole, être porté atteinte en aucun cas à l'intégrité territoriale ou à l'indépendance politique de l'État agresseur.*

Such consideration for the criminal aggressor state and its political independence would have been incomprehensible to American public opinion. Just how strongly the European governments represented in Geneva were influenced by the respect for state sovereignty shows itself here. In light of such "sanctions" that avoid any mention of a criminal punishment, a jurist of Continental European penal law will not suppose any conscious penalization nor any sufficient foundation for a criminal punishment. The "crime" that the war of aggression is designated as in such declarations is really a special kind of delict of international law. It corresponds with the hitherto existing tradition of European international law to differentiate the delict. Even the use of the word "crime" would not have meant a penalization according to previously purely domestic penal law. I will speak about a possible parallel with piracy in another separate section (under 3). But piracy is not mentioned in the Geneva Protocol.

One has to suppose that wide circles of public opinion in the United States of America considered the words "outlawry" of war and "crime" to be sufficient penalization and criminalization, even in the sense that the responsible initiators of the war of aggression could be criminally punished without further thought. Yet the facts of the case of the new crime "war of aggression" were never unambiguously explained. When one envisions today the circumstantial efforts of the Geneva Protocol of 1924 and the Disarmament Conference of 1932/34, the opposition that separates the methods of Continental European jurists from the ways of thinking of American public opinion becomes clear as soon as one considers the problem of the abolition of war. This deep opposition can be explained only by clarifying the juridical question of the real facts of the case of the new international crime. Reviewing all the strivings towards an outlawry of war, one must pay exacting and careful attention to the question of whether one is talking about the war of aggression as a war in its entirety (in which case the further question of whether the further developments of war, coalition wars, etc. connected with such a war form a unitary whole is raised), or whether the aggression itself is taken as the specific facts of the case that one then juridically differentiates from the roughly connected war. To deliver the first shot or to be the first to

---

* Nonetheless, in view of Article 10 of the Pact, it cannot, as a result of the sanctions intended in the present Protocol, do harm under any circumstance to the territorial integrity or the political independence of the aggressor state.

overstep the boundary is clearly not the same thing as being the initiator of the war in its entirety. The crime of war, the crime of the war of aggression, and the crime of aggression are clearly three different crimes with three different facts of the case. For a complex judgment of war, they nonetheless overlap with one another, and their separation seems to a large section of public opinion a mere juridical artifice.

The differentiation of a war of aggression from an act of aggression appears artificial and formalistic only upon first glance. As soon as one raises the question of what the acts of men who are being punished as criminals actually are, a certain legal specification becomes necessary. Juridically speaking, this discrimination is in itself not difficult to understand, and, in principle, indispensable. Every war, even the war of aggression, is, as a war, normally a bilateral process, a fight on both sides; aggression, on the contrary, is a unilateral act. The question of the justice or injustice of war, even a war of aggression, amounts to something completely different from the question of the justice or injustice of a certain act of aggression, regardless of whether this act of aggression leads to a war or is duly stopped. Aggression and defense are not absolute moral concepts but rather events determined by the situation.

Nonetheless, this actual situation is often unconsciously obscured by the fact that in English language usage the "aggressor" is understood as the "violator" and is understood to be identical with the "offender." This is how Blackstone's Commentaries of the Laws of England depicts it, for example: "And indeed, as the public crime is not otherwise revenged than by forfeiture of life and property, it is impossible afterwards to make any reparation for the private wrong; which can only be had from the body of goods of the aggressor." The same is true in the French: "*Attaque est l'acte, le fait; agression est l'acte, le fait considéré moralement et pour savoir à qui est le premier tort.*"* Thus defines Littré's renowned *Dictionnaire de la langue française*. In spite of this, aggression and defense can be mere methods that change with the situation. In all great martial conflicts first one side, and then the other side, is on the offensive or on the defensive. Whoever delivers the first shot or first oversteps the border – in other words, whoever is the aggressor in a certain moment of a contested conflict – must therefore not necessarily remain the aggressor throughout the further course of the entire conflict. Nor must he, as we have already said, always be the initiator, the causer, or the guilty party and always be wrong. Just as little must the party who is pushed in a certain moment and certain situation onto the defensive always be on the defensive and be right.

---

* Attack is the act, the deed; aggression is the act, the deed considered morally and in order to know who the first offender is.

We have to keep this linguistic meaning of aggression and defense in mind because the ban on aggression signifies something else from the ban on the war of aggression. I am in the position to substantiate that in the nineteenth century, one originally spoke of the "crime of aggression" as a *"crime de l'attaque"* (not of *"de l'agression"*), in which case the juridical situation becomes clearer than in the German, where "aggression" has both the meaning of aggression (burdened with shame and degradation) as well as designating the (value-free) category of *"attaque"* or "attack." Of course, both are unjust when they are forbidden. In spite of this, the crime of the first shot remains something apart from the crime of the unjust war. When war as such ought to be legally forbidden, then it goes without saying that only the unjust war is meant. The ban on the war of aggression is only a case of the ban on unjust war. The question of the justice of a war in its entirety cannot be detached from the question of the *justa causa*, in other words, the causes of war and the entire context of foreign politics. All efforts towards the abolition of war which are discussed here – the negotiations about a guarantee pact in 1923,* the Geneva Protocol of 1924, and the Kellogg Pact of 1928 – immediately ran into the connection of the three great concrete problems, which represented more political problems than juridical problems: security, disarmament, and peaceful change. The English government referenced these three concrete problems when it rejected the Geneva Protocol of October 1924 and, in doing so, brought about its downfall. In the government declaration already mentioned above that Sir Austen Chamberlain gave before the League of Nations on March 12, 1925, Chamberlain articulates with total clarity:

> The brooding fears that keep huge armaments in being have little relation to the ordinary misunderstandings inseparable from international (as from social) life – misunderstandings with which the League is so admirably fitted to deal. They spring from deep lying causes of hostility, which for historic or other reasons divide great and powerful States. These fears may be groundless; but if they exist they cannot be effectually laid by even the most perfect method of dealing with particular disputes by the machinery of enquiry and arbitration. For what is feared in such cases is not injustice but war – war deliberately undertaken for purpose of conquest or revenge.

---

* In June 1923 Lord Robert Cecil proposed a guarantee pact for the League of Nations according to which all signatory members would agree to immediate and effective assistance in the case of an aggressive war against one of the member states. The proposal for the pact also specified "that war is an international crime." The guarantee pact was only accepted by 18 members of the League, as Great Britain, the United States of America, the Soviet Union, Germany, and other powers essentially rejected the proposal as inadequate.

The question of the justice or injustice of a war on its own merits and of the deeper context of war guilt naturally leads to difficult historical, political, sociological, and moral debates whose end cannot be awaited if one wants to arrive at a practical result. In contrast to this, the question of the justice or injustice of an individual act of aggression is easier to answer, at least if it proves successful to isolate the act of aggression as a juridical legal circumstance, to precisely determine this act, and to ban the act as such.

The decades-long efforts towards a juridically useful definition of aggression and an aggressor can be explained through this greater determinability of the act of aggression, not through a tendency towards formalism. One searches for a precise anchor point in order to determine aggression and the aggressor as clearly and as simply as possible. Should, for example, the aggressor be the party who first moves towards the use of military force, or the party who first violates the territorial inviolability of the opponent, or the party who declares war without having abided by previously determined waiting periods or a certain procedure? The ideal here is to find a simple criterion that can be cleanly applied to a set of circumstances in such a way that it is, as far as possible, *ipso facto* clear who the aggressor is without the complex and often opaque circumstances of foreign affairs having to be researched. The limitation to the act of aggression itself is appropriate and even necessary in order to avoid the problem of the war justified on its own merits and war guilt.

The unique nature and idiosyncrasy of this method most notably represented by French jurists rests, then, on the fact that an ordered legal proceeding begins without consideration for the justice or injustice of an externally pacified status quo for the sake of juridically usable further proceedings. The external and formal nature of this method is tolerated in order to stop the act of aggression and the application of violence as quickly as possible and to hinder the outbreak of war itself. The method is concerned, in other words, with a provisional protection of assets, an *interdictum uti possidetis.** The momentary state of assets is legally protected without regard for the question of whether the aggressor perhaps has a reasonable right or even moral claim to a change in the present situation.

The members of the League of Nations had already agreed to a protection against such an "aggression" in Article 10 of the Geneva Pact. This was, of course, to serve towards the final result of a prevention

---

* A ban on the violent disturbance of possessions. The principle is usually applied in international law both as a guarantee of the status quo as well as the basis for the drawing of borders of successor states. The borders of the successor states to European colonies in Africa, for example, corresponded to colonial borders.

of war, but the legal circumstances of "aggression" were still clearly differentiated from those of a "war." In Article 16 of the Pact already mentioned, it was determined that the members of the League would take economic, financial, and military sanctions against a member that "resorted to war." Here there stands, however, the word "war" and not "aggression." All the same, it quickly became obvious that the word "war" here did not mean "war," but rather aggression, since the entire point was to avoid war and to stop aggression before it came to war. Aggression itself had, therefore, to be set apart from war as an independent legal circumstance because the contractual obligations for sanctions and to aid that referred to aggression were to come into effect without waiting for war itself. In the Locarno Pact of 1925 and in the numerous non-aggression pacts that even non-members of the League, such as the Soviet Union, have concluded since then, the unique juridical nature of the act of aggression compared to the war of aggression had to be made clear. The discussions about the definition of aggression and the aggressor at the disarmament conference of 1932–4 were unusually expanded and deepened in the report of the Greek delegate and press correspondent Politis and in a Soviet Russian draft declaration presented by Foreign Commissar Litvinov.* But the legal core of the great question has remained unchanged all the same.

This discussion touches on facts that are fully well known to every jurist of international law, but just as unknown and alien to wide swaths of public opinion. Indeed, it seems necessary to me to remind the reader of the practical meaning of this differentiation between aggression and a war of aggression, since it is precisely here that the far-reaching difference between a purely juridical and a purely political way of thinking becomes obvious. One cannot disregard the fact that the ban on the act of aggression, with all of its circumstantial compromises and efforts towards a definition of aggression and aggressor, should serve towards the result of a prevention of an unjust war, even if these efforts consciously make abstract the justice of war itself and the *justa causa*. One of the first and most well-regarded pioneers for a peaceful regulation of all international disputes, Lord Robert Cecil, the initiator of an important draft for a guarantee treaty (1923), formulated this difference with great clarity. He makes clear the need for a quick and simple determination of the aggressor. The aggressor should be established through the Council of the League of Nations with a majority of three-quarters of the votes. The guarantee treaty to be concluded should designate those as the aggressor who intentionally and with premeditation violate the territory of another. The famous English champion of peace emphasizes:

* Maxim Litvinov (1876–1951) was a Soviet diplomat.

La question à trancher par le Conseil n'est pas de savoir où est le bon droit dans le litige, mais de savoir qui a commis le premier acte d'hostilité. Le traité spécifiera à cet effet que tout État qui violera de propos délibéré le territoire d'un autre État sera considéré comme l'agresseur[*]

A jurist will easily understand how in this way the precise definition of aggression is entirely and intentionally separated from the question of the objectively just war. The difference between a *possessorium* and a *petitorium* has been familiar to juridically educated nations for centuries.[†] The same is true of the separation of a so-called abstract or formal legal event from its cause. A jurist will do well to make note of such differences when the specification of the circumstances of a case are intended to lead not only to economic and military sanctions against a state, but also to the threat of criminal punishment against specific persons – when the facts of a case, in other words, are concerned with a genuine penalization where the principles of *"nullum crimen"* and "due process of law" are also respected. However, the great problem of war occupies not only jurists but also the public opinion of wide circles and great masses, and these groups find these juridical efforts an artificial formalism or even a sophistic diversion from the genuine great task at hand.

The dilemma between a juridical and political way of thinking reveals itself here in an especially difficult and dangerous way. On the one hand, the juridical specification is necessary if the great goal of a penalization of war is to be truly achieved; on the other hand, objective (at least as is widely viewed by great swaths of the masses) justice or injustice and war guilt recede, and the deeper causes of war – for example, universal armament and the lack of security – remain disregarded with such definitions of the aggressor. The dilemma between, on the one hand, a juridical-formal treatment of the ban on war in a way that would correspond to the Geneva Protocol of 1924, and, on the other hand, a political-moral-objective solution to the great problems of the causes of war, such as armament and security, becomes ever more fervid. As soon as one thinks of the practical application concerning such a monstrous problem as that of war, the difficulties become a true nightmare. In this dilemma, the mere state citizen in a chaotic situation like that in Europe from 1919–39

---

[*] The question to be decided by the Council is not to know where the right is in the suit, but rather to know who committed the first act of hostility. To this effect, the treaty specifies that every state that violates the territory of another state with deliberate purpose will be considered as the aggressor.

[†] A claim to possession (*possessorium*) is the claim resulting from possession ("*Besitz*," i.e. actual practical possession in reality of something regardless of the legality of that property), whereas a claim to petition (*petitorium*) is the claim resulting from ownership, i.e. the state of exclusive rights and control over property.

had the feeling that the bans on war and the declaration of war as a crime were connected with difficult juridical reservations and did not actually amount to the elementary simple abolition of the danger of war. This is the main experience that all European nations, revisionists as well as anti-revisionists, had of the period from 1919 to 1939. All the efforts of the Geneva Protocol failed in the face of this.

The already mentioned official declarations of the English government from March 12, 1925 that brought about the downfall of the Geneva Protocol frankly articulate this difficulty and this dilemma. The English declaration shows that such "paper" declarations about the aggressor cannot decide whether military operations can serve the purpose of defense.

> It may be desirable to add that, besides the obvious objections to those clauses already indicated, their great obscurity, and the inherent impossibility of distinguishing, in any paper definition, military movements genuinely intended for defence, and only for defence, from movements with some ulterior aggressive purpose, must always make them a danger to the unwary rather than a protection to the innocent. They could never be accepted as they stand.

In this declaration by the English government it is further stated that such formal determinations of aggression and the aggressor do not accelerate the solution of the real problem, that of the causes of war, in particular disarmament; rather, they hinder such a solution because they make preparations towards a battle against a possible aggressor necessary and, as a result of the obligation to aid, introduce an expansion of war, which will then become especially dangerous when this aid is directed against those non-members of the League of Nations whose economic power of resistance is not insignificant.

The Geneva Protocol, with its ideal of an automatic ban on aggression, had to make its starting point the then current territorial status quo. It had to, therefore, enter into the fervid argument between revisionism and anti-revisionism. In order to avoid this, it is precisely the English pacifists who have worked to position the problem of peaceful change at the center of the debate in order to effect not only a formal-juridical but also an objective-political hindrance of war through the abolition of its causes. The universally (at least in Europe) and thoroughly dominant expression of those formal efforts of the Geneva Pact articulated itself in the well-known phrases that such formal definitions of aggression and aggressor become "a signpost for the guilty and a trap for the innocent."[279]

The Geneva Protocol of 1924 failed in the face of the fact that it did not respond to and did not want to respond to the objective contexts of the question of the just war. The impression that this failure made upon the views of the European nations and governments, especially the impression made by the declaration of the English government from March 12, 1925, was very great. It hindered the stabilizing of a European legal conviction concerning the establishment of a new international crime. The American promoters of an "outlawry of war" nonetheless did not allow themselves to be misled by this failure and reached, in 1928 through the Kellogg Pact, a formal condemnation, a "renunciation of war as an instrument of national policy." We still must examine whether this "condemn the war" strategy of the Kellogg Pact is to be viewed as a criminal penalization in the sense of "*nullum crimen, nulla poena.*"

2) *The Kellogg Pact of August 27, 1928* is a (in some respects) typically American answer to the question of the abolition of war, an American backlash to the European failure of the Geneva Protocol of 1924. One can find the typical expression of a Continental European way of thinking in the juridical-formal methods of the Geneva Protocol. Sir Austen Chamberlain's previously cited declaration from March 12, 1925 – with its stark indication of the problem of armament and the real causes of war – is a document of English behavior. The Kellogg Pact, however, comes from the American outlawry movement, founded by S.O. Levinson* and finding its standpoint authentically formulated in a resolution brought before the American Congress by Senator Borah on December 12, 1927. In the resolution, it was stated that the genius of civilization had only discovered two methods of regulating human disputes, namely law and war; that in light of today's civilizational state war is a barbarism; that needs, federations, and plans based on war as a possibility of enforcing peace bring about a military rule hostile to peace; that war should therefore be despised and shunned; that, simultaneously, a jurisdictional substitute for war should be created in the form of an international tribunal whose judgments will be executed through the compelling force of an enlightened public opinion without war, similar to the judgments of the Supreme Court of the United States of America.

This resolution of Senator Borah shows not only how different the conceptions of the methods towards the arrangement of peace and towards the abolition of war were. The resolution also shows, above all, the great differences in America's and Europe's state of awareness. Public opinion in the United States of America was strong and potent; in Europe, it was riven and split. Since the retreat of President Wilson from Europe, the decisive event of European history between 1919 and

---

* Salmon Levinson (1865–1941) was the founder of the "outlawry of war" movement in the United States.

1939, there was no longer an arbitral authority for the consciousness of European nations. The authority of an international tribunal upon whose establishment Senator Borah made the abolition of war dependent, seemed to the Europe of the time only a bold hope, not the realization of universal disarmament and other presuppositions of peace. Above all, the public opinion of the European governments and nations was used to paying less attention to public opinion than it was to the official behavior of the United States of America. This is important for the judgment of the Kellogg Pact.

The Kellogg Pact is, still, not identical with the Borah Resolution. While the Pact is often described as an "Outlawry of War Pact" and regarded as such, it does not contain the word "outlawry." Still, the Kellogg Pact does not ride on the juridical rails of the Geneva Protocol. It does not speak of aggression but rather of a condemnation of war itself; it abstains from the juridical judgments that the Geneva Protocol sought in a limitation to the ban on aggression. There is no definition for war itself. This was not unimportant for the European consciousness of the time. Whereas a precise juridical definition of the act of aggression seemed possible and achievable, a juridical definition of war that could be valid as the foundation for a genuine penalization became ever more difficult and problematic after 1919. The occupation of the Ruhr by French and Belgian troops in January 1923 was, of course, not treated as a war. Nor was the occupation of Corfu by Italy in August 1923 valid as a martial act or even as aggression that would have ushered in the sanction proceedings of Article 16 of the League of Nations Charter. The terms "war," "military reprisals," "sanctions," and "peaceful compulsory measures" threatened to dissolve into one another. When in 1931 Japan, then still a member of the League of Nations and even a permanent member of its Council, occupied great regions of East Asia, one did not want to see in these facts a "resort to war," even when faced with the great battles around Shanghai. A famous pioneer of pacifism, Professor Hans Wehberg of Geneva, showed in January 1932 in an essay in the leading pacifist magazine *Die Friedenswarte* with much argumentation that there could be no talk of a war led by Japan in the juridical sense, only of peaceful measures that were accompanied by battles of greater or lesser scale. Professor Hans Wehberg expressly took back this view several years later.* The point here is not to focus on Wehberg. But as a symptom of the concept of war in international law these comments cannot remain unmentioned. If a candid pacifist who stood for decades

---

* Hans Wehberg, "Hat Japan durch die Besetzung der Mandschurei das Völkerrecht verletzt?" *Friedenswarte* 32 (1932), 1ff.; Hans Wehberg, "Das Kriegsproblem in der neueren Entwicklung des Völkerrechts," *Friedenswarte* 38 (1938), 129, 140ff.

in the front line of efforts towards the abolition of war and who had, as a scholarly jurist, an objectivity that the active statesman or politician does not have at his disposal – if, in other words, a leading jurist and pacifist – evinced such an uncertainty towards fundamental legal concepts, what sort of uncertainty and confusion in a legal sense may one expect from politically agitated nations and their public opinions?

Both with respect to the juridical definitions of the Geneva Protocol of 1924 as well as with respect to the English rejection of this protocol on March 25, the Kellogg Pact of August 27, 1928 has the virtue of simplicity. It abstains both from a determination of the term "aggression" as well as from a determination of the term "war," as well as a mention of the causes of war. War, insofar as it is an instrument of national policy, is condemned. Naturally, this condemnation only applies to a war conducted in violation of the Kellogg Pact – only to the unjust war. The word "war" is used without further stipulation, although already by then the great dilemma between the juridical ban on an act of aggression and the political ban on war itself had already been ripped open by the League of Nations Pact of 1919 and the Geneva Protocol of 1924. The word "to condemn," as it appears in the text of the Kellogg Pact, was immediately regarded by jurists of European governments from the point of view of the question of where the exact legal obligation to which the signatory states of the pact subjected themselves lay. Did this obligation contain only a contractual abdication from war as an instrument of national policy on the part of the state or a complete outlawry? A mere abdication is, of course, not a penalization of the circumstances of "war." The view of the Kellogg Pact dominant in Europe held to the recognized reservation that the Kellogg Pact was not able to contradict the League of Nations Pact. Already by virtue of this fact, the Kellogg Pact could be only an abdication from war. The word "outlawry" does not, as already stated, appear in the Kellogg Pact. But even if the word had been used, it still would not have effected, just as little as would have the corresponding phrases in the Geneva Protocol of 1924, any penalization to the mind of a Continental European jurist. The Continental European way of thinking demands determinate regulations with regard to legal circumstances, perpetrators, penal threats, and penal court. It is not familiar with any universal outlawry – at the least no outlawry in the sense of primitive and medieval law. An outlawry can only, if it is to be juridically carried out, refer to determinate persons who have fulfilled certain legal conditions. Modern law knows of an outlawry of certain persons in only one specific case, namely that of piracy. The pirate is, however, an outlaw from the perspective of international law. In current praxis, this means nothing other than that the pirate can be condemned in certain proceedings by the judiciary of any state without regard for the usual borders of state jurisdiction. I shall return again to this theme in the discussion of the concept of the perpetrator (Section III, p. 164).

Yet neither can the parallel of the concepts of war and piracy be carried out, since the condemnation of the war in the Kellogg Pact was not absolute in the sense of an unconditional abolition of war without regard for just and unjust wars. The history of international law is familiar with cases of the abolition of certain legal institutes. The Paris Declaration Respecting Martial Law of April 16, 1856, for example, abolished privateering with the words: *"La course est et demeure abolie."** The abolishment of slavery as an institution is further known to legal history. The Kellogg Pact of 1928 does not, however, say anything along the lines of *"La guerre est et demeure abolie."* It condemns only a certain kind of war which it, in doing so, presupposes to be an unjust war, while it even sanctions just war through this same act. The Kellogg Pact does not declare every war to be a crime in a radical-pacifistic sense. Just war is, just as before, not only allowed, but even rather necessary. War was, therefore, not abolished in the legal consciousness of European peoples; on the contrary, a possibly just war was recognized anew. Rearmament remained, as a result, thoroughly permitted, indeed, even necessary. The entire problematic that had been granted by the differentiation between just and unjust war remained, along with the dilemma of a decision between a precise juridical ban of war on the one hand, and, on the other hand, a universal condemnation of war laden with many reservations.

The Kellogg Pact is a pact without definitions, without sanctions, and without organization. One will fundamentally quickly agree with the fact that war is baleful. But as long as there was no secure and well-functioning process for the immediate determination of the justice of an individual concrete war, every state had to pull itself into a chaotic Europe gaping at its weapons and participate in the universal rearmament. Every state had in particular to ensure that in such a situation it would decide the question concerning the justice of a war for itself and at its own peril. The reservation that every state decides for itself on its own right to self-defense is stressed again and again in the Kellogg Pact. In the note of the USA to the other states on June 23, 1928 it is expressly stated:

> There is nothing in the American draft on an antiwar treaty which restricts or impairs in any way the right of self-defense. That right is inherent in every sovereign state and is implicit in every treaty. Every nation is free at all times and regardless of treaty provisions to defend its territory from attack or

---

* Privateering is and remains abolished.

invasion and it alone is competent to decide whether circumstances require recourse to war in self-defense.

The fact that the Kellogg Pact contains no, not even one, moral obligation to a penal action against the aggressor was explained by Secretary of State Kellogg before the Committee on Foreign Relations of the American Senate on December 7, 1928 in the following statement:

> But how there can be a moral obligation for the United States to go to Europe to punish the aggressor or punish the party making war, when there never was such a suggestion made in the negotiation, where nobody agreed to it, and where there is no obligation to do it, is beyond me. I cannot understand it.
>
> As I see it, we have no more obligation to punish somebody for breaking the antiwar treaty than for breaking any one of the other treaties which we have agreed to.

The Chair of this Committee on Foreign Affairs, Senator Borah,[*] explained on January 3, 1929, verbatim before the Senate:

> The treaty is not founded upon the theory of force or punitive measures at any place or at any time [. . .] There are no sanctions; the treaty rests in a wholly different philosophy [. . .]
>
> In other words, when the treaty is broken the United States is absolutely free. It is just as free to choose its course as if the treaty had never been written.

In the report that the Committee presented to the Senate on January 15, 1929, the report stated the following with reference to sanctions and penal measures:

> The committee further understands that the treaty does not provide sanctions, express or implied. Should any signatory to the treaty or any nation adhering to the treaty, violate the terms of the same, there is no obligation, or commitment, express or implied, upon the part of any of the other signers of the treaty, to engage in punitive or coercive measures as against the nation violating the treaty. The effect of the violation of the treaty is to relieve the other signers of the treaty from any obligation under it with the nation thus violating the same.

On March 1, 1929, Briand explained in the French chambers:

---

[*] William Borah (1865–1940) was a Republican Senator.

*Il leur eût été impossible de mener à bon terme la conclusion d'un contrat aussi parfait que vous le pourriez souhaiter, contre la guerre, avec une organisation arbitrale et des sanctions.**

Secretary of State Stimson said before the Council of Foreign Relations on August 8, 1932 that the Kellogg Pact contains no other sanctions than a condemnation through public opinion:

> The Briand-Kellogg Pact provides for no sanctions of force. It does not require any signatory to intervene with measures of force in case the Pact is violated. Instead it rests upon the sanction of public opinion, which can be made one of the most potent sanctions of the world. Any other course, through the possibility of entangling the signatories in International politics, would have confused the broad, simple aim of the treaty and prevented the development of that public opinion upon which it most surely relies. Public opinion is the sanction which lies behind all international intercourse in time of peace.

What interests us here is the question of whether such a pact without definitions, without sanctions, and without organization, one that is designed only on the basis of moral condemnation through public opinion, can serve as the legal foundation for the criminal punishment of particular persons for a totally new kind of international crime, especially when considering the principle "*nullum crimen, nulla poena sine lege*" and with regard to the requirements of a "due process of law." One cannot suppose this on the basis of the quoted explanations of the pact, all the less because they only referred to states or nations, just as the Geneva Protocol, too, directed its sanctions only against the aggressor state as such.

Moreover, so many fundamental reservations have been added to the Kellogg Pact during its creation and its signing that it can for this reason barely be valid as a penalizing norm in the sense of criminal law. All the signatory states declared these reservations, some expressly, others tacitly. In doing so, they placed the condemnation of war under fundamental conditions. Already at the beginning of the discussions, the French government formally declared in its note dated January 21, 1928 that it could only agree to the renouncement of war if the Kellogg Pact contained no contradiction to the obligations of the Geneva Pact. The government added, in a note dated March 28, 1928, a further reservation by making the renouncement of war dependent on the preservation of the right to

---

* It would have been impossible to conclude a contract against war as perfect as you would wish with an arbitral organization and sanctions.

self-defense, and by stressing that the signatory of the Kellogg Pact was no longer bound to the Geneva Pact if its opponent violated its own obligations and the Pact. These reservations were expressly mentioned in the American accompanying note from June 23, 1928, which was added to the revised draft of the treaty. Other states made numerous reservations, especially England, which had reservations concerning not only the security of transportation routes of the British world empire but also concerning national honor.

The particulars of these reservations have been fundamentally discussed in the criticisms of the League of Nations, especially those of esteemed American authors (Edwin Borchard and William Potter Lage).* What matters for us here is not the criticism of the Kellogg Pact, however, but rather the question of how far an agreement weighted with such reservations could dispose of legal convictions that had existed for centuries, and how it could produce the legal foundation for a criminal punishment of unpolitical state citizens – how it could do all of this not only in the opinion of its authors but also in the view of wide swaths of European nations, and given the contemporary condition of the international legal consciousness of 1928 to 1939.

The Kellogg Pact was not only a regulation endowed with strong reservations, without definition, without sanction, and without organization. It also stood, apart from the other reservations, under the reservation of the determinations of the League of Nations Pact. A resolution of the 12th Federal Meeting on September 25, 1931 resolved to constitute a commission composed of representatives of all the members of the League of Nations who were to meet during the course of the disarmament conference and make suggestions. This commission never met. The question of accommodating the Kellogg Pact to the League of Nations Charter has been delayed year on year ever since this resolution.

In contrast to this, an unofficial association, the International Law Association, resolved upon a series of "Articles on an Interpretation of the Kellogg Pact" at its 38th Conference in Budapest in September 1934. These articles have been discussed many times in American public opinion as authentic and positive principles, as principles that are authoritative under international law. The opposition between an official statement and an unofficial private statement – an opposition that we continue to run into – becomes meaningful here. It can lead to many misunderstandings when the European juridical way of thinking runs into the convictions of American jurists. The Budapest Articles

---

* Edwin Borchard (1884–1951) was an American scholar of international law and an opponent of foreign intervention. William Potter Lage was an American attorney who was a co-author of Borchard's.

were edited into the draft of a convention concerning "Rights and Duties of States in case of aggression" that Harvard University published in 1939. The American Secretary of State Stimson pointed to these articles during his examination before the Foreign Committee of the American Senate and treated them as a kind of authentic and positive interpretation of the Kellogg Pact.* Especially as regards the fundamental question of the extent to which the old international law of neutrality in war is abolished through the Kellogg Pact, the Budapest Articles are often cited as the decisive piece of evidence for the abolition of the old concept of neutrality. The old right to neutrality made no distinction between the just and unjust war. As a result of this, a penalization of the war of aggression is impossible under international law as long as one holds to the old right of neutrality. In light of the great significance of this matter, I include here the complete text of the Budapest Articles:

> Whereas the Pact is a multilateral law-making treaty whereby each of the High Contracting Parties makes binding agreements with each other and all of the other High Contracting Parties, and
>
> Whereas by their participation in the Pact sixty-three States have abolished the conception of war as a legitimate means of exercised pressure on another State in the pursuit of national policy and have also renounced any recourse to armed force for the solution of international disputes or conflicts:
>
> (1) A signatory State cannot, by denunciation or non-observance of the Pact, release itself from its obligations thereunder.
>
> (2) A signatory State which threatens to resort to armed force for the solution of an international dispute or conflict is guilty of a violation of the Pact.
>
> (3) A signatory State which aids a violating State thereby itself violated the Pact.
>
> (4) In the event of a violation of the Pact by a resort to armed force or war by one signatory State against another, the other States may, without thereby committing a breach of the Pact or of any rule of International Law, do all or any of the following things:
>
> > (a) Refuse to admit the exercise by the State violating the Pact of belligerent rights, such as visit and search, blockade, etc.;
> >
> > (b) Decline to observe towards the State violating the pact the duties prescribed by International Law, apart from the Pact, for a neutral in relation to a belligerent;

---

* Schmitt is referring throughout this paragraph to Henry Stimson's hearings of January 27–February 3, 1941 before the Senate Committee on Foreign Relations, in which Stimson justified the Lend-Lease policy on the basis of international law. See *Hearings Before the Committee on Foreign Relations United States Senate,* 77th Congress, 1st Session, Part 1, 85, 89–90.

(c) Supply the State attacked with financial or material assistance, including munitions of war;

(d) Assist with armed forces the State attacked.

(5) The signatory States are not entitled to recognize as acquired *de jure* any territorial or other advantages de facto by means of a violation of the Pact.

(6) A violating State is liable to pay compensation for all damage caused by a violation of the Pact to any signatory State or to its nationals.

(7) The Pact does not affect such humanitarian obligations as are contained in general treaties, such as the Hague Convention of 1899 and 1907, the Geneva Conventions of 1864, 1906 and 1929, and the International Convention relating to the Treatment of Prisoners of War, 1929.

Even these Budapest Articles speak only of the "violating state." With respect to them, too, a question continues to exist: do the Articles contain a penalization of the war of aggression with reference to specific people in the sense of "*nullum crimen*"? A jurist of the Continental European way of thinking will surely respond in the negative. It would be self-evident to any European jurist that such an interpretation of the International Law Association from 1934, which never made any official governmental statement, cannot after the outbreak of war be perceived in the sense of a positive, valid rule binding upon all states and even directly upon state citizens. A European jurist would draw from the previously cited declarations – among which it transpires that the Kellogg Pact was unambiguously concluded as a pact without sanctions – the conclusion that an ex post facto introduction of sanctions of any kind is impermissible after the outbreak of war. This must be valid in any event for sanctions concerning criminal law. Indeed, it is probably here at this point that the previously mentioned, always resurfacing opposition that separates the way of thinking of the Western Hemisphere from that of Europe becomes acute once more. Yet even if this way of thinking should emerge victorious, it would be an injustice to draw the individual state citizen of a European state into this opposition and make him into a criminal on the basis of this conflicting foundation. It should again be repeated here that this only relates to the war of aggression as an international crime, not the participation in atrocities or war crimes in the classic sense.

Just how inadequately the problem of the new crime was resolved for the legal consciousness of nations is finally revealed by the fact that in previous discussions of war as a crime it was not once clarified whether the war of aggression should stand as a political or common crime. The concept of the political crime as a special crime different from the common criminal crime is familiar to every jurist. The concept of the political crime led to a series of special formations in domestic law that were, for example, constitutionally connected to the accusation against a minister or to the problem of a "bill of attainder." This problem is familiar in international law in the special treatment of political crimes in asylum and extradition law. If war, which is an event of high politics, is declared a crime, then the question of whether or not this crime is a political crime must also be clarified in the sense just alluded to. The political character of the new crime must have its effect for all questions regarding the legal circumstances of a case, of the perpetrator and his judgment, and, finally, the proceedings themselves. In spite of the comprehensive scope of the discussion concerning the Kellogg Pact and the criminalization of war, I have up to this point failed to find a single discussion of this important question.

It is, then, not difficult to convince a Continental European jurist of the fact that the Kellogg Pact, with its lack of definitions, sanctions, and organization, and, finally, with its use of public opinion as a fundamental sanction, cannot be a legal foundation for the criminal punishment of a novel crime. But it is precisely on this point that the understanding with American jurists is extraordinarily aggravated, because here all of the oppositions that have come up again and again in our analysis accumulate: the opposition of juridical and moral, juridical and political, positive and legal-rational ways of thinking. To this one has to add the oppositions of a dualistic and monistic interpretation of international law as well as the opposition of official behavior and public opinion – a public opinion that the European jurist will find especially vigorous. Finally, the extensive differences between America's and Europe's political situations further deepen and aggravate all these oppositions. The real argument of the American jurists will always remain that the Kellogg Pact binds all states and nations to the universal conviction of mankind, and that according to this conviction, war is a crime that Hitler and his accomplices doubtlessly committed. In opposition to this, there remains only the possibility of again reminding one anew that we are not speaking here of the participation in atrocities, but rather only of whether unpolitical state citizens who did not take part in such atrocities can be punished as participants in the new international crime of the war of aggression because of a war conducted by their own government.

For the adherents of the outlawry movement, war is a crime like piracy, and whoever is party to war is the same as a pirate. For the radical believer in outlawry this is no mere rhetorical move, but rather law based on the modern and universal consciousness of mankind. The deep oppositions that operate within this comparison will come to light in our following discussion of piracy as a parallel to war.

3) *Piracy as* exemple-type *of an international crime.* The question of whether an individual can be the perpetrator of or participant in an

international crime seems to have found a positive answer through several important examples. One finds, particularly in several discussions of international law, especially among Anglo-Saxon authors, a certain category of "international crimes" that are not "delicts of international law" in the sense of a pure relation of states, as with the typical so-called delicts of international law. Rather, their unique nature consists in the fact that norms of international law are differently applied to individual people. The perpetrator here is an individual of any nationality who violates not a domestic law but rather a norm of international law. He is made legally – and even criminally – responsible for this. It must be remarked, however, that this penal jurisdiction concerns not international but rather national courts of a given individual state. All the same, even today these special cases are still often spoken of as "international crimes." They typically concern the following circumstances: piracy (to which other circumstances, like the slave trade, can be equated), harm of oceanic cables; blockade-running and trade in contraband in a maritime war on the part of neutral nationals. The case that is important for our discussion, indeed, in a certain sense decisive, is piracy. Blockade-running and contraband trade belong to the neutrality law of maritime war and are not decisive for our problem, all the less so as blockade-runners and contraband dealers act, according to a widespread interpretation, not contrary to law and illegally, but rather only at their own danger, "riskily." I leave this case aside and treat the question of how far it is possible to bring criminal punishment on account of piracy into an analogy and parallel with criminal punishment on account of aggression or a war of aggression.

The difference in Anglo-Saxon legal thinking from Continental European legal thinking becomes especially clear in their interpretation of piracy as an international crime. Continental European thought tends to make law into a positive law. In penal law this positivization, which is simultaneously a nationalization, leads to the conviction that only a state law can be the basis for a punishment. Among Continental European jurists this has become an almost self-evident view, one often barely aware of its opposition to other views. In the course of this positivization, the jurist of Continental European penal law regards robbery at sea as a case of robbery, an event that is threatened with punishment among other cases of robbery in the penal law books of numerous states. In Article 250, Point 3 of the German *Strafgesetzbuch*, for example, piracy is treated as "robbery in the open sea" in the same sentence as "robbery in public ways, streets, a train" – in other words, as a qualified clear case of robbery, one not recognizable in any particular way as an international crime. The fact that robbery is committed on the high seas – in other words, outside the realm of a state eminency – nonetheless leads to certain practical consequences for the responsibility of other states. The pirate can be punished by any state of the world. But this, according to the leading Continental European interpretation of piracy over several centuries, does not make piracy into an international crime in a special sense. According to Continental European jurists, it only amounts to, to use a commonly recognized formulation, an "expansion of the realm of competence of domestic norms and authorities."

The specifically international character of the crime of piracy has been lost to the Continental European interpretation as a result of this. In contrast to this, the English interpretation is familiar with a kind of piracy under Anglo-Saxon law insofar as the circumstances of the crime fall under English statutes. Alongside this, the traditional "piracy *jure gentium*" is retained, which is fundamentally distinct from state piracy as an international crime. The pirate *jure gentium* is an enemy of all humanity. He is, as the saying goes, *hostis generis humani*. His predatory intentions are directed indiscriminately against all states. Every state can, therefore, dispense with him. No state, not even the state whose nationality he holds, may retain him. The pirate is denationalized as a consequence of his piracy. He cannot call upon the protection of his state, and the state to which he belongs loses the right to protect him.

This is extraordinary, at least for the legal consciousness of a Continental state jurist. In light of the cited phrases relating to the enemy of humankind and "denationalization," it is understandable that the efforts to proscribe war and declare it an international crime connect with the piracy *jure gentium*. War, at least the unjust war and the war of aggression, should be treated as an international crime following in the example of piracy. The perpetrator of the new international crime "war" is himself a pirate and is as such an outlaw. Many opponents of war find this a thoroughly illuminating parallel. Piracy becomes in this way an example and even an ideal type of an international crime, the "*exemple-type*," as N. Politis calls it. Numerous practical proposals for the penalization of war make reference to the concept of piracy. The equal treatment of pirate and war criminal is easily made propagandistically comprehensible to public opinion. But even jurists see here, if not a precedent, then an analogous example, an "*exemple-type*" – one with whose help the capture of individual state nationals over the heads of their state and government becomes possible both from the perspective of international law and direct criminal law.

I need to go into further detail here concerning so-called piracy in international law in order to make reference to a certain possibility of a penalization of war that has gone completely unnoticed in Germany. At the same time, the connection of piracy with the question of war crimes must not remain misunderstood for any longer. This concerns not only theoretical constructions for drafts and regenerations of international law. More than that, the great symptomatic meaning of the use of the concept of piracy can be made clear through four examples of which I would like to remind the reader. The first two of these four examples date to the period of the First World War of 1914–18 and both concern the question of international law of U-boat warfare. According to an interpretation that became widespread in England, the commandants and crews of U-boats were to be treated as pirates because they had sunk merchant ships without having obeyed the established rules of naval war. They were differentiated from other prisoners of war, and if one did not want to litigate against them in a criminal trial, they would be interned in special camps and at the very least discriminated from other prisoners of war. The second example is the speech of President Wilson from April 2, 1917. The expression "piracy" may not be used as such in this speech, but the German U-boat war is described using the formulations common for piracy, as a "war led against mankind" – a war, that is, against all nations. The term "piracy" comes up for the third time in a context important for us in the agreement of the Washington Conference from February 6, 1922. There, the principle that war-conducting U-boats are liable to the universal rules of naval war concerning the seizure of merchant ships is postulated. In Article 3, it then expressly states that any person employed in the service of any power that violates these rules, "whether or not such person is under orders of a governmental superior" is made responsible "as if for an act of piracy." Here, a war crime in the sense of an offense against the rules of war is formally equated with piracy. The 1922 Washington Accord was not ratified, but its symptomatic meaning is obvious. This meaning is strengthened through the fourth example. The Conference of Nyon, which convened on September 11, 1937, was called a "Conference on Piracy." The official text of the conference resolution signed on September 14, 1937 spoke of the fact that certain sinkings of merchant ships through U-boats should be treated as "acts of piracy."

It is, therefore, not to be overlooked that the concept of piracy is the point at which the international criminalization and penalization of war can be accessed. In several proposals of the *Association internationale du droit pénal* and in the writings of several authors, such as Nicolas Politis, this has already been done with reference to the fact that, of course, not national courts but rather an international criminal court specially created for this task is to be responsible for this. In spite of this, neither the Geneva Protocol of 1924 nor the Kellogg Pact of 1928, nor any other official document or even an official proposal was used to this end. The parallel of war and piracy has its own tight borders. If war is forbidden and declared a crime, this still does not cover the war of defense. Even the Kellogg Pact judges only unjust war. War is not, therefore, *ipso facto* and absolutely declared a crime. Rather, one differentiates between just and unjust war. Only for some radical pacifists and members of an unconditional "no-resistance" philosophy is war always a crime, without reference to justice or injustice, in every case and on both sides. In the case of piracy, however, it is not possible to distinguish between just and unjust piracy. Piracy is a "*malum in se*" and not permitted as an act of defense.

A further difference lies in the fact that war has both an interior and exterior political character. Unpolitical wars are unthinkable. In contrast, it belongs to the essence of piracy that piracy is of an unpolitical character. The pirate acts, at least according to the traditional interpretation, out of unpolitical motives. He acts out of a pure lust for acquisition. He is a robber, a thief, and a plunderer. He has the *animus furandi*.* As soon as he acts out of political motives, he is no longer a pirate. He who is guilty of high treason is not a pirate. Treason is not piracy. Revolutionaries, insurgents, and rebels who commandeer a warship of the legal government are therefore still not pirates in the sense of international law as long as they do not rob and plunder the ships of other nations on the high seas. Only because of the unpolitical nature of piracy was it possible for it to be recognized as an international delict and, in spite of this, have its punishment left to the national courts of individual states.

It is fundamental to the hitherto existing interpretation of piracy that the action of the pirate is not a war in the sense of international law, just as little as, conversely, the action of a state directed against the pirate is not a war. By punishing the pirate as a common criminal, the opposition of piracy to war in the sense of international law was stressed in the hitherto existing interpretation. The fact that war was something different from a crime according to the previous conviction of international law cannot be shown anywhere more clearly than through this opposition of war and piracy.

But the real opposition that we run into here is too deep for it to be overcome with such juridical arguments. Here, certain convictions of progress, civilization, and humanity become potent. For the outlawry movement, war in its current form is nothing other than a barbarity and an atavism, and it must stop with immediate effect just as much as earlier piracy had to stop. A sentence from the author of "principles of maritime strategy," Sir Julian Corbett, clarifies this important parallel better than any juridical discussion: "piracy is the pre-scientific stage of the conducting of naval war."† Through this statement it becomes clear what the parallel of war and piracy really means. A country that does

---

* Intent to steal.

† Julian Corbett (1854–1922) was a British naval historian and geostrategist.

not abdicate from war and a martial disposition places itself outside the modern "*conscience universelle*" and makes itself into a debased enemy of humankind, just as the pirate did before his methods were civilizationally superseded. Germany's real crime is found in this violation of the *conscience universelle*. But in reality, this can only concern the real atrocities. For one cannot seriously suppose that the real guilt of which Germany should be accused lies in the fact that it was too scientifically backwards to invent the atom bomb in due time.

4) *International penal jurisdiction.* To date, there has been no single international penal court. In the case of piracy and similar international crimes, national courts decided. The difficulties and reservations of an international jurisdiction and international arbitration in today's international law are well known. Political disputes are fundamentally not litigable or arbitral. The fact that war is a political and even highly political affair goes without saying. If reservations of a political nature are already largely valid for the non-criminal jurisdiction and arbitration in an affair, then the difficulties that will arise for an international *penal* jurisdiction as a result of the new crime of the war of aggression will be even greater and more obvious.

There have been some proposals for the establishment of an international criminal court. The attempt to punish Wilhelm II (Article 227) never led to the formation of a tribunal. In a consultation concerning the statute of the Permanent International Tribunal in The Hague in 1920, Baron Descamps proposed an International Criminal Court that was to decide on international crimes. Although the proposal was recommended with some reservations by the Jurists' Committee of examination to the Council of the League of Nations, the question of an international criminal court was shelved upon the first meeting of the League of Nations as too difficult and not pressing enough of a problem. A proposal was then suggested from the side of the Americans through Mr. S.O. Levinson in Chicago in 1921, which in 1923 gave Senator Borah occasion to begin the already mentioned project regarding the outlawry of war. This was a project according to which war should be proscribed as a crime against international law, and by which all nations should be given the obligation to punish their own war profiteers based on similar prescriptions of the Constitution of the United States of America that give Congress the authority for punishment in cases of international law.[280] The International Law Association occupied itself several times with this issue and adopted a proposal of Professor Bellot*

---

* Hugh Bellot (1861–1928) was one of the leading champions for an international criminal court to accompany the League of Nations.

in its meeting in Vienna in August 1926. The Interparliamentary Union handled the question in 1924 at its conference in Bern, and in 1925 at its conference in Washington, and it formed a permanent committee for the examination of the question on the basis of a proposal by the Romanian professor Pella, who was planning a universal international criminal code. The well-known jurist of the League of Nations, Nicholas Politis, suggested in his 1926 lectures at Columbia University that a penal chamber with five judges be formed at the Permanent Criminal Court in The Hague. The idea of making the International Court at The Hague into a criminal court has often been articulated. There exist a number of older and more recent common proposals that, while they may have brought forward a wide-ranging literature, have not led to the institution of an international criminal court. The efforts towards a conforming of the Kellogg Pact to the League of Nations Charter have led neither in this regard nor in any other regard to a practical result. With respect, moreover, to the organization of a jurisdiction, here, too, the attempts at a penalization of the war of aggression have failed to reach completion.

An international criminal court belongs to an international criminal law. The ban on ex post facto laws also contains, at least with regard to controversial and unclear norms, the ban on an ex post facto criminal court. It should be repeated here that we are concerned only with the war of aggression as "international crime" and not of the inhumanities and atrocities.

5) *The deciding facts.* The legal convictions of nations are determined in times of transition only by simple, elementary experiences. The oppositions of the different opinions and the complicated compromise formulations of numerous international pacts have only served to confuse the convictions of the European peoples to date. Several deciding facts have made a strong impression, however. I shall name only two examples here.

a) The first and, until now, only case of a *proclaimed aggressor* concerns the conquest of Abyssinia by Italy in the years 1935–6. The events are well known. Italy was designated the aggressor by most members of the League of Nations in carefully thought out juridical formulations, an aggressor against whom a coordinated system of sanctions was directed. Not one word was spoken of an international crime in the criminal sense. After Italy's occupation of Abyssinia, the sanctions against the aggressor were overturned by a resolution of the assembly of the League of Nations on July 4, 1936. Several members of the League of Nations, above all Great Britain and France, recognized Italy's annexation of Abyssinia. Other members could not make up their mind. The English government not only *de facto* recognized the annexation of Abyssinia in December

1936 and *de jure* in April 1938; it also obligated itself with respect to Italy to bring its influence to bear on the next meeting of the Council of the League of Nations so that the hindrances standing in the way of a recognition of Italian sovereignty over Ethopia by other members of the League of Nations would be resolved (see the exchange of notes on the English–Italian Treaty from April 16, 1938).* Upon the request of Italy, the following point was raised on the agenda for the meeting of the Council on May 12, 1938: "Consequences that result from the current situation in Abyssinia." The debate was opened by the English Foreign Minister Lord Halifax, who, in the name of his government, turned the attention of the Council to the "unnatural situation" that would result from the fact that several members of the League of Nations had already recognized the Italian annexation, while others still could not make up their mind as to the matter. The English Foreign Minister expressly added that his government did *not* share the view that the relevant measures of the League of Nations issued during the Abyssinian War had obligated League members to wait to grant recognition to the Italian annexation until a unanimous decision by the League to that effect had been reached. It was, in contrast, the view of the English government that League members were justified in granting recognition to the Italian situation at a time of their own choosing without, in doing so, violating the League Charter. While the English government, Halifax continued, was not obligated to counsel with other League members on this question before it recognized the Italian annexation, the final recognition of the Italian conquest of Abyssinia by a single League member was, as a result of the common actions of the League members in the Abyssinian War, an affair that concerned all League members. In doing so, Lord Halifax referred to the actual situation in Abyssinia, where there no longer existed any organized native authority that had any hopes of reconquering the country. He added that the interest of the maintenance of peace was more important than the unshakeable devotion to a sublime goal and the endless adherence to an abstract principle of international law. If one, he continued, did not wish to live in a world of fantasy, one had to, sooner or later, recognize the fact that Italy had all of Abyssinia under its control. This declaration by the English government from May 12 can be found in the *Journal Officiel* of the League of Nations

---

* Schmitt is referring here to an agreement negotiated in 1938 between the Italian Foreign Minister, Lord Ciano, and the British Ambassador to Italy, Lord Perth, concerning future relations between Italian East Africa and Egypt as well as Great Britain's intention to urge the League of Nations to recognize Italian sovereignty in Abyssinia. See *Keesings Archiv der Gegenwart*, VIII (1938), 3517f. Gian Galeazzo Ciano (1904–44) was Mussolini's son-in-law and the Italian Minister of Foreign Affairs from 1936–43. Eric Drummon, 16th Earl of Perth (1876–1951) was the British Ambassador to Italy from 1933–9.

(pp. 333–45).* The protest of the Negus did not change the fact that the remaining members of the League of Nations Council, with the exception of the representatives of China, Bolivia, the Soviet Union, and New Zealand, shared the view of the English government. The president of the Council, Munters (Latvia), explained that the discussion of the question in the Council had proved that the great majority of the Council members regarded the question of the recognition of the Italian position in Abyssinia as an affair of the decision of every individual member of the League.

> *Il est clair que, malgré les regrets qui ont été exprimés, la grande majorité des membres du Conseil sont d'avis qu'en ce qui concerne la question actuellement en discussion, il appartient aux Membres individuels de la Société des Nations de déterminer leur attitude d'après leur propre situation et leurs propres obligations.†*

Already in September 1936, a report by the Commission for the Examination of Extraordinary Powers was accepted, according to which "the effective exercise of state authority through the head of state attempting to issue it" was designated as a criterion for the validity of the extraordinary powers of a government. The further argument concerned the question of whether the Negus really had such an *"exercice suffisamment réel"* for their legal title. Lord Halifax said the following about this affair in the meeting of the English House of Lords on November 3, 1938:

> With all respect I would say that it is really no good crying over spilt milk that no human agency can put back into the jug. It [sc. the practical sovereignty of Italy] is a fact, let us recognize it as a legal fact, and clear up once for all the innumerable outstanding questions that arise.

Only after Italy's entry into the war against England did the English government declare, following requests in the House of Commons (June 19, 1940) and in the House of Lords (August 13, 1940), that it regarded itself as justified in guaranteeing Ethiopia's full freedom to trade. It is hardly surprising that this behavior of the English government and other governments in the Abyssinian Question most strongly influenced the views and convictions of other nations, at least the European nations, in the years 1938 and 1939.

---

* Edward Frederick Lindley Wood Halifax, *Journal Officiel – Société des Nations* (1936), No. 5–6, 333–5.

† It is clear that in spite of the regrets that have been expressed, the large majority of the members of the Council are of the opinion that as far as the current question of discussion is concerned, it behoves individual members of the League of Nations to determine their attitude according to their own situation and their own obligations.

b) The conviction that, in spite of the efforts of the Geneva Protocol of 1924 and the Kellogg Pact of 1928, it has still not been possible to give war a new legal status through a new order of international law has deepened ever since in 1936 a cardinal institution of hitherto existing international law, *neutrality*, was completely redefined. Switzerland, whose exemplary propriety in questions of international law is universally recognized, declared in 1937 that it would no longer take part in any sanctions of the League of Nations and retreated to a position of integral neutrality. "The experience of the past years forces us to declare the maxims of neutrality even with respect to the League of Nations." Thus explained the President of Switzerland, Motta, on August 1, 1937.* The well-regarded Swiss scholar of international law Professor Dietrich Schindler wrote in 1938: "the belief that it is possible to distinguish according to a criterion relevant to international law between just and unjust wars cannot be maintained following the failure of the League of Nations."† The Swiss *Bundesrat* sent a memorandum to the Council of the League of Nations on April 29, 1938 that declared Switzerland's intention. In light of its continuing neutrality, Switzerland would not take part in any sanctions of the League of Nations Pact, not even any to which it was obligated after the declarations of 1920. The Council of the League of Nations formulated a resolution on May 14, 1938 that gave notice that it had received this intention and explained that Switzerland would not be called upon to participate in sanctions.

In the fall of 1939, all neutral states, including the United States of America, confirmed their neutrality in the sense of old international law. This contradicted the above-mentioned Budapest Articles and shows that up until the summer of 1939, the Kellogg Pact had not succeeded, at least for Europe, in replacing the traditional view of war with a new order.

IV. Principals and Accessories of the International Crime "War of Aggression"

Every war, the just war as well as the unjust war, the war of aggression as well as the war of defense, is by its very essence a collective process. The modern war in which millions of men are engaged, both militarily as combatants as well as economically as manufacturers and workers, is, to a special degree, the most intensive manifestation of the collective capture of every individual person, whose individual stake seems that much smaller the larger and more monstrous the total event is. When one speaks of the totality of the modern world war, one must note that

---

* Giuseppe Motta (1871–1940) was a Swiss politician.
† Dietrich Schindler (1890–1948) was a Swiss legal scholar.

such a war brings with it domestic and foreign political situations that cannot be fairly compared with the situation of the individual criminal murderer, thief, or of any other criminal. It must be reiterated here that we speak here of the war of aggression as the facts of the case of a new criminal act and not of war crimes in the sense of atrocities.

The criminal court judge who presides in court over a modern world war as an international crime, and who does not want to content himself with the determination of a summary collective responsibility, must establish those individuals who are to be regarded as the real perpetrators and participants of such a collective event. The criminal court judge must concretely determine the level of participation of each of these perpetrators of and participants in the causation of an enormous global event at both an objective and subjective level. In some cases and for certain politically decisive persons, this can be easy. Some people can be punished as the lead criminal on the basis of a notorious guilt. As soon, however, as a further circle of perpetrators or participants beyond such an individual are put on trial, as soon as people who were fundamentally not politically but rather economically and unpolitically active are to be judged, unusual questions are raised, at least they are if the "due process of law" is to be preserved. The obligation to obedience in the face of an unlawful order is clearly the subject of a completely different legal question than that of whether there exists a right or an obligation to refuse to obey when faced with an order contrary to martial law, or an inhuman order. The problem of insubordination with respect to orders contrary to law arises, in other words, for each of the three kinds of war crimes we have identified, in completely different ways.

A legal examination of the situation of the individual state citizen with respect to a war of aggression led by his government mainly concerns two points: one, the general question of the relation between state and individual in international law, especially the mediation of the individual state citizen through his state, and two, the separation of the circle of perpetrators or participants who come under scrutiny for the international-legal delict of a war.

1) According to a well-known theory that dominates the textbooks of international law, *the state* is the sole subject of international law, at least the normal and typical subject. This theory most sharply separates interior from exterior. International law is differentiated from domestic law as a special and separated circle of law. Individual state agencies and the individual state citizen are cut off from every direct responsibility of international law. They do not have any interstate (international), but rather only an intra-state (national) status. For the strictly dualistic interpretation that dominates in both theory and praxis in Germany and

other Continental European countries today, the individual state citizen cannot, as a result of this theory, commit an international crime. Only as an organ of the state can he effect an international responsibility for his state as such, with respect to other states. The lone perpetrator of a delict of international law can, therefore, only be the state as such. That which was called a "delict of international law" in the hitherto existing praxis and theory is therefore something fundamentally different from a delict in the criminal sense of the word. It is only the facts of a case that trigger certain financial, economic, or political consequences in international law (liability for damages, sanctions, backlashes, war) in the relations of state to state. States as such exist as equal and sovereign subjects of international law. This equal status consists fundamentally in the fact that every party has the same right to war (*jus ad bellum*) and the same right to neutrality. An international jurisdiction existed only on the foundation of the free contractual subjection of one state to another, and only according to the exact stipulation of arbitral or jurisdictional contracts. An international *criminal* jurisdiction in the criminal sense was truly unthinkable according to this interpretation. There has hitherto not existed an international criminal jurisdiction, and if one were to exist, it would only be possible on the basis of a special and expressly contractual subjection.

The concept of the equality of sovereign states formed the basis of the 1907 Hague Convention Respecting the Laws and Customs of War on Land as well as the 1919 Geneva Pact. It did so thoroughly, in the sense that the hitherto existing structure of international law remained unchanged. Only the state as such, not a political party or any other organization, nor the individual state citizen, conducted war. Only the state as such was the aggressor in the sense of the Geneva Protocol or object of sanctions. One observed in the eighteenth and nineteenth centuries the fact that war was an affair purely between states as the greatest progress that international law had ever achieved for mankind. The individual state citizen was, particularly in war, if not absorbed, then mediated for by his state. Practically, this meant that a norm of international law could never directly reach him. Rather, in all cases a commutation, a transformation of the norms, rights, and obligations of international law into intra-state norms, rights, and obligations of the individual state citizen had to be awaited.

Since 1919, the sharp division between interior and exterior, between international law and national law, has often been treated as an object of scholarly discussion. So-called monistic theories, many of which represent the primacy of international law, have achieved progress against the dualism of international law and intra-state law. Under these monistic theories, a direct inclusion of intra-state organizations and individual state citizens in international law is most often, but not always, understood. In many cases, the discussion is very theoretical and seemingly abstract. Its practical meaning lies in the fact that the individual state citizen is no longer, as was formerly the case, cut off from every responsibility of international law through intra-state legislation and government. This strict dualism has never corresponded to the Anglo-Saxon interpretation. This Anglo-Saxon interpretation holds to the principle: "international law is a part of the law of the land." It was more concerned with seeing the problem from the side of the individual and stressing that the individual, even in international law, is and must remain the bearer of all rights. I mention as a typical example a great authority from the time before the First World War, Westlake, who coined the formulation that while the state may be "the immediate," the individual is "the ultimate subject of international law."* Many statements by Anglo-Saxon authors sound even more individualistic.

In light of such antitheses of state and individual, one must not overlook the fact that even the leading English textbook of international law, Oppenheim's, represented, in all clarity and in exactly the same way as the German authors, the strict dualism of international law and state law and the full mediation, even absorption, of the individual. The phrase "international law is a part of the law of the land" does not have to exclude the possibility that the English judge, when in a conflict between a state order and a rule of international law, will abide by the state order. In the Geneva Protocol of 1924, only states, as already mentioned, are spoken of as aggressors. Only states as such are made responsible. Nor does the Kellogg Pact contain a word that negates this concept of war grounded in states. It is, further, a common fact that in all countries' praxis of international law, state and individual are sharply distinguished from one another for reasons of clarity. American praxis recognizes, too, the difference between national claims and individual claims. It developed this difference in numerous decisions of the American Mixed Claims Commissions. Likewise, the difference between state responsibility and individual guilt (private malice) is of course practically indispensable. Fundamentally, only states can appear as parties before international courts and international arbitral courts, if no other special arrangements are made. And according to Article 34 of the Statute from 1920, only states can appear as parties before the International Court of Justice in The Hague.

Yet the typical adherent of the outlawry of war will regard these examples of a sharp juridical separation of state and individual, of international law and intra-state law, of exterior and interior as examples of a purely

---

* John Westlake (1828–1913) was an English scholar of international law.

juridical and technical construction. As soon as the question ceases to be juridical and technical, and as soon as it contains moral meaning, as it does in relation to the question of a modern world war, the question of the relation between state and individual is raised to a fundamental and moral intensity. At this point, the question of this relation can easily descend into moral-philosophical, ideological, or even religious debates. American authors in particular are eager to underscore with strong moral pathos that only man, and not a state organization or any other organization, can be regarded as the upholder of international rights and obligations. If one turns the question in this universality towards the fundamental question of the opposition of state and individual, collectivity and individual, then the atmosphere changes completely. The charge of the deification of the state, Hegelianism, and militarism has been raised against Germany and the German nation for centuries. Concepts and constructions that refer to the state would then appear as the expression of a statist philosophy, if not as the sign of bondage and a slave-like disposition. The old problem gains a new trenchancy through the connection with the question of the criminalization of war. The difficulties must, in fact, seem incalculable, if metaphysical and moral oppositions are brought into connection with the horrible responsibility for the task of annihilation posed by a modern war.

Such deep oppositions were already held great sway at the time of the discussion of Wilhelm II's guilt (Article 227 of the Treaty of Versailles). Then, in 1919, there still existed in Europe a strong tradition of state sovereignty and an equality of states based upon equal sovereignty. It was, therefore, relatively easy to juridically demonstrate that a criminal punishment of one government by another government was impossible from the perspective of international law. Even Article 227 of the Treaty of Versailles itself still placed value upon the contractual agreement of defeated Germany. One did not want to forego the signature of the German state, nor was there assumed to be a directly valid norm of international law that would have directly provided the foundation for a criminal court of international law ruling on the individual "Wilhelm II of Hohenzollern." But since the First World War, all these questions have been advanced by American jurists. The attempt that then miscarried with reference to the German *Kaiser* is being repeated today with increased bitterness with reference to the guilty parties of the previous world war. If Wilhelm II's responsibility under criminal law failed in 1919 because of the then existing concepts in international law of state and sovereignty, then the great precedent for this interpretation shall be created today. The *novum crimen* shall not again fail because of the principle "*nullum crimen*." This is the firm resolution of the victors of this world war. One can only countenance them with juridical arguments to remind them of the fact that this attempt concerns not only a new, but rather a totally *novel* crime – not only a *novum crimen*, but rather, in light of its international character, a *crimen novi generis* that is separated from offenses against the rules of the laws of war and the real atrocities through its great legal and moral particularities.

If it is, then, fully correct according to hitherto existing international law to point out that, according to international law, only the state as such can conduct war, and that only the state as such can become an aggressor, then it is still hardly practical to put such an argument at the center of things in the attempt to clearly delineate the new international crime of war from the other kinds of war crimes, and to raise up this crime in its entirely specific particularity. Every war, including the war of aggression and the just war, is by its very nature such a collective process in the eminent meaning of the word "collective." Guilt and punishment, meanwhile, are, according to the modern interpretation of penal law, no longer collective guilt and collective punishment. They should only affect the individual, guilty, human being. If such a marked collective process is penalized and criminalized in this way, then the criminal court judge stands before a novel attempt. Even if war is a crime, mankind has still become used to saying that a war is being "committed" in the same way that one commits murder or theft. The relation of the perpetrator to his act is, in the case of war, a peculiar, completely novel problem. This becomes particularly evident when the question of the delineation of the circle of perpetrators of and participants in such a new international crime is considered.

2) Who is the *perpetrator of the international crime "war,"* and from which points of view can a delineation of the circle of perpetrators be carried out? The *state* as such, as a juridical person, should be winnowed out here as the perpetrator. The representatives of a criminalization of the war of aggression, however, universally reject this construction. They declare it a gimmick that serves only to free the real evil-doers from punishment.

Besides the state in its juridical sense, the *nation* as a whole could still come under consideration as the perpetrator of the crime, namely, if it were in agreement with the war under a democratic regime. This collective responsibility of the nation would lead to a situation where every soldier, every munitions worker, every taxpayer – in short, every member of the nation – would have to be punished, should he or she not be able to individually exculpate him- or herself. If one makes a parallel between war and piracy, then it stands to reason to use this parallel to arrive at such collectivistic implications. That is to say, the real upholder of piracy is not the individual pirate, be he leader or an inferior. The pirate is, according to an old interpretation, the ship as a whole. Everyone who is found aboard the pirate ship is treated as a pirate, if it is not obvious that he was there as a prisoner or as a victim of the pirates.

Such a kind of collective punishment of an entire nation would be a primitive interpretation. It is a mere matter of strict liability, not a liability corresponding to actual guilt, and is rejected universally today. Respected jurists see the mark of the primitive character of this law in the fact that in hitherto existing international law only the state as such held parties strictly liable. The modern interpretation expresses itself in the often cited and well-known phrase, "you cannot in(ter)dict a nation." A total collective responsibility is, moreover, suited to depriving the real guilty and responsible parties of punishment. An expression of Napoleon's is cited in this regard: "*Les crimes collectifs n'engagent personne.*"* The task of determining the perpetrators of and participants in the new crime therefore remain unsolved.

One cannot disregard the political character of war when determining the real perpetrators of the new international crime. War is both internally and externally a process of high politics. All important decisions that lead to war are political decisions and concern persons in their political function. As a result of this, the head of state who declares the war of aggression is responsible above all. Moreover, members of the government who declared war are also made responsible. If war is declared, according to the constitution of the war-conducting state, in the form of a law (in other words, through a resolution of parliament), then the members of the legislative body will also be directly responsible, at least if they have not expressly voted against the war. One finds this politically determined circle described in the literature as that of the "*gouvernants.*"

Already with these first deliberations concerning the delineation of the circle of perpetrators, it becomes evident that it is necessary to keep in view the inner constitutional conditions of the state that conducts the war of aggression. Through doing so, it becomes clear – and not only in a formal sense – who the head of state, the government, and the remaining responsible perpetrators are. The real responsibility for the political resolution to wage war as well as the causal context, without the clarification of which a penal judgment is not possible, can only be determined with regard to the concrete constitutional situation of the state conducting war. The words "head of state" and "government" politically mean something completely different in an absolutist system as opposed to in a constitutional state, where responsible ministers take over the political responsibility for the orders of the head of state through their own signature. How far this constitutional responsibility reaches is another question. In the case of Wilhelm II, the head of state alone was

---

* Collective crimes involve no one.

made responsible under international law, without the inclusion of the constitutionally responsible *Reich* Chancellor Bethmann-Hollweg.[281] This was, however, only an expression of the conviction that Wilhelm II led a personal, authoritarian, and arbitrary regiment. It was precisely this personal regiment that was treated as a fundamental component of his guilt in the world war.

If one shifts this point of view towards the Hitler regime, then Hitler would have to be, by virtue of the concentration of all power and all responsibility in Hitler's hand, the lone war criminal of the last world war, as far as Germany is concerned. Obviously, the circle of perpetrators of the new crime against international law should also be persecuted. Not only Hitler himself personally, but also his "regime" must be made criminally responsible. The expression "regime" is, in this case, characteristic and, I believe, unavoidable. In using the expression "regime," a unique kind of political and social rule is distinguished from other forms of state and government. The expression is common, but it is still used in a particular way both for the Fascist regime as well as for the National Socialist regime to describe a particular method of political decision-making. The specific idiosyncrasy of both regimes was based on the fact that political decision-making was concentrated in the head of a party who, with the help of the party, penetrated and subjected the state and the entire remaining polity to his will. Such a regime rests upon the differentiation between leaders and the led, governing and the governed. Only those who belong to the center of decision-making of the regime are party to political decision-making. This means, with respect to the question of the perpetrator and the circle of perpetrators of the international crime "war," that only those who are really in the regime in the sense that they are party to the formation of political ideas should come into view as perpetrators.

Here, too, the judgment as to which persons come into view must depend on the concrete interior political situation within the regime. The Hitler regime showed, after all, that political decision-making in the case of such a concentration of power in one person is a particularly interesting but often opaque affair. It is a part of the essence of such a regime that many power groupings fight amongst one another behind the closed façade of the unconditional unity of the regime. A tight circle forms around the central point of formal omnipotence, a circle that does not deliberately come forward within the state or in public, but a circle that nonetheless blocks access to the peak in a most effective way. During the absolutism of the eighteenth and nineteenth centuries this was called the *Camarilla* and the *Antichambre*, and in the Hitler regime it was not difficult to see that the much-touted *Führer* principle had become an *Antichambre* principle to the fullest degree. Here, in the milieu around the *Führer*, there formed the real complot in a criminal sense, the real conspiracy. It is of symptomatic significance for the legal judgment of such a situation that Hitler had a special predilection for speaking of a "sworn community." I am of the view that the perpetrators in the sense of the international crime "war" in such a regime can only be those who belonged to this "sworn community" that built itself around Hitler. If one cannot succeed in determining this real complot, this "gang," this politico-criminal association, this entirely concrete "sworn community" as such and showing it to the world, that which the public opinion of the world and the feeling of justice of many millions of people expects from a criminal case against the Hitler regime will be most tragically disappointed, even in spite of massive protests.

The specific idiosyncrasy of such a regime must, then, be kept in view. If not, it is almost unavoidable that the juridical concepts of other constitutional conditions will become mixed up in the proceedings of such a trial, and will render the real circumstances of the case entirely beyond recognition. This danger can best be recognized in the word "government." In general, one understands by the term "government," apart from the head of state, the ministers – both individuals and also as a council in their capacity as bearers of the highest offices of state and the highest functions of state. I do not wish in any way to excuse or defend the ministers of the Hitler regime. However, for an objective evaluation of the real perpetrators, one cannot ignore the fact that many ministers in the Hitler regime were something completely different from those responsible leading persons who, in the sense of a hitherto exist-ing state law, be it that of a constitutional-monarchic or a republican constitution, be it even that of an enlightened monarchical absolutism, are called "ministers." Minister, in the sense of the constitutional-legal terms of the past century, is the only person who can be responsible for his portfolio because he is exclusively responsible for his portfolio. Such a minister has direct access to the head of state in questions concerning his portfolio as well as the great right of immediate and direct presenta-tion. He can refuse to tolerate, he can rebuff meddling and influence from a third, irresponsible party that interferes with the decision-making of the head of state. He is, with regard to his portfolio, "master in his own house" insofar as he himself can determine the functionaries, from the under-secretary to the last usher, of his ministry and his portfolio without outside influence.

This was not the case for many "ministers" of the Hitler regime. "Access to the *Führer*" was a particular problem. Interference and influence from other parties, especially from the side of the Party Chancellery, the *Reichleiters*, *Gauleiters*, and numerous other persons was a matter of course and inevitable. The naming of functionaries, including functionaries of the ministries, required the agreement of the Party Chancellery. The leader of the Party Chancellery had fundamental and more intensive ways of interfering in such processes than did the minister himself. The leaders of the Chancelleries (Party Chancellery, *Reich* Chancellery, Presidial Chancellery, Chancellery of the *Führer*) were, depending on the issue at hand, authorities beyond the ministerial level. A meeting of the *Reich* Cabinet never took place after the first few years. Numerous special deputies ruled over the various portfolios with varying amounts of actual power. The minister often waited for months for an audience before he could get access to the head of state. It is, then, a fair question to ask whether one can make the ministers responsible for the fact that they tolerated such a state of affairs. But as for answering the question of who the perpetrator of an international crime is, no further clarification of these circumstances of which I remind the reader is necessary in order to show that it is impermissible to declare a penal judgment against a large number of individual men on account of an international crime, "war," without having a clear picture of the inner conditions of such a regime and the methods of the formation of its political decision-making.

The word "party," too, has a different meaning in different political contexts and cannot be used as a criterion without a further objective examination. In the three well-known cases of a one-party system – the Communist Party in the Soviet Union, the Fascist Party in Italy, and the National Socialist Party in Germany – the party had a different function in each case. An organization that had swelled up to ten million members, like the National Socialist Party in Germany, cannot, simply by sheer virtue of its size, be an "order" or an "elite" in the same way as a party chastised through continual "purifications," like the Communist Party, or in the same way as the far less numerous Fascist Party in Italy. In comparison with the party in the Hitler system, an organization like the SS had far more the character of an "order." I want to allude to this general sociological problem of the "order" and the "elite" here only because it is of interest for answering the question of who belongs to the "regime" and to the "*équipe*" of the regime.

A sociology of these new parties that share only their name with the parties of a liberal constitutional system based on free promotion and publicity is unfortunately still lacking. The foreign literature, in particular the American literature, is not accessible to me, and the investigations in the German literature prior to 1933 (such as Robert Michels, *Soziologie des Parteiwesens*, 1910) have unfortunately not been continued.* One finds, as far as I can see, an interesting monographic treatment in a

---

* Robert Michels (1876–1936) was a German sociologist.

dissertation from the Berlin *Handelshochschule*, J. Kendziora's 1933 "The Concept of the Political Party in the System of Political Liberalism,"* which, as its title already shows, restricts itself to the constitutional conditions of those years, and then only to the transitional type of action parties. It does not address the particular, unanticipated, and often non-transparent developments of the Hitler regime. Several insights and formulations from earlier authors, such as Max Weber, Georges Sorel (on the politico-criminal organization), and Vilfredo Pareto are useful. I cite here, for example, Pareto's definition of the "elite:" "Elite are those who pay the lowest charges while receiving the greatest income." This formulation, limited to financial categories and typical for the sociologist Pareto, contains an important criterion for the reversed situation of the numerous victims who, without having any political influence, had to pay in the form of donations, contributions, and other tributes *"pour se racheter de l'invasion."*† I must content myself with only this brief mention of the sociological side of the new problem in this more general discussion.

The actual consequences of a war impact the entire nation and every individual. Blockade, occupation, revenge, and other effects of an operation affect the good and the evil, the just and the unjust without discrimination. The just and the unjust are affected without discrimination through both war and defeat. This is a great misfortune, but it does not amount to a jolting of the concepts of law and morality. As soon as the question concerns earthly criminal justice organized by men for other men, however, it becomes necessary to differentiate between the two (good and evil). If a criminal judicial case proceeding in a solemn form commits such a mistake on a decisive point, this is no everyday error of justice that one can put up with as a human mistake. The injustice and the calamity of such an error would correspond to the greatness of the global crime towards whose atonement the great trials were arranged.

3) A war of aggression is a matter of *foreign affairs*. If the war of aggression is an international crime, then it becomes a crime that concerns not only domestic affairs but also foreign affairs. This means that all questions of delinquency, complicity, and participation are also raised as foreign political questions. The aggressor state can have auxiliaries. The members of the leading political class of the auxiliaries become, through their actions, participants in the international crime. Depending on the case, they are principals of the first degree or principals of the second degree, or are guilty of aiding and abetting. The Anglo-American theory and praxis concerning participation in criminal acts differ in many

---

* Johanna Kendziora (1903–?) was a German student of political theory.
† To redeem the invasion.

respects from that of German jurisprudence. One main difference is due to the lack of a codified penal law. A common section of penal law separate from the special section is lacking, and there is, therefore, no theory of the facts of the case in the German sense. Older English jurisprudence differentiates the actual perpetrator from the accessories. As for the differentiation of the participants, one still holds to the old, common law-based point of view that differentiated between participation in a crime committed before, during, and after the crime itself (*concursus antecedens, concomitans,* and *subsequens*). The differentiation between perpetrator and participant is, however, not made in the first class of crimes, treasons. In the second class of crimes, felonies, this differentiation has been abolished ever since the 1861 Accessories and Abettors Act, with the result that for all kinds of crimes in Anglo-American law, every form of participation, insofar as it is not causally important, is valid as delinquency and is punished with the penalty for delinquency. Conspiracy can, of course, be punished alongside the committing of the crime itself, but is not (as is a "complot" in current German penal law) an entirely independent delict, but rather an expansion of the regulation of participation, indeed, in the same way as the complot in common penal law (complot means "*conspiratio*" in Latin). The main aim here was to capture the mutual strengthening of criminal intent without regard for the equal application of force. The term "conspiracy" allows one to punish all participants equally, even for uncompleted crimes. "The conspiracy is a partnership in criminal purposes;" according to the classic definition of judge Willes in the English decision Mulcahy v. The Queen (1866): conspiracy is "the agreement of two or more to do an unlawful act." Aid after a committed act is treated, just as in German penal law (Article 257 of the German *Reichsstrafgesetzbuch*), not as an act of participation, but rather as a particular delict. The earlier actor or perpetrator who actually commits the offense is designated today as the "principal of the first degree," the former "accessory at the fact," who was present at the committing of the act. The party who aids and abets the offense is designated as the "principal of the second degree."

We need not delve further here into the theory of participation and involvement in crimes in penal law. But when one speaks of crimes, one cannot avoid mentioning participation in crimes. When crimes of an international – in other words, of a foreign-political character – are at stake, then the question of foreign accomplices, participants, and abettors raises itself with all of the accompanying difficulties of such a problem of foreign affairs. What this practically means for a criminal trial becomes immediately evident as soon as one begins to apply the above-mentioned penal categories of accessory and conspiracy to the foreign political situation of 1939. I had, therefore, to remind the reader of a few elementary terms of the theory of participation, all the more so since this aspect of the problem has come up in recent discussions of war as an international crime with an often astonishing consistency with regard to the fundamentals, yet without any consequence as regards the concrete, foreign affairs-related side of the question.

The pioneers of the criminalization of the war of aggression speak, therefore, of the foreign "*complices*" of the new crime. They are aware that a neutrality in the old sense of international law is no longer acceptable when international law allows the just war and treats the unjust war as a crime. They go so far as to consider the neutral state that, under reference to the previous law of neutrality of the 1907 Hague Conventions, does not forbid its citizens from economically supplying the state conducting the unjust war as a participant in the injustice of the war of aggression. "A State aiding a violating State is itself guilty of violating the Pact," as it says in the interpretation of the Kellogg Pact in the Budapest Rules of the Conference of the International Law Association from September 1934, mentioned above. If even the neutral state becomes a participant in the international crime in this way, then clearly so must the state that concludes a non-aggression pact with the aggressor state. For under the circumstances, the non-aggression pact covers the aggressor's back. And if not the state as such, but rather the responsible initiators are to be made criminally responsible, then the investigation would have to be expanded correspondingly to the inner constitutional condition of the neutral state or of the state obligating itself to non-aggression.

From the point of view of the new international crime, therefore, all non-aggression pacts from the summer of 1939 would have to be investigated as to whether the partners distanced themselves from the crime. Germany had, at that time, concluded the treaty of August 23, 1939 with the Soviet Union, which expanded and developed the neutrality treaty of April 1926. The treaty was described on the German side as a "firm and immovable foundation upon which both states can build and reach close collaboration." This non-aggression treaty was regarded as a treaty of great international meaning and historical importance, indeed, as a turning point in the history of Europe and beyond. The German–Soviet Border and Friendship Treaty of September 28, 1939 followed this treaty and established the borders of both sides' *Reich* interests in the area of the former Polish state, recognized these borders as final, and rejected "any and every interference of a third power in this arrangement." In a German–Soviet exchange of letters from September 28, 1939, it was agreed, on the basis and with the intention of the desired political understanding, to develop via all means the economic relations and trade of goods between Germany and the USSR and to develop an economic program according to which the Soviet Union would provide

Germany with raw materials in exchange for industrial products. In pursuance of this plan, in February 1940 an economic agreement was concluded between the two countries, and on January 10, 1941, an expanded economic agreement. The government of the United States of America expressly declared its neutrality in September 1939. These remarks may suffice to make the point clear. It is not possible, in light of the connections between intentionalization and penalization upon which the novelty of the crime of war rest, to entirely disregard the foreign political situation and the resulting questions concerning complicity and participation.

V. The Situation of the Individual State Citizen, Especially that of the Economically Active Ordinary Businessman

The individual state citizen who does not belong to the circle of leading political figures and who has taken part neither in offenses against the rules of the law of war nor in barbarities would normally be regarded neither as a perpetrator of nor as a participant in the international crime of the war of aggression. Some authors have nonetheless represented the view that the individual state citizen can be made responsible to object to military service and obedience to the government that conducts an unjust war through the direct obligation of international law.

In Germany, the problem of penal law regarding the direct legal situation of the individual in international law was handled through the question of whether the individual state citizen, in spite of domestic penal prescriptions against treason, had the right to report secrets concerning actions contrary to either international law or existing treaties with foreign governments. This right of the state citizen was particularly represented after 1919 by the Hamburg scholar of penal law Moritz Leipmann.[*] A student of Leipmann's, Artur Wegner, came to the conclusion in the piece "Criminal Injustice, State Injustice, and National Injustice" (Hamburg, 1925) that the individual, regardless of the respective domestic prescriptions against treason, was not permitted to report to a foreign government acts of his own government contrary to international law, but that he could do so to the international community as such, which in this case would be represented by the League of Nations.[†] According to this view, then, an industrialist or businessman would have the right to share his state's military secrets with the League of Nations, were he of the opinion that the arming of his state violated international obligations. As concerns our question touching on international penal

[*] Moritz Leipmann (1869–1928) was a German scholar of criminology and penal law.
[†] Artur Wegner was a German scholar of international law.

law, we are, however, not so much concerned with the justification through international law of acts normally prohibited by domestic law, especially concerning treason, but rather with the question of whether the individual state citizen is, in the event of an unjust war, responsible under international law to refuse any and every act of cooperation and obedience if he himself is not to be a participant in the new international crime of war. In this regard, the well-known pacifist scholar of international law Hans Wehberg has (among other writings) in his piece "The Proscription of War" (Berlin, 1930) represented the thesis that it is a consequence of the Kellogg Pact "that henceforth in the event of a war of aggression, all citizens of all states which have ratified the Kellogg Pact are qualified and obligated to refuse military service."

This interpretation remained entirely isolated and without influence in Europe. The dominant view and praxis in all states of the earth stand in opposition to it – namely, that the individual is obliged, in the event of war, to loyalty and obedience to his national government, and that the decision about the justice and injustice of a war is to be put not to the individual but rather to the national government. Here, too, one must note that this does not concern taking part in atrocities, in barbarities, but rather the question of the international crime of war as such. The fact that the extreme pacifist view of an author like Hans Wehberg led to no change in the common conviction, let alone in current positive law, is evident from the remarks of a well-known jurist of the League of Nations, Nicolas Politis, who gave lectures on this theme at Columbia University in New York and later published these lectures in 1926 under the title *"Les Nouvelles Tendances du Droit International."* Politis emphasizes that the direct obligation of the individual to international law leads both to large practical difficulties and runs contrary to a *"tradition séculaire."* This secular tradition has, to be sure, been attacked in some challenges and proposals by private authors, but it has yet to be brought into doubt by any official declaration or by the praxis of any government. All governments of the earth have, up to this point, adhered to the idea that the state citizen, even when he does not approve of the conduct of his government, is obligated to loyalty and obedience in the event of a war.

Nor has this universal praxis and theory been abolished through the argumentation of Scholastic natural law. In the discussion about just war, many distinguished authors have made reference to the doctrine of Scholastic thinkers from the Middle Ages and the sixteenth century. This has been done above all in the work of a leading American jurist of international law, James Brown Scott, the President of the American Society for International Law as well as the president of the International Law Division of the Carnegie Foundation and professor of International Law at Columbia University. James Brown Scott has, in numerous lectures and publications, particularly celebrated the Spanish Dominican Francisco de Vitoria and the Neo-Thomist Jesuit Suárez* as founders of modern international law and of an interpretation of war appropriate to their time. J.B. Scott already played a prominent role at the Paris Peace Conference of 1919 with regard to the question of the prosecution of Wilhelm II and war guilt, through the doctrine of "just war." In light of his extraordinary influence on public opinion in America and the entire world, it is expedient to discuss further this Renaissance of the Scholastic doctrine and to make the reader aware of the limits of its usefulness.

Scholastic theologians universally assumed one of two situations. One was that of medievally organized polities, strongly feudal- or estate-based in character, with a constitutional right to resistance. The other was the situation of the confessional civil wars of the sixteenth and seventeenth centuries. In the event of a manifestly unjust war, they supposed that the individual (whom they most often conceived as being in the bonds of the estate system) had the right to resistance and to refuse his obedience, but that he also had a corresponding responsibility. When such theories are cited today, one cannot disregard the fundamental change in the situation and in social organization. Scholastic thinkers stand in the fixed *ordo spiritualis*† of their church and argue under the presupposition of a recognized trans-national authority, the *potestas spiritualis*‡ of their church. The individual who refuses his obedience had in his church – in other words, in his confessor and its church authority – a determined, supernatural footing. One refers not to the empty space, to his individual judgment, but rather to clear institutions, and even with regard to his conscience, the individual has a represented, secure *forum internum*§ in the form of his confessor.

One needs only to compare this entirely concrete presupposition of those Scholastic teachings with the present situation on the earth in order to recognize the *punctum saliens*.¶ It is clearly not possible to postulate a clear state of affairs in international law for the individual that obligates him to resistance against his own country and its government in the event of a war, as long as fixed international institutions that the individual can turn to for information and protection are not created. The Scholastic theologians who speak with great caution of the right to resistance and the right to deny obedience in the event of the unjust war

---

* Francisco Suárez (1548–1617) was a Spanish Jesuit priest, philosopher, and theologian who made major contributions to seventeenth-century metaphysics, theology, and legal philosophy.
   † Spiritual order.
   ‡ Spiritual power.
   § Internal forum.
   ¶ Salient point.

(here, we are not concerned with the refusal of obedience with respect to a single order to commit punishable acts) were not jurists of a state government, but rather church advisers of conscience and church teachers of church advisers of conscience. They lectured as part of a teaching vocation, a *missio canonica** that they had received from a godly institution set high above all national states and governments. Every one of their words was spoken against the secure background of religious belief and within the firm framework of a well-organized church. Modern authors who envision such direct, international rights and responsibilities of the individual with respect to his government would therefore have to be able to refer to corresponding international institutions of analogous authority, firmness, and supra-political spirituality. The League of Nations has not succeeded in rising to become such an institution, in the opinion of the European nations. The preparation of such an institution, which was granted with the arrival of President W. Wilson in Europe, immediately went for naught with Wilson's departure from Europe. The International Court of Justice in The Hague was not responsible for questions of war. Moreover, the governments of Great Britain, France, Australia, New Zealand, South Africa, and India disassociated themselves from the obligations of the Facultative Clause (Article 36 of the Statute of the Permanent International Court of Justice) immediately after the outbreak of war in their correspondence (from September 7–27, 1939) with the General Secretary of the League of Nations. To date, there still does not exist any universally international penal court that could have decided on the justice or injustice of a war at the outbreak or beginning of the conflict without having to await the outcome of the conflict. Not once, in the case of Italy in 1935–6, the only case of a "proclaimed aggressor," did it manage to make any declarations, appeals to the citizens of the aggressor state, or to prosecute a citizen as a participant in an international crime.

The history of the efforts aimed at the prevention of war from 1919–39 shows, then, that today's world is far removed from an order that could be reasonably compared with the "*ordo spiritualis*" of the Christian church of the Middle Ages. Above, we have exhaustively discussed the question of whether the concept of the war of aggression existed in the consciousness of European peoples and governments in the summer of 1939 not only universally as an injustice, but also as a crime that belonged to the jurisdiction of other states in a criminal sense. We have not been able to answer this question with a "yes." In September 1939, all the governments of all the states that were not conducting war formally declared their neutrality and enacted several neutrality laws for

---

* Canonical mission.

their citizens. In doing so, they, at least with respect to concepts of the European state, expressed the fact that they regarded the decision as to the justice or injustice of a war as an affair of governments and not of individual citizens. It may be true that the champions of the theory of just war spiritedly criticized this behavior of perfect neutrality. Indeed, already in 1938, John B. Whitton charged the American legislation concerning neutrality with placing the aggressor and its victim on the same level and of not once attempting to guard the rights of a collective security system.* In doing so, he expressed the opinion of numerous distinguished Anglo-American authors. But the difference between the official behavior of the US government and the public opinion of anti-neutrality revealed itself here, too. This contrast must have made a citizen of a European state engaged in war come to a certain realization: his direct status under international law was only a project and a postulate, while in practical reality he was, incidentally, left to his own fate, and, indeed, a fate that was decided nationally, not internationally.

The individual state citizen who, in 1939, resolved to resist the war led by his government as an unjust act could find neither in domestic opinion nor in domestic law any footing or protection. He was inserted into the highly specialized organization of a modern industrial polity marked by the division of labor. Even though he was not in the position to obtain information, he should, according to the theory of some authors, have nonetheless come, at his own risk, to a decision about unforeseeable foreign political consequences for his country and his nation. Who could have imposed on the individual citizen such a legal responsibility of international law, one sanctioned by criminal punishments, in the face of an imminent world war in such a global situation – in a Europe, moreover, whose entire situation had been marked by the civil war of international parties, by an impenetrable system of mutual assistance and non-aggression pacts, and by the obvious collapse of the League of Nations?

In this situation, the individual citizen, especially the economically active businessman and industrialist, who did not belong to the political circles of the regime, had to leave the judgment as to the justice and injustice of a war to his national government. This corresponded to the secular tradition, a tradition that had prevailed among all nations of the European continent for centuries, and which can be abrogated only through secure, new institutions. This tradition has deep-rooted causes and reasons to exist of both a religious and a moral nature. It can call upon a theological doctrine that was extraordinarily strong in the

---

* John B. Whitton (1892-?) was a professor of international law at Princeton University.

Lutheran section of the German people (Romans 13:1).* In consideration of the fact that the name of the great philosopher Kant is cited as an authority against war in all of the pacifist literature, one cannot ignore the fact that even Kant rejects any right to resistance against the government and speaks of the responsibility of the people "to bear even the unbearably issued misuse of the utmost violence." On the other hand, as concerns the citizen directly, the status quo today is such that up to this point no state in the world has abdicated from retaining the decision as to the justice and injustice of a war. A citizen who, in the event of war, refuses his obedience and disturbs mobilization, or one who attempts to place himself in a position of understanding with a foreign country in order to provide himself with the necessary information for a moral and juridical evaluation of war, has hitherto been treated by every European government as a traitor, as guilty of high treason, a saboteur, or made liable for the most severe criminal punishments. Here, again, this does not concern the question of a right or a responsibility, or of refusing one's obedience to certain orders contrary to law. This concerns the decision about justice and injustice of a war in its entirety and the implications in criminal law that result from such a decision.

The secular tradition that binds the individual citizen especially strongly to his national government in the event of a war has strong historical roots. The modern state of the European continent resulted from the fact that it disposed of the medieval right to resistance and replaced it with its own legality and legal judicial remedies. All legality of a modern state rests on the assumption of the legality of all government and administrative acts. The modern state of the European Continent has, as a result, a unique prerogative that all scholars of state and administrative law accentuate, and that the great French Jurist Maurice Hauriou designates as the right of "*obéissance préalable*."† The citizen is obligated with respect to a formal legal order, subject to the possibility of judicial remedy. In the event of a war, this obligation to obedience is endlessly raised, while the possibility of legal means and judicial remedies no longer applies in the broadest sense. All modern states have created judicial remedies against state ordinances. But in practically all states there is a valid, in one form or another, principle that has been named the "doctrine of political questions" due to the famous decision of Chief Justice Marshall in *Marbury v. Madison* (5 US Cranch 166/67). This means that government acts – especially, however, those of a highly political nature,

---

* Romans 13:1: Everyone must submit himself to the governing authorities, for there is no authority except that which God has established. The authorities that exist have been established by God. (New International Version)

† Maurice Hauriou (1856–1929) was a French jurist and legal theorist.

such as a declaration of war – are not subject to any judicial control. Most European countries, especially France, Italy, Spain, and Romania, recognize this doctrine of the independence of political acts vis-à-vis the judiciary and have developed a praxis of "*actes de gouvernement*," acts that are litigable neither for a civil-judicial nor for an administrative-judicial reexamination. In no country does there exist a judicial remedy for the individual citizen against a declaration of war issued by his government.

I remind the reader here again of the unique character of "political questions" in order to show that the domestic situation of the individual citizen was in no way prepared for a direct claim under international criminal law. The states and governments of the world adhered to the principle that objection to military service in a war was an act contrary to law threatened with severe penalties. Nonetheless, the citizen who objected to military service for reasons of conscience, the conscientious objectors, are especially provided for and treated with respect in some countries. But the cases of refusal that refer to the justice or injustice of a certain war are fundamentally different from the cases of universal refusal of armed service for religious motives. The intention of the citizen who objects to military service on the grounds that a particular war is unjust directs himself not towards every war as such and every armed operation as such, but rather towards the fact that this specific, present war represents injustice on the side of his own state and justice on the side of the foreign opponent. Here, then, the individual citizen makes not a specific religious decision, but rather a specific political decision directed against his own country that benefits the foreign adversary of his country.

The praxis of the United States makes, as far as I can see, no exception in this regard. It may be true that the attempts connected with the Kellogg Pact to give the individual a right to resistance are especially strong as far as public opinion is concerned. Nonetheless, the final result is that the behavior of the authorities and the highest courts is unambiguous. This becomes apparent in the following cases.

In the naturalization affair of a woman, Schwimmer, the United States Supreme Court declared in a decision on May 27, 1929, that it was a basic principle of the Constitution of the United States of America that citizens of the United States are obligated to defend the government with armed force whenever the need should arise. In its grounds for this decision, the Court stressed the fact that the influence of the conscientious objector against the use of military force in defense of the principles of the Constitution and the government was more harmful than mere refusal to bear arms. One has to concede that along with this decision three Justices, under the leadership of Justice Holmes, formed a dissenting minority, referring to the principle of the freedom of thought and the doctrine of the Sermon on the Mount, which grants the right to refuse military service. The decision in Schwimmer's case did not, however, really concern our question, because the decision speaks only of the religiously motivated refusal of armed service. Nonetheless, the decision is precisely for this reason directly of great argumentative force, because the case of a religiously motivated refusal to bear arms lacks the real political trenchancy that a refusal to bear arms on account of the injustice of a *particular* war contains in the highest degree. In contrast to Schwimmer's case, the judgment of the Supreme Court from May 25, 1931 in the matter of MacIntosh precisely concerns our question. The decision has become well known to jurists from every country because it was reproduced in the *Annual Digest of Public International Law Cases 1929–1930*, edited by Prof. Lauterpacht. Because of its great practical significance, I shall cite the case at greater length.

The professor of theology, MacIntosh, who was born as a Canadian citizen and was resident in the United States for some time, applied for his naturalization. According to the naturalization laws (34 US Sta. L. 596, 598), MacIntosh was to give a declaration in the form of an oath "that he would support and defend the Constitution and laws of the United States of America against all enemies, foreign and domestic." At this point, MacIntosh declared "that he would do everything that in his conviction corresponded to the interests of the country, but that he would, in the event of war, reserve the right to judge the war and that he was not obligated to enter into every war without regard for his judgment of the war." The attempt was rejected by the first authority, because the reservation of a judgment of war proved that the applicant was not devoted to the principles of the Constitution of the United States. The applicant then appealed to the Circuit Court of Appeals. In a decision made on June 30, 1930, the Court of Appeals reversed the decision of the first authority and ruled that the applicant must be naturalized. Upon the announcement of this decision, Justice Manton explained: "a citizen who has intents that amount to scruples of conscience or religion against a war that he regards as unjust is to be handled similarly as one who has reservations towards all wars. International law recognizes a distinction between a morally justified and unjustified war. In the recently concluded Kellogg Pact just such a recognition was articulated." The Justice added that someone who objected to military service must not necessarily have religious scruples, as long as the scruples are honest. However, this decision of the Circuit Court was reversed by the Supreme Court in its decision of May 25, 1931, although four of the nine Justices issued a dissenting opinion. The Supreme Court's decision reads:

> whether any citizen shall be exempt from serving in the armed forces of the nation in time of war is dependent upon the will of Congress, and not upon

the scruples of the individual, except as Congress provides. That body, thus far, has seen fit, by express enactment, to relieve from the obligation of armed service those persons who belong to the class known as conscientious objectors, and this policy is of such long standing that it is thought by some to be beyond the possibility of alteration. Indeed, it seems to be assumed in this case that the privilege is one that Congress itself is powerless to take away. [. . .] The privilege of the native-born conscientious objector to avoid bearing arms comes not from the Constitution, but from the acts of Congress. He is unwilling to rely, as every native-born citizen is obliged to do, upon the probable continuance by Congress of the long established and approved practice of exempting the honest conscientious objector, while at the same time asserting his willingness to conform to whatever the future law constitutionally shall require of him, but discloses a present and fixed purpose to refuse to give his moral or armed support to any future war in which the country may be actually engaged if, in his opinion, the war is not morally justified, the opinion of the nation as expressed by Congress to the contrary notwithstanding. If the attitude of this claimant, as shown by his statements and the inferences properly to be deduced from them, be held immaterial to the question of his fitness for admission to citizenship, where shall the line be drawn?

The individual citizen has, then, absolutely no legal possibility within his own state to assert his own judgment on the injustice of a war against his own government. His conscience stands in the conflict between an old national obligation sanctioned by secular traditions and a completely new international obligation – one, however, that claims to be an obligation not only of conscience but also of law. In the realm of international law, however, he finds no ordered authority or institution to which he can turn. All that remains for him is to resolve himself to an attempt at civil war or to martyrdom. This is the terrible conflict between a national and international obligation in which the individual citizen is placed if one gives him a directly international status with consequences for international criminal law. The citizen of a totalitarian one-party system, however, finds himself in an even more difficult position than that of the citizen of a polity with a liberal constitution. In the totalitarian one-party system, every resistance against the regime means instant annihilation on the grounds of treachery and sabotage. If one so obligates the individual citizen subject to such a totalitarian system, this would indeed mean nothing else than imposing on him the legal responsibility of a hopeless attempt at civil war on the one hand, or the legal responsibility of martyrdom on the other.

Such obligations cannot, of course, simply exist for the wartime enemy of the national state. They can only be imposed by an international authority. This international authority would not only have to give unambiguous declarations and orders to all state citizens upon the outbreak of war. It would also be obligated under all laws of justice and morality to provide for a reasonably sufficient protection of those men who abide by its orders. One cannot draw up obligations and, in doing so, push those obligated towards a murderous fate. One who is not in the position to protect is, in the long run and in the event of emergency, also not in the position to obligate. This corresponds to the connection, stressed by scholars of natural law, between protection and obedience, the "mutual relation between obedience and protection."* The idea that he who protects also obligates, and that, too, reciprocally, there cannot exist any legal responsibility in the long run without protection, belongs to the elementary fundamentals of all human community. The well-known English socialist and representative of a pluralist theory of the state, G.D.H. Cole, who often refers to this connection and makes the obligatory force of a polity dependent on its effective power to protect, has a phrase for this: "*Protego, ergo obligo.*"†

This is not only a memorable formulation but also an important legal and moral principle. It is valid for national and international law, but especially so for a conflict of national and international obligations, as arose in our case. An obligation of international law lacking a precise *corpus delicti*, lacking a precise delineation of the circle of perpetrators, lacking a judicial organization for the decision of doubtful cases, lacking an organization for the effective protection of the obligated, cannot from this point of view be the foundation for a conviction under criminal law, especially when the case concerns the unpolitical individual citizen, who, faced with the conflict between national law resting on firm institutions and a highly controversial (with respect to the war of 1939) international law, placed himself on the side of his national government. This is valid, and indeed, to an even higher degree, if this regime was a terrorist regime. For this would, in this case, result in the event that the punishment of an individual citizen would declare not only the terrorists but also the terrorized, the victim of the terror, a criminal.

Conclusion

As far as the legal concepts of the citizen and the ordinary business-man of a European state are concerned, the war of aggression as such could not have been valid as a criminal injustice subject to international jurisdiction in the summer of 1939. The concept of the criminalization and penalization of the war of aggression had not yet become positive

---

* A quotation from the final chapter of Hobbes' *Leviathan.*
† I protect, therefore I obligate.

law in the difficult circumstances of the time from 1919 to 1939. The loyal citizen who was not party to the political leadership could not, in summer 1939, yet place the new international crime of a war of aggression on the same level as the hitherto existing crimes of national penal law, high treason, treason, or sabotage against one's own government. The citizen's conceptions of his obligations of loyalty in war rested on a secular tradition, the same tradition that justified the high penalties for high treason and treason. Up to that point, the organization of a judiciary handling criminal law had a purely domestic and not an international character. Should such hitherto exclusively national and domestic institutions and concepts be relocated out of the national purview and into the international purview, the entire legal position of the individual citizen would be changed. Acts that before then were the fulfillment of a domestic obligation would become crimes, and acts that before then were punished as criminal in the domestic sphere, for example, high treason, treason, resistance, and sabotage, would now belong to the fulfillment of international obligations, acts whose non-fulfillment would make the loyal citizen into an international criminal. A conflict of obligations arises, a conflict of such trenchancy and cruelty as was previously only imaginable in situations of the most terrible civil wars. To bring a normal citizen who does not belong to the political ruling class into such a conflict, and to add on top of this a retroactive effect for the past, would violate every equity. In light of the creation of a not only new but also completely novel international crime, the power of the principle "*nullum crimen, nulla poena sine lege*" grows. It is not only a principle of valid positive law, but also a maxim of natural law and morality that the citizen who is not party to atrocities can unconditionally call upon.

Note

The problem of war in general, and especially that of the war of aggression, has a long and complicated history. In the discussion concerned with the Geneva Protocol of 1924 and the Kellogg Pact of 1928, as well as in the many years of travel searching for a definition of the aggressor, for disarmament and peaceful change, only part of these difficulties have become obvious.

It goes without saying that – at the end of this second world war – mankind is obliged to pass a sentence upon Hitler's and his accomplices' "*scelus infandum.*" This sentence must be solemn in its form and striking in its effect. After the defeat of Napoleon in 1815, the European government found a solemn and effective form for the condemnation of Napoleon. Today, the condemnation of Nazism ought to be to such a degree more strict and impressive as the crimes of Hitler are greater than those of Napoleon.

Furthermore, it is evident, that Hitler's "*scelus infandum*," and especially the monstrous atrocities of the SS and the Gestapo, cannot be classified in their real essence by the rules and the categories of the usual positive law; neither with the help of the old municipal criminal or constitutional law, nor with the help of the present international law, that has its origins in the *jus publicum Europaeum*, i.e. the relations between the Christian sovereigns of Europe from the sixteenth to the nineteenth century.

But it is just the abnormity of such a type like Hitler and of an organization such as the SS that makes it clear that there are several different questions regarding the legal side of this matter. Above all, the general international problem of the war of aggression as an international crime must be distinguished from other crimes of the Hitler regime. The statement that in September 1939 Hitler resorted to a war of aggression in the sense of the Geneva Protocol or the Kellogg Pact is evidently not identical with the much greater, specific task of openly branding and condemning Nazism and the SS and their atrocities *in toto*.* These two things are not identical. Moreover, it does not seem advisable to combine them, thus shifting that trial's center of gravity and the viewpoints of the Geneva Protocol or the Kellogg Pact. Hereby, attention would largely have been drawn away, both when preparing the trial and still further during the trial itself, from the specific task and removed to a complicated problem of international law. Even in the precisely formulated tenor of the verdict a delusion would be the consequence. Hitler and his accomplices' actions would be comprised under rules and notions that would obliterate that which makes the abnormity and monstrosity of their actions unique.

A "*scelus infandum*" must by no means become a precedent. A term such as "crime" belonging to criminal law evokes the use of other terms of criminal law such as principals and accessories, aids and abets, complicity, concealment, etc., terms that, when applied to actions of foreign policy – e.g. the partition of Poland in September 1939 – imply further questions of unheard of consequences.

Berlin, August 25, 1945
Carl Schmitt

---

* In total.

Further Reading

Works by Carl Schmitt in English

The Concept of the Political. Translated by George Schwab. Chicago: University of Chicago Press, 2006.

Constitutional Theory. Translated by Jeffery Seitzer. Durham: Duke University Press, 2007.

The Crisis of Parliamentary Democracy. Translated by Ellen Kennedy. Cambridge, MA: MIT Press, 1988.

Hamlet or Hecuba: The Intrusion of the Time into the Play. Translated by David Pan and Jennifer R. Rust. New York: Telos Press, 2010.

Legality and Legitimacy. Translated by Jeffery Seitzer. Durham: Duke University Press, 2004.

The Leviathan in the State Theory of Thomas Hobbes: Meaning and Failure of a Political Symbol. Translated by George Schwab and Erna Hilfstein. Chicago: University of Chicago Press, 2008.

The Nomos of the Earth in the International Law of the Jus Publicum Europaeum. Translated by G.L. Ulmen. New York: Telos Press Publishing, 2006.

Political Romanticism. Translated by Guy Oakes. Cambridge, MA: MIT Press, 1986.

Political Theology: Four Chapters on the Concept of Sovereignty. Translated by George Schwab. Chicago: University of Chicago Press, 2004.

Political Theology II: The Myth of the Closure of any Political Theology. Translated by Michael Hoelzl and Graham Ward. Cambridge: Polity Press, 2008.

Roman Catholicism and Political Form. Translated by G.L. Ulmen. Westport, CT: Greenwood Press, 1996.

Theory of the Partisan. Translated by G.L. Ulmen. New York: Telos Press, 2007.

English–Language Secondary Literature (Focusing Primarily on Schmitt and International Law)

Balakrishnan, Gopal. *The Enemy. An Intellectual Portrait of Carl Schmitt.* New York/London: Verso, 2000.

Bendersky, Joseph. *Carl Schmitt. Theorist of the Reich.* Princeton: Princeton University Press, 1983.

Gross, Raphael. *Carl Schmitt and the Jews: The "Jewish Question," the Holocaust, and German Legal Theory.* Translated by Joel Golb. Madison, WI: University of Wisconsin Press, 2007.

Hooker, *Carl Schmitt's International Thought: Order and Orientation.* Cambridge: Cambridge University Press, 2009.

The International Political Thought of Carl Schmitt: Terror, Liberal War, and the Crisis of the Global Order. Edited by Louiza Odysseos and Fabio Petito.

Scheuermann, William E. *Carl Schmitt: The End of Law.* Lanham, MD: Rowman & Littlefield, 1999.

Schwab, George. *The Challenge of the Exception: An Introduction to the Political Ideas of Carl Schmitt between 1921 and 1936.* Greenwood, CT: Greenwood Press, 1989.

Shapiro, Kam. *Carl Schmitt and the Intensification of Politics.* Lanham: Rowman & Littlefield, 2008.

Slomp, Gabriella. *Carl Schmitt and the Politics of Hostility, Violence, and Terror.* Basingstoke: Palgrave Macmillian, 2009.

German-Language Secondary Literature (Focusing on Schmitt and International Law)

de Benoist, Alain. *Carl Schmitt und der Krieg.* Berlin: Junge Freiheit, 2007.

Blindow, Felix. *Carl Schmitts Reichsordnung: Strategie für einen europäischen Großraum.* Berlin: Akademie Verlag, 1999.

Campagna, Norbert. *Carl Schmitt. Eine Einführung.* Berlin: Parerga, 2004.

Eberl, Matthias. *Die Legitimität der Moderne: Kulturkritik und Herrschaftskonzepte bei Max Weber und Carl Schmitt.* Marburg: Tectum Verlag, 1994.

Gross, Raphael. *Carl Schmitt und die Juden: eine deutsche Rechtslehre.* Frankfurt am Main: Suhrkamp, 2000.

Großraum-Denken: Carl Schmitts Kategorien der Großraumordnung. Edited by Rüdiger Voigt. Stuttgart: Steiner, 2008.

Heuer, Andreas. *Carl Schmitt: Die Dialektik der Moderne: Von der europäischen zur Welt-Moderne.* Berlin: Duncker & Humblot, 2010.

Koenen, Andreas. *Der Fall Carl Schmitt: sein Aufstieg zum "Kronjuristen des Dritten Reiches."* Darmstadt: Wissenschaftliche Buchgesellschaft, 1995.

Maschke, Günter. *Der Tod des Carl Schmitt: Apologie und Polemik.* Vienna: Karolinger, 1987.

Mehring, Reinhard. *Carl Schmitt – Aufstieg und Fall. Eine Biographie.* Munich: Verlag C.H. Beck, 2009.

Meier, Heinrich. *Carl Schmitt, Leo Strauß und "Der Begriff des Politischen." Zu einem Dialog unter Abwesenden.* Stuttgart: Metzler Verlag, 1988.

Noack, Paul. *Carl Schmitt: eine Biographie.* Frankfurt am Main: Propyläen, 1993.

Quaritsch, Helmut. *Complexio Oppositorium. Über Carl Schmitt.* Berlin: Duncker & Humblot, 1988.

Quaritsch, Helmut. *Positionen und Begriffe Carl Schmitts.* Berlin: Duncker & Humblot, 1995.

Schmoekel, Matthias, *Die Großraumtheorie. Ein Beitrag zur Geschichte der Völkerrechtswissenschaft im Dritten Reich, insbesondere der Kriegszeit.* Berlin: Duncker & Humblot, 1994.

Notes

Introduction

1. A serious review of all of the varying interpretations of Schmitt and a full literature review would on its own exceed the reasonable length of what is intended to be a short introduction to only three of Schmitt's works. For an impressive overview of the scholarly literature on Schmitt, see Peter C. Caldwell, "Controversies Over Carl Schmitt: A Review of Recent Literature," *The Journal of Modern History* 77 (June 2005), 357–87.

2. Jacob Taubes, *The Political Theology of Paul*, trans. D. Hollander (Stanford: Stanford University Press, 2004), 69; Wiliam Hooker, *Carl Schmitt's International Thought* (Cambridge: Cambridge University Press, 2009), 10.

3. For a brief survey of the uses of Schmitt's thought, see Kam Shapiro, *Carl Schmitt and the Intensification of Politics* (Lanham, MD: Rowman and Littlefield Publishers, 2009), Chapter 1.

4. For the major work affiliated with this line of argument, see Joseph Bendersky, *Carl Schmitt: Theorist for the Reich* (Princeton: Princeton University Press, 1983).

5. This brief biography of Schmitt is largely taken from Tracy Strong's new foreword to Carl Schmitt, *The Leviathan in the State Theory of Thomas Hobbes: Meaning and Failure of a Political Symbol* (Chicago: University of Chicago Press, 2008), vii–viii. For a more exhaustive biography, see Reinhard Mehring, *Carl Schmitt. Aufstieg und Fall* (Munich: C.H. Beck Verlag, 2008).

6. For more on this theme, see Mark Lilla, *The Reckless Mind: Intellectuals in Politics* (New York: New York Times Books, 2001).

7. This was George Schwab's phrasing in his introduction to Schmitt's 1938 study *The Leviathan in the State Theory of Thomas Hobbes: Meaning and Failure of a Political Symbol* (Chicago: University of Chicago Press, 2008). As he notes there, the view that 1936 constituted a breaking point for Schmitt's relationship with National Socialism was advanced in his own *The Challenge of the Exception: An Introduction to the Political Ideas of Carl*

Schmitt Between 1921 and 1936 (New York & London: Greenwood Press, 1989), 141–3, 146–50 as well as in Joseph W. Bendersky, *Carl Schmitt: Theorist for the Reich* (Princeton: Princeton University Press, 1983), 235–43. Reinhard Mehring's recent biography of Schmitt, *Carl Schmitt. Aufstieg und Fall* (Munich: C.H. Beck Verlag, 2008), presents a rich reading of Schmitt's *Nachlass* concerning this question.

8. George Schwab, Introduction to Carl Schmitt, *The Leviathan in the State Theory of Thomas Hobbes: Meaning and Failure of a Political Symbol* (Chicago: University of Chicago Press, 2008), xxxi. Obviously, not all Schmitt scholarship is admiring: see, for example, William E. Scheuermann, *Carl Schmitt: The End of Law* (Lanham, MD: Roman & Littlefield, 1999). For a critical response to Scheuermann, see Ellen Kennedy, Review of *Carl Schmitt: The End of Law*, *The American Political Science Review* 94: 3 (September 2000), 713–15.

9. I am grateful to Peter Caldwell for encouraging me to emphasize this point in the text.

10. *Völkerrechtliche Großraumordnung mit Interventionsverbot für raumfremde Mächte: ein Beitrag zum Reichsbegriff im Völkerrecht* and *Das internationalrechtliche Verbrechen des Angriffkriegs und der Grundsatz* "nullum crimen, nulla poena sine lege" are presented here for the first time in English translation. The translator would like to emphasize his gratitude to Professor George Schwab for authorizing the translation presented here. *Die Wendung zum diskriminierenden Kriegsbegriff* was illegally published as an unauthorized translation as *War/Non-War: A Dilemma*, trans. Simona Draghici (Washington, D.C.: Plutarch Press, 2004). I comment on Draghici's translation in my notes on the translation.

11. The other major works Schmitt produced during the years of Nazism were *The Leviathan in the State Theory of Thomas Hobbes*, trans. George Schwab (Westpore, CT: Greenwood Press, 1996), and *Land and Sea*, trans. Simona Draghici (Plutarch Press, 1997), a fable-like discussion of some of the issues about conceptions of space raised in *Großraum*.

12. Some crucial articles to start with for the 1920s would include "Das Rheinland als Objekt internationaler Politik" (1928), "Status Quo and Peace" (1925), "Völkerrechtliche Probleme des Rheingebiets" (1928), "Völkerbund und Europa" (1928), and "Das Zeitalter der Neutralisierungen und Entpolitisierungen" (1929). All these works appear in both Carl Schmitt, *Positionen and Begriffe* (Berlin: Duncker & Humblot, 1940), or in Carl Schmitt, *Staat, Großraum, Nomos: Arbeiten aus den Jahren 1916–1969*, ed. Günter Maschke (Berlin: Duncker & Humblot, 1995).

13. I am indebted to John P. McCormick's writings on Schmitt and European integration for making me aware of this problem: "Carl Schmitt's Europe: Cultural, Imperial, and Spatial Proposals for European Integration, 1923–1955," in *The Darker Legacy of European Law: Legal Perspectives on a*

"European Order" in the Fascist Era and Beyond, ed. Christian Joerges and N.S. Ghaleigh, (Hart, 2004) 133–42. For an essay on the link between *Großraum* and *Lebensraum* that takes a different position from mine in this introduction, see: Julien Freund, "Schmitt's Political Thought," *Telos* 102 (1995), 36.

14. This background history to *The Turn to the Discriminating Concept of War* is condensed for reasons of brevity. Günter Maschke provides his own extensive footnotes to the text as well as an exhaustive history of the text and its reception in Carl Schmitt, *Frieden oder Pazifismus: Arbeiten zum Völkerrecht und zur internationalen Politik, 1924–1978*, ed. Günter Maschke (Berlin: Duncker & Humblot, 2005).

15. Schmitt, *Frieden oder Pazifismus? Arbeiten zum Völkerrecht und zur internationalen Politik. 1924–1978*, ed. by Günter Maschke (Berlin: Duncker & Humblot, 2005), 50.

16. Carl Schmitt, "Die Rheinlande als Objekt internationaler Politik," in *Positionen und Begriffe*, 27–8.

17. Ibid., 31.

18. Schmitt, "USA und die völkerrechtlichen Formen des modernen Imperialismus," in *Positionen und Begriffe. Im Kampf mit Weimar-Genf-Versailles* (Hamburg: Hanseatische Verlagsanstalt, 1940), 162–80.

19. Ibid., 177.

20. Schmitt, "Die Rheinlande als Objekt internationaler Politik," in *Positionen und Begriffe*, 33.

21. Ibid., 34.

22. For more on Schmitt's relationship with Catholicism, see Manfred Dahlheimer, *Carl Schmitt und der deutsche Katholizismus* (Paderborn: Ferdinand Schöning, 1998).

23. Günter Maschke notes Schmitt's use of the predominantly Protestant term of *Obrigkeit* in this lecture before a Catholic audience to come, tentatively, to the conclusion that Schmitt may have been suggesting the permissibility, if not responsibility, of Christians to levy resistance against unjust authority. At the same time, Maschke notes an ambivalence in Luther's writings on the limits of the Christian's responsibility to obey an unjust prince.

24. Schmitt, "Die Rheinlande als Objekt internationaler Politik," in *Positionen und Begriffe*, 33.

25. Specifically, Schmitt refers to an order issued by the French occupation government in the Saarland on March 7, 1923 that threatened speech against the League of Nations, any members of the League of Nations, or the signatory powers of the Treaty of Versailles with up to five years in prison. See: *Amtsblatt der Regierungs-Kommission für das Saargebiet*, No. 167 (1923), 49ff.

26. For a different approach to *The Turn to the Discriminating Concept of War* that connects the piece to Schmitt's notion of *nomos*, see:

Martti Koskenniemi, *The Gentle Civilizer of Nations: The Rise and Fall of International Law 1870–1960* (Cambridge: Cambridge University Press, 2001), 424–6. Koskenniemi situates his short discussion of *The Turn to the Discriminating Concept of War* in a larger essay about Carl Schmitt and Hans Morgenthau that constitutes Chapter 6 of the cited book.

27. George Scelle, *Précis du droit des gens, principes et systématique* (Paris: Recueil Sirey, 1932–4); Sir Hersch Lauterpacht, *The Function of Law in the International Community* (Oxford: The Clarendon Press, 1933). For more on Lauterpacht in particular but also on the history of international law during this period, see Koskenniemi, *The Gentle Civilizer of Nations*.

28. For a more detailed analysis of *The Concept of the Political*, see Gopal Balakrishnan, *The Enemy: An Intellectual Portrait of Carl Schmitt* (New York: Verso, 2002), 101–15.

29. Schmitt, *The Concept of the Political*, trans. with an introduction by George Schwab (Chicago: The University of Chicago Press, 1996), 50–1.

30. Ibid., 52.

31. Ibid., 53.

32. Ibid.

33. Ibid., 54.

34. Gopal Balakrishnan, *The Enemy: An Intellectual Portrait of Carl Schmitt*, 107.

35. *The Turn to the Discriminating Concept of War* (abbreviated hereafter as *TDCW*), 67f.

36. For a further discussion of some of the same themes I discuss here, see Koskenniemi, *The Gentle Civilizer of Nations*, 426–36.

37. Schmitt, *TDCW*, 87.

38. Ibid., 88.

39. Ibid., 49.

40. Gopal Balakrishnan, *The Enemy: An Intellectual Portrait of Carl Schmitt*, 109.

41. For more general remarks on *The Turn to the Discriminating Concept of War*, see Jean-François Kervégan, "Carl Schmitt and 'World Unity'," in *The Challenge of Carl Schmitt*, ed. Chantal Mouffe (Verso: New York, 1999), 58–62.

42. Schmitt, *TDCW*, 67f.

43. Schmitt, *Theorie des Partisanen* (Duncker & Humblot: Berlin, 1975, 2nd edition), 60.

44. Gopal Balakrishnan, *The Enemy: An Intellectual Portrait of Carl Schmitt*, 231.

45. Schmitt, "Die deutsche Rechtswissenschaft im Kampf gegen den jüdischen Geist," *Deutsche Juristen-Zeitung*, Volume 41, Issue 20, October 15, 1936, 1193–9; *TDCW*, 40.

46. Andreas Koenen, *Der Fall Carl Schmitt* (Darmstadt: Wissenschaftliche Buchgesellschaft, 1995), 786.

47. Ibid., 784.

48. Quoted in Andreas Koenen, *Der Fall Carl Schmitt* (Darmstadt: Wissenschaftliche Buchgesellschaft, 1995), 823.

49. The publication history of *Großraum* as presented here represents only a condensed summary of the full story. For an exhaustive history of the origins of the text as well as its reception, see Carl Schmitt, *Staat, Großraum, Nomos*, ed. Günter Maschke (Berlin: Duncker & Humblot, 1995), 343–51.

50. John P. McCormick, "Carl Schmitt's Europe: Cultural, Imperial, and Spatial Proposals for European Integration, 1923–1955," in *The Darker Legacy of European Law: Legal Perspectives on a "European Order" in the Fascist Era and Beyond*, ed. Christian Joerges and N.S. Ghaleigh (Hart, 2004), 133–42.

51. Mark Mazower, *Hitler's Empire: Nazi Rule in Occupied Europe* (New York: Allen Lane, 2008), 577.

52. Quoted in Joseph H. Kaiser, "Europäisches Großraumdenken: Die Steigerung geschichtlicher Größen als Rechtsproblem," *Epirrhosis*, 542.

53. Frank-Rutger Hausmann, *Frankfurter Allgemeine Zeitung*, March 13, 1999. Ritterbusch was the rector at Kiel during the time of the Kiel School, one of the centers of National Socialist legal thought; he later committed suicide in April 1945.

54. Gopal Balakrishnan, *The Enemy: An Intellectual Portrait of Carl Schmitt* (New York: Verso, 2002), 234.

55. For other opinions on *Großraum*, see: Mathias Schmoeckel, *Die Großraumtheorie. Ein Beitrag zur Geschichte der Völkerrechtwissenschaft im Dritten Reich, insbesondere der Kriegszeit* (Berlin, 1994); Felix Blindow, *Carl Schmitts Reichsordnung: Strategie für einen europäischen Großraum* (Berlin: Akademie Verlag, 1999); *Großraum-Denken: Carl Schmitts Kategorien der Großraumordnung* (Stuttgart: Steiner, 2008); William Hooker, *Carl Schmitt's International Thought: Order and Orientation* (Cambridge: Cambridge University Press, 2009).

56. Schmitt, *Großraum*, 87.

57. Ibid., 101.

58. Ibid., 99.

59. Ibid., 111.

60. Ibid., 100–1.

61. Schmitt, *Staat, Bewegung, Volk: Die Dreigliederung der politischen Einheit* (Hamburg: Hanseatische Verlagsanstalt, 1933).

62. Ibid., 150.

63. Gopal Balakrishnan, *The Enemy: An Intellectual Portrait of Carl Schmitt*, 236.

64. Alfred Mischke, Introduction to Werner Daitz, *Der Weg zur völkischen Wirtschaft. Ausgewählte Reden und Aufsätze von Werner Daitz.* (Munich:

Verlag der deutschen Technik GmbH, 1938), 3–8; Werner Daitz, "Echte und unechte Großräume" (1941), in *Lebensraum und gerechte Weltordnung. Grundlagen einer Anti-Atlantikcharta. Ausgewählte Aufsätze von Werner Daitz* (De Amsterdamsche Keurkamer: Amsterdam, 1943), 23–31.

65. Daitz, "Echte und unechte Großräume," in *Lebensraum*, 43.

66. Franklin D. Roosevelt, "President Roosevelt to the Chancellor of Germany (Hitler) [Telegram], April 14, 1939," in *Peace and War: United States Foreign Policy, 1931–1941* (Washington, D.C.: United States Government Printing Office, 1943), 455–8.

67. *Der Führer antwortet Roosevelt. Reichstagsrede vom 28. April 1939* (Munich: Zentralverlag der NSDAP, Franz Eher Nachfolger, 1939), 51.

68. Joseph Bendersky, *Carl Schmitt: Theorist for the Reich* (Princeton: Princeton University Press, 1983), 258–9.

69. Of course, many other approaches are possible. While the focus here remains on Schmitt within a German context, Mark Mazower's recent work on thinking about the international system in the 1940s is suggestive for the broader global context in which Schmitt's ideas existed, as well as how his advocacy of population transfers and skepticism towards minority rights had something of an afterlife after 1945. See Mark Mazower, *No Enchanted Palace: The End of Empire and the Ideological Origins of the United Nations* (Princeton: Princeton University Press, 2009).

70. Carl Bilfinger, "Streit um das Völkerrecht," *Zeitschrift für ausländisches öffentliches Recht und Völkerrecht* 12 (1944), 1–34.

71. Werner Daitz, "Die europäische Großraumwirtschaft," in *Lebensraum und gerechte Weltordnung. Grundlagen einer Anti-Antlantikcharta. Ausgewählte Aufsätze von Werner Daitz* (Amsterdam: De Amsterdamsche Keurkamer, 1943), 99.

72. Mazower, *Hitler's Empire*, 232–8.

73. Ibid., 239, 241.

74. Ibid., 243–5.

75. *Großraum*, 99.

76. Werner Best, "Völkische Großraumordnung," *Deutsches Recht*, Jahrgang 10, Issue 25 (June 22, 1940), 1006–7; Roger Diener, "Reichsverfassung und Großraumverwaltung im Altertum," *Reich, Volksordnung, Lebensraum*, Jahrgang 1, Volume I (1941), 177–229; Günther Küchenhoff, "Großraumdenken und völkische Ideen im Recht," *Zeitschrift für ausländisches öffentliches Recht und Völkerrecht*, Volume XII, No. 1 (September 1944), 34–82.

77. Schmitt, *Großraum*, 100.

78. Ibid., 122.

79. Werner Daitz, "Echte und unechte Großräume," (1941), in *Lebensraum und gerechte Weltordnung. Grundlagen einer Anti-Atlantikcharta. Ausgewählte Aufsätze von Werner Daitz* (De Amsterdamsche Keurkamer: Amsterdam, 1943), 23.

80. Schmitt, *Großraum*, 100.
81. Schmitt, *Glossarium. Aufzeichnungen der Jahre 1947–1951*, ed. Eberhard Freiherr von Medem (Berlin, 1991), 167 (June 20, 1948).
82. Carl Schmitt, *The* Nomos *of the Earth in the International Law of the Jus Publicum Europaeum*, trans. G.L. Ulmen (New York: Telos Press Publishing, 2006). For more on European jurisprudence of the period, see Martti Koskenniemi, *The Gentle Civilizer of Nations: the Rise and Fall of International Law, 1870–1960* (Cambridge: Cambridge University Press, 2001).
83. Schmitt produced several articles on international law between the publication of *Land and Sea* in 1942 and his consulting work in the summer of 1945, one of which, "Die geistgeschichtliche Lage der europäischen Rechtswissenschaft," has been translated into English by G.L. Ulmen. See: Carl Schmitt, "The Plight of European Jurisprudence," *Telos* 72 (summer 1987). For the articles themselves, see Schmitt, *Frieden oder Pazifismus? Arbeiten zum Völkerrecht und zur internationalen Politik 1924–1978*, ed. Günter Maschke (Berlin: Duncker & Humblot, 2005) and Schmitt, *Staat, Großraum, Nomos: Arbeiten aus den Jahren 1916 bis 1969*, ed. Günter Maschke (Berlin: Duncker & Humblot, 1995).
84. Schmitt, *The International Crime of the War of Aggression and the Principle "Nullum crimen, nulla poena sine lege,"* (abbreviated in further notes as *ICWA*), 186.
85. Quaritsch, "Ein Gutachten für die Nachwelt," in Schmitt, *Das internationalrechtliche Verbrechen des Angriffskrieges*, 144–5.
86. Schmitt, *Großraum*, 122.
87. Ibid., 111.
88. Schmitt, *ICWA*, 120.
89. Ibid., 197.
90. Schmitt, *ICWA*, 195.
91. Schmitt, "Die Rheinlande als Objekt internationaler Politik," *Positionen und Begriffe*, 34.
92. I am grateful to Peter C. Caldwell for pointing this application of the 1925 lecture out to me. For more on Schmitt's relationship with Catholicism, see Manfred Dahlheimer, *Carl Schmitt und der deutsche Katholizismus 1888–1936* (Paderborn: Schoningh, 1998).
93. For a deeper discussion of Schmitt's anti-Semitism, see: Wolfgang Palaver, "Carl Schmitt on Nomos and Space," *Telos* 106 (1996), 105–27; Raphael Gross, "'Jewish Law and Christian Grace' – Carl Schmitt's Critique of Hans Kelsen," in *Hans Kelsen and Karl Schmitt. A Juxtaposition*, eds. Dan Diner and Michel Stolleis (Gerlingen: Bleicher, 1999), 105–7; Heinrich Meier, *The Lesson of Carl Schmitt: Four Chapters on the Distinction Between Political Theology and Political Philosophy* (Chicago: University of Chicago Press, 1998); Raphael Gross, *Carl Schmitt and the Jews: The*

"Jewish Question," the Holocaust, and German Legal Theory (Madison, WI: University of Wisconsin Press, 2007).

94. Schmitt, *ICWA*, 183.

95. Ibid., 197.

96. Martin Heidegger, "Das Gestell," cited in Wolfgang Schumacher, *Technik und Gelassenheit* (Freiburg: Alber, 1983) 25. "Das Gestell" was an unpublished lecture given by Heidegger as part of a lecture series before the Bremen Club (*Bremer Club*) on December 1, 1949.

97. Schmitt, *ICWA*, 127.

98. For Pompey's death and Lucan's commentary, see Lucan, *Pharsalia*, Book VIII, lines 481–711.

99. I am grateful to Peter Caldwell for expanding on the arguments in this paragraph.

100. Schmitt, *ICWA*, 145, 186.

101. Ibid., 127.

102. Quaritsch, "Ein Gutachten für die Nachwelt," 141. See also Hans-Heinrich Jescheck, *Die Verantwortlichkeit der Staatsorgane nach Völkerstrafrecht – Eine Studie zu den Nurnbürger Prozessen* (Bonn, 1952), 345.

103. Konrad Kaletsch, Letter to Carl Schmitt, January 3, 1951, Nordrhein-Westfälisches Landesarchiv, File RW 265-220, Number 176; Carl Schmitt, Letter to Konrad Kaletsch, January 8, 1951, Nordrhein-Westfälisches Landesarchiv, File RW 265-220, Number 180.

104. Joseph Bendersky is eloquent on this point in his criticism of William E. Scheuermann's *Carl Schmitt: The End of Law* in *Central European History*, 34:1 (2000), 116–20.

105. Gary Ulmen, "Just Wars or Just Enemies?" *Telos* 109 (fall 1996), 99–113; Michael Walzer, *Just and Unjust Wars. A Moral Argument with Historical Illustrations* (New York: Basic Books, 1992).

106. Ibid., 292.

107. Michael Walzer, "The Politics of Rescue," in *Dissent* (winter 1995), 35–41.

108. Gary Ulmen, "Just Wars or Just Enemies?"

109. Schmitt, *TDCW*, 31.

110. Carl Schmitt, "USA und die völkerrechtlichen Formen des modernen Imperialismus," in *Positionen und Begriffe*, 179.

111. Schmitt, *TDCW*, 676.

112. Václav Havel, "Moi aussi je me sens albanais," *Le Monde*, April 29, 1999.

113. Schmitt, *The Concept of the Political*, 28, translation modified.

114. For a history of humanitarian interventions, see: Gary J. Bass, *Freedom's Battle: The Origins of Humanitarian Intervention* (New York: Knopf, 2008).

115. Schmitt, *TDCW*, 72.

116. This was Michnik's phrasing to describe Schmitt in a spring 2007 seminar on twentieth-century intellectuals that the author attended.

117. For more on the last instance, see Craig Murray, *Murder in Samarkand: a*

British Ambassador's Controversial Defiance of Tyranny in the War on Terror (Edinburgh: Mainstream, 2007).

118. My comments in this paragraph largely expand on Tracy B. Strong's foreword to *The Leviathan in the State Theory of Thomas Hobbes*. At the time of Strong's writing, however, the so-called Bybee Memo of August 1, 2002 had not been made available for public consumption.

119. Jay S. Bybee, "Memorandum for Alberto S. Gonzales, Counsel to the President. Re: Standards of Conduct for Interrogation Under 18 U.S.C. §§2340–2340A," August 1, 2002, 31.

120. Ibid., 33.

121. Mark Mazzetti, "U.S. Is Said to Expand Secret Actions in Mideast," *New York Times*, May 24, 2010. Mark Mazzetti, Scott Shane, and Robert Worth, "Secret Assault on Terrorism Widens to Two Continents," *New York Times*, August 16, 2010. For more on this topic, see Micah Zenko, *Between Threats and War: U.S. Discrete Operations in the Post-Cold War World* (Palo Alto: Stanford University Press, 2010). For more on CIA activities involving Predator Drones and targeted assassinations, see: Jane Meyer, "The Predator War," *The New Yorker*, October 26, 2009.

122. John Brennan, "Remarks by Assistant to the President for Homeland Security and Counterterrorism John Brennan at CSIS," available online at: http://www.whitehouse.gov/the-press-office/remarks-assistant-pres ident-homeland-security-and-counterterrorism-john-brennan-csi.

123. Carl Schmitt, *The* Nomos *of the Earth in the International Law of the Jus Publicum Europaeum*, trans. G.L. Ulmen (New York: Telos Press Publishing, 2006), 354.

The Turn to the Discriminating Concept of War (1937)

124. For more, see the essay: "Totaler Feind, totaler Krieg, totaler Staat" in the journal *Völkerbund und Völkerrecht* IV (1937), 139–46, as well as the unusually interesting essay of Baron Julius Evola, "La guerra total," *La Vita Italiana (Il Regime Fascista)* XXV (1937), 567.

125. Georges Scelle in *Völkerbund und Völkerrecht* (1934), 7. See also Carl Bilfinger, *Völkerbund und Völkerrecht* (1937), 345.

126. For more on this literature and its "dominating perspective," see J. Kunz, "Die Staatenverbindungen," *Handbuch des Völkerrechts* II (Vienna, 1929), 505. For more on the literature cited in that article, consult Claudio Baldoni, *La società della Nazioni* I (Padua: Studi di Diritto Pubblico, diretti da Donato Donati 10: 1936), 74.

127. Carl Schmitt, "Nationalsozialismus und Völkerrecht," *Schriften der deutschen Hochschule für Politik* 9 (Berlin: Paul Meier-Benneckenstein, 1934). See also Herbert Kraus' discussion of the topic in *Niemeyers Zeitschrift für Internationales Recht* 50, 151. With regard to p. 11 of my lecture

"Nationalsozialismus und Völkerrecht," Professor A. von Verdroß has made me aware of the fact that he himself has dubbed the maxim *pacta sunt servanda* the "basic norm of the unified order of international law" in his book *Die Verfassung der Völkerrechtsgemeinschaft* (Berlin, 1926). However, Verdroß in no way means to recognize the Paris *Diktat*s through this statement. As his other essays "Heilige und unsittliche Staatsverträge," *Völkerbund und Völkerrecht* II (1935), 164 and "Der Grundsatz pacta sunt servanda und die Grenze der guten Sitten," *Zeitschrift für öffentliches Recht* XVI (1936), 79, make clear that the Paris *Diktat*s are invalid, being immoral treaties. I gladly recognize Verdroß' contribution and use this occasion to add these comments from my Viennese colleague.

128. W. Ziegler, *Der Zerfall des Versailler Vertrages, eine geschichtliche Darstellung, Veröffentlichung der Forschungsabteilung der Deutschen Hochschule für Politik* I (Berlin, 1937).

129. This formulation comes from the title of the 1932 Sir John Fischer Williams work, "International Change and International Peace." More can be found on this topic in Heinrich Rogge, *Das Revisionsproblem, Theorie der Revision als Voraussetzung einer internationalen wissenschaftlichen Aussprache über "Peaceful Change of Status quo,"* (Berlin, 1937). For information on the International Conference on Collective Security in London from June 2–June 8, 1935, consult F. Berber's report in *Bruns Zeitschrift* V (1935), 803–18. This topic inspired the Akademie für Deutsches Recht to host a lecture by Prof. Arnold Toynbee (London) on February 28, 1936 in Berlin, which can be read in *Jahrbuch der Deutschen Akademie für Deutsches Recht* (1936), 225. For information on the International Conference held in Paris from June 28–July 3, consult the reports by F. Berber and D. von Renvers in the *Monatshefte für Auswärtige Politik* (August 1937). For more on Werner Gramsch's book *Grundlagen und Methoden internationaler Revision* (Stuttgart/Berlin, 1937), consult Bertram's discussion in the journal *Völkerbund und Völkerrecht* IV (1937), 398–9.

130. Carl Schmitt, "Die Kernfrage des Völkerbundes" (1926), 11 and "Völkerrechtliche Probleme im Rheingebiet," *Rheinische Schicksalsfragen* 27/28 (Berlin, 1928), 86–7. The latter essay also appeared in the *Rheinischer Beobachter* (1928), 340.

131. For more on Kelsen's pure legal theory in the tradition of Austrian state theory, see Erich Voegelin, *Der autoritäre Staat* (Vienna, 1936), 127. It goes without saying that Alexander Hold-Ferneck's textbook on international law (1930–2) does not belong in this context.

132. The following report limits itself to French and English publications. The American literature (Quincy Wright, Hudson, etc.) that would complete a total picture should be discussed in an American-specific report.

133. See H. Raschofer's analyses "Die Krise der Minderheitenschutzes" in *Bruns Zeitschrift* VI (1936), 238f, in which certain individualistically constructed

freedoms are treated as "base de l'organisation sociale dans tous les États de l'Europe" and "the standard of the state structure."

134. See pp. 69 and 73 of this work.

135. William Guerdan de Roussell, "Demaskierung des Staates," *Europäische Revue* (1936), 799.

136. Triepel's "unification," which remains based in a psychologism of the will, were for us finally explained in Gustav Adolf Walz' *Völkerrecht und staatliches Recht* (Stuttgart, 1933), 19–27.

137. Alfred von Verdroß, *Enzyklopädie der Rechts- und Staatswissenschaft, Abteilung Rechtswissenschaft* (Berlin: E. Kohlrausch and H. Peters, 1937).

138. Pierre-Joseph Proudhon, *Du principe fédératif* (Paris, 1863), 109. There, Proudhon refers to the oft-repeated parallel (Spengler, for example, made mention of this) of the present with the beginning of the "Actian Era," which began 30 years before Christ with a long period of peace ushered in by the Battle of Actium.

139. On the difference between the concept of the *Rechtsstaat* that results depending on whether a commonwealth is built upon common law and judges, or whether a *Gesetzesstaat* with administrative justice is in question, see *Bruns Zeitschrift* VI (1936), 268. For more on the dependence of the formation of concepts of international law on the development of domestic legal concepts, see Dickinson, *American Journal of International Law* 26 (1932), 239.

140. For more on this pluralistic social theory, see Carl Schmitt, *Der Begriff des Politischen*, 3rd edition (Hamburg, 1933), 20ff. See also *Kant-Studien* XXXV (1930), 29f.

141. Walter Schiffer, "Die Lehre vom Primat des Völkerrechts in der neueren Literatur," *Wiener rechts- und staatswissenschaftliche Abhandlungen* XXVII (Vienna, 1937), 104f. See also Heinrich Drost, *Grundlagen des Völkerrechts* (Munich/Leipzig, 1936), 97.

142. *Recueil des Cours de l'Académie de Droit International* 40, II (1932), 529–639. Feinberg, who was the secretary of the committee for the Jewish delegation in Paris for several years, argued in his petition of request (*pétition-vœu*) for a universal legitimacy of international law based on developments of customary law. In practice, however, this was not to be allowed to contradict a state law. In his petition of grievance (*pétition-plainte*), Feinberg claimed, based on the praxis of the Council of the League of Nations in opposition to the positions of the inhabitants of the mandated territories, the members of minorities, and the inhabitants of the Saar, the following position: all parties designated as such through a decision of the Council of the League of Nations have a direct international legal right to a petition of complaint with respect to the decisions of the Council of the League of Nations. Every member state of the League, he continues, must accommodate its internal legislation to this right to petition. According to p. 48 of Alfred von

Verdroß' *Völkerrecht* (1936), minorities' right to petition has as its basis the principle that the members of League member states remain subordinate to their states, albeit "a bit loosened" from them at the same time.

143. In opposition to Scelle's essay in the *Revue* critical of international law (*Europäische Revue* [1934], 63ff), which represents the same viewpoint, consult Baron Schenk Graf von Stauffenberg in *Bruns Zeitschift* IV (1934), 261–76.

144. *Recueil des Cours* II (1925), 35. See also *Recueil des Cours* IV (1928), 290 and p. 96 of this report.

145. For more on Scelle's earlier comments against a world state, consult the evidence presented by Walter Schiffer in ibid., 145.

146. The lecture "The Development of International Law by the Permanent Court of International Justice" before The Hague Academy in 1934 represents the fundamentally identical thoughts and methods, as does the explication of a "law behind the case."

147. Article 20 reads: "the Members of the League severally agree that this Covenant is accepted as abrogating all obligations or understandings inter se which are inconsistent with the terms thereof, and solemnly undertake that they will not hereafter enter into any engagements inconsistent with the terms thereof."

148. Charles Rousseau, "De la compatibilité des normes juridiques et contradictoires dans l'ordre international," *Revue générale de droit international public* 39 (1932), 132–92, especially p. 161 on Article 20 of the League of Nations Charter, with the caveat of the League of Nations' contract as a contract "with reinforced power" with "preeminence" over all other contradictory contracts, regardless of whether they pre- or postdate the League; regardless of whether these other contracts are bi- or multilateral.

149. In connection with Secretary of State Stimson's January 7, 1932 note on Japan and China, according to which the United States would not recognize any situation contradicting the League of Nations Charter or the Kellogg Pact (the so-called Stimson Doctrine), the March 11 resolution of the League of Nations assembly claims that all League of Nations members have a responsibility not to recognize any contract or agreement contrary to either the League Charter or the Kellogg Pact. For more, see *American Journal of Law* XXVI (1932), 342, 499; Sir John Fischer Williams, "The New Doctrine of Recognition," *Grotius Society* XVIII (1933), 109.

150. Charles Rousseau, "L'application des sanctions contre l'Italie," *Revue de Droit International et de Législation comparée*, 3rd Series, XVII (1936), 5–64.

151. A short essay by J.G. Starke on "Monism and Dualism" (66–81) from the same volume of this annual should be mentioned here, not as though it were of the same weight as the two essays of the famed publisher of that highly esteemed legal publication, but rather as a symptom of the simple

naïveté with which concepts of a normativistic monism can contain empirical reality and, with the help of federalistic analogies, can help "to institutionalize" a trans-state organ. Starke gives the "hypothetical original norm"
an empirical reality. In his opinion, an international constitution is, as a
result of this, already possible today: a constitution with constitutional, or,
as Starke says, "functional" norms of international law. These are the "original norms" of the formerly international legal norms and intra-state norms.
Denial of the primacy of the international legal constitutional norm appears
to Starke to be denial of international law itself. The obsolete dualist theory
is "anarchy and fiction;" "state law is conditioned by international law."
(477). The fact that the praxis of international law still proceeds from the
will of states, and the fact that the Permanent Court of International Justice
adheres to the principle that "limitations of the sovereignty of states are not
suspected" in its report on the *Lotus* case (Case A10), is "more the declaration of a historical fact than the analysis of a true legal situation." (81).
This essay best shows how plausible and influential federalistic analogies
are to support, expand, and propel the League of Nations and the universal
international order. Starke's knowledge of Australian federal constitutional
law comes to his aide. The primacy of the federal constitution over the individual constitution represents for him "a perfect example" of the hierarchy
of concrete norms and, as a result thereof, real institutions. The analogy
with federal law also allows the differentiation between the international
legal constitutional norm and the mere international legal norm. For
there is also a simple federal legal order besides the federal constitutional
order. "Certain differences" nonetheless emerge from the fact that in the
"normal" federal system a written federal constitution outlines the division
of responsibility between federation and state. The universal international
community is then accomplished in the course of a longer historical development. And it is natural that current "functional norms," such as those
of the League of Nations, reflect this slow development. Moreover, this
interesting essay therefore reveals the typical picture: institutionalization of
the League of Nations and the universal order of international law through
federalization; bridging of the manifest discrepancy between current reality
and universalistic constructions through an ecumenical belief in progress
and development.

152. The report presented to the League of Nations Council on October 7,
1935, written by the Committee of Six on the question of a breach of the
League of Nations councils Charter in the sense of Article 16 with regards
to the conflict in Abyssinia, is reproduced in *Bruns Zeitschrift* V (1935)
920–2. The resolutions and suggestions on the application of measures
accordant to Article 16 and the suggestions of the coordination committee from October 11–19, 1935 can be found in ibid. VI (1936), 137–48
(the reports of the legal subcommittee are to be found on pp. 143–6). The

protest of the Italian regime, meanwhile, is in ibid., 377; the hearings on mutual assistance in the Mediterranean are on p. 380. With regards to the legal "method of sanctions" from a German perspective, E. Woermann's essay in *Völkerbund und Völkerrecht* II, 605–11 is noteworthy as a pregnant summary of the inner contradictions of the attempt at sanctions. Moreover, A. Mandelstam's 1937 "Le conflit italo-éthiopien devant la Société des Nations" proposes to bring the decision on the question of the breach of the peace before the Permanent Court of International Justice in The Hague; Mandelstam argues that court proceedings of the fall 1935 were rushed and unobjective. The fact that the path to the just must lead deeper to legal discrimination and, in doing so, to the nullification of the concept of war, will become clearer through later remarks in our report (namely, p. 67). The principle "our heart tells us the law" that Briand said in front of the League of Nations Council in order to bring the question of the German-Austrian customs union before the Permanent Court of International Justice has failed to amount to much.

153. Rudolf Smend, Commemorative Paper for Otto Mayer (Tübingen, 1916), 260f. See also Rudolf Smend, *Verfassung und Verfassungsrecht* (Munich/ Leipzig, 1928), 170–1; Carl Bilfinger, *Der Einfluß der Einzelstaaten auf die Bildung des Reichswillens* (Tübingen, 1923), 52f.

154. Sir John Fischer Williams, *Some Aspects of the Covenant of the League of Nations* (London: Oxford University Press, 1934).

155. With respect to the publications of J.L. Brierly relevant to this context, his recently appeared lectures ought to be mentioned: "Règles générales du droit de la paix," *Recueil de l'Académie de Droit International* IV (1936), 109f ("the just and unjust war").

156. See the documents in the collection: *Political Contracts*, Volume II, edited by Georg von Gretschaninow (Berlin, 1936), in particular those materials in the book's "Part I: Materials on the Development of the Security Question Within the Framework of the League of Nations (1920–1927):" the Geneva General Act of September 26, 1928 in the *Recueil des Traités de la Société des Nations* XXII, 272. On further proposals, see in particular M. Bourquin's report on the London Conference on collective security from June 3–8, 1935 in *Société des Nations, Coopération Intellectuelle* 53/53. See also Bourquin's lecture "Le Problème de la Sécurité Internationale," *Recueil des Cours*, Volume 49 (1934). On German criticisms, see Baron von Freytagh-Loringhoven, "Die Regionalverträge, fünf Vorlesungen an der Haager Akademie für Völkerrecht" (German edition in the journals of the Akademie für Deutsches Recht, *Völkerrecht* Group #4); Asche Graf von Mandelsloh, "Politische Pakte und völkerrechtliche Ordnung," *25 Jahre Kaiser Wilhelm-Gesellschaft*, Volume III: The Humanities (Berlin, 1937); Carl Schmitt, "Über die innere Logik der Allgemeinpakte auf gegenseitigen Beistand," *Völkerbund und Völkerrecht* II (1935), 92–8.

157. Alfred von Verdroß, *Recueil des Cours de l'Académie de Droit International* IV (1932), 680.

158. Alfred von Verdroß, *Völkerrecht* (Berlin: 1937), §45, 192–3 explains war as permissible only as a coercive measure of international law in connection with a *justa causa*. This, too, is based on Article 15, Paragraph 7 of the League of Nations Charter. On p. 88 of Verdroß' work, a connection between a compulsory peace treaty and a legal war is suggested; because the state of course remains sovereign and remains the decider of the justness or unjustness of war, we remain with the old, non-discriminating concept of war. On p. 320, Verdroß' work thus reads with respect to the tenet of neutrality: "This principle of non-partisanship is the thread that weaves the entire right to neutrality."

159. Ernst Wolgast's *International Law* (Berlin, 1934), which stands out through its many striking and original observations, is quite restrained when it comes to this point. It may be said in §493 (934–5) that it is impossible to depict exactly the present state of the right to neutrality ("just as much as the League of Nations, the Kellogg Pact and the Stimson Doctrine, have made the right to neutrality questionable in its whole.") See also §475 and §477. But in the "Highest Principles," this means that the responsibility to "consistent" practice excludes the supposition of "benevolent neutrality." Wolgast has, in other words, clearly recognized the dilemma: neutrality or not neutrality?

160. Josef Kunz, *Kriegsrecht und Neutralitätsrecht* (Vienna, 1935).

161. The question of the neutrality of Switzerland should not be discussed here: I mention it only to note that in the case of its neutrality does the compulsory character of the dilemma "neutrality or not neutrality" become visible. In contrast with this, a "differential" neutrality (such as that which is defended by Dietrich Schindler in *Völkerbund und Völkerrecht* II, 524) is untenable. The connection with a decision about the justness or unjustness of a war-conducting party excludes the legal essence of neutrality, namely non-partisanship. Semi-non-partisanship does not exist.

162. One must be reminded of the fact that the first considerable attempt to do away with the practical effects of a distinction between the just and unjust war in pursuit of a right to neutrality were undertaken by the Belgians during the world war against Germany. We can see this in Charles de Visscher's July 28, 1916 lecture, 'De la belligérance dans ses rapports avec la violation de la neutralité," *Grotius Society* II, 102: "This juridical equality, which exists between normal belligerents in the case of a regulated war, exists excluded here in proportion to the unjustness of the act of aggression."

163. Georges Scelle, *Le droit des gens*, Part II, Book 3, Chapter 1, §2 and Chapter 3; in Book 3, Chapter 3, §39 and §40, the agnostic point of view becomes most clear through Scelle's statement that when every nation

believes in its own justice, every sovereign state must itself decide by virtue of its own sovereignty.

164. Whatever practical responses the neutral state would take in response to its recognition of the justness or unjustness of another party waging war is another question. At any rate, though, a third state distinguishing between justness and unjustness is no longer neutral, even when it does not participate in military or economic methods of coercion.

165. See J. Kunz' overviews in ibid., 4f. See also Georg Kappus, *Der völkerrechtliche Kriegsbegriff in seiner Abgrenzung gegenüber militärischen Repressalien* (Breslau, 1936) for its "will theory."

166. Dag Hammarskjöld, *La neutralité en général* (Leyden: Bibliotheca Visseriana III, 1924), 59.

167. See John H. Spencer, "Die Vereinigten Staaten und die Rechte der Neutralen im Seekriege," *Bruns Zeitschrift* V (1935), 293–304. The sweeping American literature that has especially arisen in recent years revolves around the dilemma of these two extremes. The compulsory character of this dilemma arises directly from that of the other dilemmas: war or not-war, as mentioned in the text. Indeed, this is so much the case that a further treatment of the American literature is unnecessary for the purpose of this report. An informative parallel from the praxis of recognition can be found in Marakov's work from *Bruns Zeitschrift* IV (1934), 3. For more, see p. 73 of this report.

168. Norbert Gürke must take great credit for having taken a position with respect to the question of the just war with a concrete distinction, instead of resorting to the common scholastic, natural law-based universalities. And he does this by contrasting, on the one hand, a justified war with a compensation for loss of life as its goal with, on the other hand, a war of annihilation fueled by a universalistic ideology and led against a "total enemy." (*Volk und Völkerrecht* [Tübingen, 1935], 73; "Der Begriff des totalen Krieges," *Völkerbund und Völkerrecht* IV [1937], 207, 212). This distinction is fruitful and makes the opposition between a universalistic and a politically pluralistic worldview apparent. One must pay attention to the fact that the war of annihilation justified by the universalistic ideology, because of its ecumenical claim, robs the state of its former character as a closed national and spatial order. One must pay attention to the fact that it transforms the state war into an international civil war (and, thus, the so-called "civil war" of course becomes no longer the same type of war as the state war). One must pay attention to the fact that in doing so, this universalistic war of annihilation robs the concepts of the war and the enemy of their honor and value, and annihilates both concepts by making the war on the "just" side into an execution or cleansing operation and the war on the unjust side into a resistance contrary to all justice and morals led by vermin, trouble makers, pirates, and gangsters. In my tract on the "concept of the political" (1927:

1st edition; 1932: 3rd edition) to which Gürke refers, this connection of the abolition of the concept of war and enemy with a universalistic pacifism is made clear. The fact that this transformation of the "war" into "not war" has little to do with mere conceptual niceties and speaks to the efforts of those authors who have depicted the *Luftwaffe* as a weapon: a weapon in the service of sanctions or civil wars that proves that the progress of military technology corresponds to world-historical progress of the transformation of the war into a pacification action against rebellious or backwards populations. For, of course, it cannot be said to be "war" any more when bombs are dropped onto such populations. For more on this, I refer to the following comments of my report as well as to notes 178 and 179.

169. Lauterpacht attempts to unite discrimination with the obsolete concept of war on the grounds of the League of Nations Charter and the Kellogg Pact, supporting his argument by saying that the intra-state legal order, too, must reject civil war and cannot hinder the fact that successful revolutionaries are recognized as war-conducting parties, nor the fact that its citizens speak of a civil war. The argument here is important not because it applies to the case but because it allows the connection of the discriminating concept of war with the transformation of the state war into a civil war to be recognized. For more, see p. 45 of Wolzendorff's *Die Lüge des Völkerrechts* on the logically necessary negation of the legal institution of "war."

John B. Whitton's lecture in *Recueil des Cours de l'Académie de Droit International* XXVII, II (1927), 453–71 gives an interesting discussion of the League of Nations' legal diversity of interests with regard to allowed and unallowed wars and old and new neutrality. Philippe Michailides' Paris Thesis (in his 1933 *La neutralité et la Société des Nations*) asserts that while significant changes have been made to the earlier right to neutrality (because the member states of the League constitute something like a "tribal family" within which all stand in solidarity against an injustice done to any one member), there do nonetheless remain many instances of the old neutrality. German interpretations of this issue will have to wait until the publication of G. von Schmoller's summarial treatment of the question. Until then, see the following essays: Baron von Freytagh-Loringhoven's "Neue Neutralität," *Zeitschrift für Völkerrecht* XX (1936), 1–13; W. Troitzsch's "Ende oder Wandlung der Neutralität?" *Völkerbund und Völkerrecht* II (1935/1936), 237–43; K. Keppler's "Zwischen Neutralität und Sanktionen," *Deutsche Juristen-Zeitung* (1936), 1336–44; H. Rogge's *Kollektivsicherheit, Bündnispolitik und Völkerbund* (Berlin, 1937), 360f (in particular, the sections "The Return of Neutrality Politics," "Security Calculations of 'Neutrality Politics'," and "On the Sociology of Neutrality Politics.")

170. Josef L. Kunz, *Kriegsrecht und Neutralitätsrecht* (Vienna, 1935), 2, note 4: "True, there exist contractual limitations of the *jus ad bellum*. But both

the League of Nations Pact and the Kellogg Pact allow the war to exist in principle as an institution of law."

171. On tolerated lesser wars, or dogfights, see p. 70 of this text.

172. Foreword to Georges T. Elès' book, *Le principe de l'unanimité dans la Société des Nations et les exceptions à ce principe* (Paris, 1935).

173. Hans Wehberg, Lecture from *Recueil des Cours de l'Académie de Droit International* XXIV (1929); also published in the German edition of *Recueil des Cours de l'Académie de Droit International* XXIV (Berlin, 1930).

174. Thomas Hobbes, *Behemoth*, Part I (1750), 491.

175. As an example of an attempt at such a reflection, R. Genet's treatise ought to be mentioned here: "La Société des Nations et la Communauté internationale," *Revue Internationale du Droit des Gens*, Volume I (1936), 92f, 149f.

176. Viktor Bruns, *Bruns Zeitschrift* VII (1937), 295–312.

177. In this speech, Wilson even warns his countrymen against the temptation of partisanship, even when only in their thoughts and feelings ("to lead the soul into temptation, to remain neutral in name"). "We must be impartial in thought, as well as action, must put a curb upon our sentiments, as well as upon every transaction that might be construed as a preference of one party to the struggle before another." See also H. Pohl's work, still relevant today, *Amerikas Waffenausfuhr und Neutralität* (Berlin, 1917), 17f. Further interesting supporting documents for Wilson's evolving position can be found in Felix Brüggemann's 1933 dissertation from Giesen, "Woodrow Wilson und die Vereinigten Staaten von Amerika," in which further literature is referenced.

178. George A. Finch has of late in his remarks on the September 14, 1937 Nyon Anti-Piracy Agreement in the *American Journal of International Law* 31 (1937), 665, reminded his audience of the connection between Wilson's argumentation and the definition of piracy. In his April 2, 1917 speech, Wilson may not have used the expression "piracy," but he did call the German U-boats agents of a war led "against mankind," one led "against all nations." Germany was, therefore, described with a formulation common to the pirate: *hostis generis humanis*. The legal-logical consequence of all of this is that the war ceases to be a war. For one does not conduct a war against pirates; pirates are only the object of anti-criminal or maritime police actions and arbitrary methods.

179. Carl Bilfinger, "Die russische Definition des Angreifers," *Bruns Zeitschrift* VII (1937), 490 speaks of such attempts at definitions as a "circumscription and organization of the idea of the just war against the attacker." For more on the concept of piracy, see Carl Schmitt, *Völkerbund und Völkerrecht*, 4th edition (1937), 351. In J.G. Starke's essay mentioned on p. 73 (J.G. Starke, *British Yearbook of International Law* XVII [1936], 71) one finds a nice example of the fact that the concept of piracy may serve as the breach point for the "primacy of international law."

The Großraum Order of International Law with a Ban on Foreign
Intervention for Spatially Foreign Powers: A Contribution to the Concept
of Reich in International Law (1939–1941)

180. Compare the body of writings in Walter Thiele's *Großraumwirtschaft in Geschichte und Politik* (Dresden, 1938). This otherwise competent work lacks contextualization within the present agitation and turnover of global politics. It still speaks, therefore, of the *Großraum* of the British global economy, even though this network of traffic routes is not a real *Großraum*. Compare with Section III of this text, 90.

181. *Das Selbstbestimmungsrecht Europas* (Dresden, 1940).

182. "Großraum und Meistbegünstigung," *Der Deutsche Volkswirt*, December 23, 1938. "Der neue deutsch-rumänische Wirtschaftsvertrag," *Der Vierjahresplan*, April 20, 1938. "Neuordnung in Europa und Deutscher Außenhandel," *Der Deutsche Volkswirt*, May 10, 1938.

183. See, for example, "Nord- und Ostsee," *Das Meer* VI (*Kleine Wehrgeographie*, 1938); "Wehrgeographie am Beispiel Sowjetrußlands," *Zeitschrift der Gesellschaft für Erdkunde zu Berlin* (1940), 1 ff.

184. I take the word formation "achievement space" from the important work of Viktor von Weizsäcker, *Der Gestaltkreis* (Leipzig, 1940), 129. For more, see the further remarks in Section VII, "The Concept of Space in Jurisprudence," 181.

185. The sector principle for the Arctic states that "all land territories, even those which have not yet been discovered, that lie inside of the spherical triangle whose corners are formed by the North Pole and the westernmost and easternmost points of the coast of the coastal states of the northern polar sea, belong to the state territory of the relevant coastal state; likewise, that the coastal state has a preferential right to the acquisition of this territory," according to Böhmert in his treatment of this and other principles (contiguity, propinquity) for the acquisition of territories in the *Archiv für Luftrecht*, Volume VIII (1938), 272. Further, see Ernst Schmitz and Wilhelm Friede, "Souveränitätsrechte in der Arktis," *Zeitschrift für ausländisches öffentliches Recht und Völkerrecht*, Volume IX (July 1939), 219 ff; see further below in this text (Section II), 86.

186. See, for example, the article "State Borders" in the *Wörterbuch des Völkerrechts und der Diplomatie* by Karl Strupp, Volume II, 615, or Fauchille, *Traité de droit international public*, I 2 (1925), 108 (§486ff). See further, Paul de Lapradelle, *La Frontière* (Paris, 1928), and Hermann Martinstetter, *Das Recht der Staatsgrenzen* (Berlin, 1939).

187. The best-known representatives of the dominant so-called space theory are Fricker, *Vom Staatsgebiete* (Tübingen, 1867), "Gebiet und Gebietshoheit," in the *Festgabe für Schäffle* (1901), *Die Persönlichkeit des Staates* (Tübingen, 1901); Rosin, *Das Recht der öffentlichen Genossenschaft* (1866), 46;

Zitelmann, *Internationales Privatrecht,* I (1867), 82ff; Meyer-Anschütz, *Lehrbuch des deutschen Staatsrechts,* 236; G. Jellinek, *Allgemeine Staatslehre,* 394 ff; Liszt-Fleischmann, *Das Völkerrecht* (1925), 26, 129; F. Giese, "Gebiet und Gebietshoheit," *Handbuch des deutschen Staatsgebietes* (Berlin, 1933); further literature can be found among W. Hamel, *Das Wesen des Staatsgebietes* (Berlin, 1933), 89, and footnote 302; Meyer-Anschütz as cited above, 236–7. No view needs to be taken here with respect to the pure theory of competence. For an example of a position against Hamel's theory of materiality, see Hermann Held, *Gebiet und Boden in den Rechtsgestalten der Gebietshoheit und Dinglichkeit* (Breslau, 1937). More on this "space theory" can be found on p. 118 "The Concept of Space in Jurisprudence."

188. See, for example, A.W. Heffter, *Das europäische Völkerrecht der Gegenwart,* 3rd edition (Berlin, 1855), "§5: Coincidental Guarantee of International Law: The Equal Weight of States." Franz von Holtzendorff, too, devotes a special section of Volume II of his work (*Völkerrechtliche Verfassung und Grundordnung der auswärtigen Staatenbeziehungen* [1887]), §4, 14ff, to the "so-called equal weight of European states."

189. See further in Bruns, *Fontes Juris Gentium,* Series B (*Handbook of the Diplomatic Correspondence of the European States*), Volume I, Part I, 339ff (Savoy and Nice in 1860, Schleswig, Venice, South Tirol, the left bank of the Rhein, etc.); further, see B. Fauchille, *Traité de Droit International,* I 2 (1925), 100ff (§486).

190. Karl Haushofer, *Grenzen in ihrer geographischen und politischen Bedeutung* (Berlin, 1927). From the most recent literature, see especially Kurt O. Rabl, "Staat und Verfassung," *Zeitschrift für öffentliches Recht* XVIII (1938), 213ff; Ernst Wolgast, "Völkerrechtsordnung und Raumordnung," *Zeitschrift für Völkerrecht* XXII (1938), 25ff, which discusses Tallyrand's plan for Europe (Strasbourg Aide-Mémoire from 1805). K.O. Rabl has also made me aware of the important treatise by Hassinger, "Das geographische Wesen Mitteleuropas" (*Mitteilungen der K.K. Geographischen Gesellschaft Wien,* 1917). Besides these works, the purely geographic (as opposed to geopolitical) literature is of little use.

191. *Précis du droit des gens,* 3rd printing (Paris, 1900), 17ff, "Du système des frontières naturelles."

192. German edition (Hamburg, 1934). In order to recognize the total inability of the Geneva methods to make a decision and the ineffectiveness of the treatment of such questions, one should compare with this the negotiations of the Global Conference for Population Questions in Geneva from August 29 to September 3, 1927, published in the *Proceedings of the World Population Conference* (London, 1927), especially p. 257.

193. *Foreign Rights and Interests in China* (Baltimore, 1927), 409 (the birth rate will decrease until these standards become maintainable).

194. *Zeitschrift für ausländisches öffentliches Recht und Völkerrecht*, Volume VII (1937), 139.

195. Paul Barandon, *Das Kriegsverhütungsrecht des Völkerbundes*, III 4 (Berlin, 1933), 279f; Freiherr von Freytagh-Loringhoven, *Die Regionalverträge, fünf Vorlesungen an der Haager Akademie für Völkerrecht*, German edition, Writings of the Academy for German Law, edited by Reichminister Dr. Hans Frank, International Law Group, Number 4 (München/Leipzig, 1937); Asche Graf von Mandelsloh, *Politische Pakte und völkerrechtliche Ordnung*, Special printing from *25 Years of the Kaiser-Wilhelm-Gesellschaft*, Volume 3 (Berlin, 1937). See also G.A. Walz, *Inflation im Völkerrecht*, Supplement to Volume XXIII of the *Zeitschrift für Völkerrecht* (Berlin, 1939), 54f; and Georg Hahn, *Grundfragen europäischer Ordnung* (Writings of the Institute for Policy and International Law at the University of Kiel, N.F., Volume 5) (Berlin/Vienna, 1939), 160.

196. Fritz Berber, *Locarno, Eine Dokumentarsammlung mit einer Einleitung des Botschafters von Ribbentrop* (Berlin, 1936), especially 162f; Carl Schmitt, "Sprengung der Locarno-Gemeinschaft durch Einschaltung der Sowjets," *Deutsche Juristen-Zeitung* (1936), 377ff; Georg Hahn, ibid., 112 ff. On the appraisal of Locarno see the award-winning analysis by Asche Graf von Mandelsloh, ibid., 23ff.

197. Concerning the remark of the Belgian delegate Rolin at the 6th General Assembly of the League of Nations (Actes de la VI. Ass. plén. 118; Bruns, *Politische Verträge* II (2), 465): "As concerns the security pacts, they have been called regional ententes. It is true that they deserve this name to some extent since they aim to maintain peace under the terms of the Covenant and since they concern certain regions. But beyond this, as concerns their content, in particular, they differ completely from the regional ententes to which the Assembly had granted their sympathy in recent years."

198. Freiherr von Freytagh-Loringhoven, ibid., 26f; see also Freytagh-Loringhoven, *Die Satzung des Völkerbundes (Kommentar)* (1926), 221.

199. For the American standpoint, see Dexter Perkins' exposition, *The Monroe Doctrine*, Volume 3, 1867–1907 (Baltimore, 1937), 301/302.

200. One should compare, for example, Secretary of State Olney, in 1895 (cited from Reuben Clark, *Memorandum on the Monroe Doctrine* [Washington, 1930], 160), where the Monroe Doctrine is "a doctrine of American public law, well founded in principle and abundantly sanctioned by precedent" with Secretary of State Knox in 1911 (Reuben Clark, 175/176): the Monroe Doctrine is respected as long as we are in the position to maintain it; "it does not depend on technical legal right but upon policy and power"; or with Secretary of State Hughes in 1923 (Reuben Clark, 179): the Monroe Doctrine is "only a phase of American policy in this hemisphere"; only a "principle of opposition to action by non-American powers."

201. See further the declarations of Senator Root in 1914 and of Secretary of

State Hughes in 1923, in the *American Journal of International Law* XVII (1923), 611. Since then, the Monroe Doctrine is supposed to have received a "multilateral" character through the Declaration of Lima (see Fenwick, *American Journal of International Law* XXXIII [1939], 266. Against this point of view see U. Scheuner, *Zeitschrift für Völkerrecht* XXIV (1940), 193.

202. Fauchille does this, for example, in his textbook of international law, *Traité de Droit International Public*, I, 1 (1922), 646, §324.

203. Fenwick, *International Law*, 2nd edition (1934), 178. See also note 18 above.

204. Alvarez has repeatedly exposited his thoughts since 1910 (*Le Droit International Américain*), most recently in the writing *Le Continent Américain et la Codification du Droit International, une Nouvelle "École" de Droit des Gens* (Paris, 1938), especially 82/83. See also Carl Bilfinger, "*Völkerbundsrecht gegen Völkerrecht*," *Schriften der Akademie für Deutsches Recht*, International Law Group, Number 6 (Munich, 1938), 19ff; Heinrich Triepel, *Die Hegemonie, Ein Buch von führenden Staaten* (Stuttgart, 1938), 300ff; Scheuner, ibid., 186f.

205. The impressive depiction of the events at this Hague Peace Conference that Heinrich Pohl gave in his essay "Der Monroe-Vorbehalt" (*Festgabe* of the Bonn Juridical Faculty for Paul Krüger, 1911, also printed in Pohl's Collected Essays [Berlin, 1913], 132ff) remains worth reading today and is in no way outdated.

206. On the reservation regarding the Monroe Doctrine in the Kellogg Pact: David Hunter Miller, *The Peace Pact of Paris* (New York, 1928), 118, 123; James T. Shotwell, *War as an Instrument of National Policy* (New York, 1929), 20f, 75, 123, 169, 272; T.B. Whitton, *La Doctrine de Monroe et la Société des Nations* (Lecture from May 13, 1932), Institut des Hautes Études internationales, Dotation Carnegie, Volume 8, 174f; C. Barcia Trelles, "La Doctrine de Monroe dans son développement historique, particulièrement en ce qui concerne les relations interaméricaines," *Recueil des Cours de l'Académie de Droit International*, Volume 32 (1930), 557; Hans Wehberg, *Die Ächtung des Krieges*, German edition (Berlin, 1930), 112, gives the interesting reasoning that "America does not see disputed questions concerning the Monroe Doctrine as such as purely national policy." Secretary of State Henry L. Stimson said in a speech on August 8, 1932, that the right to self-defense (and with it, the Monroe Doctrine) was the only limitation of the Kellogg Pact; see further, Asche Graf von Mandelsloh, "Die Auslegung des Kellogg-Paktes durch den amerikanischen Staatssekretär Stimson," *Zeitschrift für ausländisches Recht und Völkerrecht*, III (1935), 617 ff. The most exhaustive treatment on this topic is André N. Mandelstam's exposition on the negotiations in the American Senate: *L'interprétation du pacte Briand-Kellogg par les gouvernements et les parlements des États signataires* (Paris, 1934), 32–95.

207. According to Carl Schmitt, "Der Völkerbund und Europa" (1928),

printed in *Positionen und Begriffe* (Hamburg, 1940), 88f; Carl Bilfinger, *Völkerbundsrecht gegen Völkerrecht*, 22ff.

208. Jean Ray, *Commentaire du Pacte de la Société des Nations*, 1930, 571f.

209. On the Monroe theory in its opposition to American solidarity: C. Barcia Trelles, "La Doctrine de Monroe dans son développement historique, particulièrement en ce qui concerne les relations interaméricaines," *Recueil des Cours de l'Académie de Droit International*, Volume 32 (1930), 397f; J. Quijano Caballero, "Bolivar und Fr. D. Roosevelt," *Geist der Zeit* (June 1940), 338; also, "Grenzen der panamerikanischen Solidarität," *Monatshefte für Auswärtige Politik* (March 1941).

210. Reeves, *American Journal of International Law*, Volume 33 (1939), 239.

211. Ernst Wolgast, who examines Talleyrand's Europe Plan in the essay "Völkerrechtsordnung und Raumordnung," *Zeitschrift für Völkerrecht*, Volume XXII (1938), 25–33, interprets, as it seems to me, Talleyrand's concept of Europe in the sense of what we would understand as "spatial order." Wolgast's great service in having turned his vision to such questions with this determination should in no way be underestimated. See also Wolgast's essay, "Konkretes Ordnungsdenken im Völkerrecht," in the magazine *Völkerbund und Völkerrecht*, Volume IV (1937), 74.

212. Smedal, *Acquisition of Sovereignty over Polar Areas* (Oslo, 1931), German version (Königsberg, 1931); Wolgast, "Das Grönlandurteil des Ständigen Internationalen Gerichtshofes vom 5. April 1933," in *Zeitschrift für öffentliches Recht*, Volume XIII (1933), 599 ff; Böhmert, *Archiv für Luftrecht*, Volume VIII (1938), 279; Schmitz und Friede, "Souveränitätsrechte in der Arktis," *Zeitschrift für ausländisches öffentliches Recht und Völkerrecht*, Volume IX (July 1939), 257.

213. Volume 3, in particular of the writings *Raum und Erde* published by Karl Haushofer (Leipzig and Berlin, 1934) bears the title "Space-Overcoming Powers" (*Raumüberwindende Mächte*).

214. Kurt O. Rabl speaks in his essay "Staat und Verfassung," *Zeitschrift für öffentliches Recht*, Volume XVII (1938), of the trinity: soil, nation, and idea. This comes close to my thought and seems to me an important confirmation inasmuch as Rabl's essay proceeds from totally different points of view and not, as in our exposition, from points of view specifically pertaining to international law.

215. Fauchille, *Traité* I, 1 (1922), 37 (§44, II).

216. "One could practically designate the world war as the conclusive (this has since become questionable – Carl Schmitt) confrontation of the great cultured states by way of the fact that their imperialism must remain bound up with the domestic and foreign legal reforms of the democratic parliamentary ideology." So writes Carl Brinkmann in the *Festgabe* for Lujo Brentano's 80th birthday in a very thoughtful essay, "Imperialismus als Wirtschaftspolitik," p. 84.

217. Westel W. Willoughby, ibid., 402ff ("Has Japan a Valid Right to Assert a Monroe Doctrine with Reference to China?"); C. Walter Young, *Japan's Special Position in Manchuria*, (Baltimore, 1931), 329; Johnson Long, *La Mandchourie et la doctrine de la porte ouverte* with a foreword by La Pradelle (Paris, 1933) designates, from the Chinese standpoint, the so-called Asian Monroe Doctrine as a "Pseudo-Doctrine." See further, Carl Schmitt, "Großraum gegen Universalismus; der völkerrechtliche Kampf um die Monroedoktrin," in *Positionen und Begriffe* (1940), 295ff.

218. Fauchille, ibid., I 1, 647 (§325).

219. Disraeli's policy of amity towards Turkey and hostility towards Russia received the designation "Disraeli Doctrine" in Fenwick, *International Law* (1924), 148.

220. "Italy is an island that is immersed in the Mediterranean. This sea (I turn to the English who perhaps at this moment are listening to the radio), this sea is a road for Great Britain, one of many roads, a shortcut through which the British Empire reaches its peripheral territories. If for others the Mediterranean is a road, for us Italians it is life."

221. For more on this from the English point of view: Elizabeth Monroe, *The Mediterranean in Politics* (Oxford/London, 1938) 10ff; George Slocombe, *The Dangerous Sea* (London, 1937) 266. From the Italian side: Gaspare Ambrosini, *I problemi del Mediterraneo*, Rome (Istituto Nazionale di Cultura Fascista, 1937), 164; Pietro Silva, *Il Mediterraneo dall'Unita di Roma all'Impero Italiano* (Milan, 1938), 477.

222. Whether a transference of the principles valid for maritime routes to air routes is possible should remain open here. In a talk connected to my lecture in Kiel, Norbert Gürke has convincingly represented the viewpoint of the non-transferability of these principles and the unique character of air routes as opposed to maritime routes.

223. Carl Schmitt, *Nationalsozialismus und Völkerrecht*, Schriften der Deutschen Hochschule für Politik, Volume 9 (Berlin, 1934), 23.

224. *The British Yearbook of International Law* XVIII (1937), 87.

225. Treaty Series 1937, Number 6; Exchange of Ratification Certificates in Cairo on December 22, 1936.

226. James T. Shotwell, *War as an Instrument of National Policy*, ibid., 169.

227. Materials on the Pact Towards the Proscription of War (Berlin, 1928), 49. Repeated in the note dated July 18, 1928, ibid., 94, 95.

228. Printed by Fauchille, ibid., I 2 (1925), 212, §511b.

229. For the meaning of this "general reservation," see the recent work by Herberth Monath, *Die Rechtslage am Suezkanal*, Vorträge und Einzelschriften des Instituts für Internationales Recht an der Universität Kiel, Volume 23 (1937), 38, 44ff.

230. Ernst Wolgast, *Der Wimbledonprozeß vor dem Völkerbundgerichtshof* (Berlin, 1926), especially 74 ff.

231. On the connection of the theories of freedom with colonial expansion (freedom of the seas and of commerce as a Dutch and English theory against the Spanish-Portuguese colonial monopoly of the sixteenth and seventeenth centuries), see the excellent essay by Ulrich Scheuner, "Zur Geschichte der Kolonialfrage im Völkerrecht," *Zeitschrift für Völkerrecht*, Volume XXII (1938), 442ff, 463.

232. "It is an expression of genuine political power when a great nation determines the ways of speaking and even the ways of thinking, the vocabulary, the terminology, and the concepts of other nations on its own terms." Carl Schmitt, "Die Vereinigten Staaten von Amerika und die völkerrechtlichen Formen des modernen Imperialismus," Königsberg Lecture from February 20, 1932, published in *Positionen und Begriffe*, (Hamburg-Wandsbek: Hanseatische Verlagsanstalt, 1940), 162f.

233. Carl Schmitt, *Die Wendung zum diskriminierenden Kriegsbegriff*, Schriften der Akademie für Deutsches Recht, Gruppe Völkerrecht, Nr. 5 (Munich, 1938).

234. Carl Bilfinger, *Völkerbundsrecht gegen Völkerrecht*, Schriften der Akademie für Deutsches Recht, Gruppe Völkerrecht, Nr. 6 (Munich, 1938).

235. Georg H.J. Erler, "Mißverstehen, Mißtrauen und Mißerfolg im Genfer Minderheitsschutzsystem, Zeitschrift für Völkerrecht," Volume XXII (1938), 5.

236. Hermann Raschhofer, *Die Krise des Minderheitenschutzes, Zeitschrift für ausländisches öffentliches Recht und Völkerrecht*, Volume VI (1936), 239–40; G.A. Walz, "Inflation im Völkerrecht der Nachkriegszeit," Supplement to Volume XXIII of *Zeitschrift für Volkerrecht*, (1939) 70–1; G.A. Walz, *Artgleichheit gegen Gleichartigkeit, Die beiden Grundprobleme des Rechts*, Schriften der Akademie für Deutsches Recht, Gruppe Rechtsgrundlagen und Rechtsphilosophie, Nr. 8 (Hamburg, 1938).

237. For more on this, see Carl Schmitt, "Neutralität und Neutralisierungen, Verfassung und völkerrechtliche Bemerkungen zu dem Buch von Christoph Steding, *Das Reich und die Krankheit der europäischen Kultur*," *German Jurisprudence*, Volume IV (1939), Issue 2; also in *Positionen und Begriffe*, as cited above, 271f; for more, see *Zeitschrift für Völkerrecht* XXIV (1940), 164f.

238. On the systematic connection between liberal individualism and universalism in international law, see: Carl Schmitt, *Die Wendung zum diskriminierenden Kriegsbegriff*, as cited above, p. 58.

239. The most recent monographic treatment of the problem of intervention in international law by Gerhard Ostermeyer, *Die Intervention in der Völkerrechtstheorie und -praxis unter besonderer Berücksichtigung der Staatenpraxis des 19. Jahrhunderts* (Abhandlungen der Hanischen Universität, published by L. Raape and R. Laun, Volume 36 [1940]), contains good attempts at a concrete way of thinking about orders, although it

overlooks the global-political space problem and misses the real question, which cannot be solved with the general term "emergency intervention." Instead of doing this, the structure of the concrete order of "European international law" and the meaning under international law of the "concert of the great powers" should have been worked out. Whoever speaks of "a state of emergency" and intervention in international law, should never forget the *Quis judicabit?* Using pseudo-juridical general terms, one remains in a grey area between the unlimited permission of totally unexpected "humanitarian" interventions and the just as unlimited rejection of even the smallest "interference" which then must appear, wrongly so, as a "delict of international law."

240. A confrontation with this concept of imperialism and its comprehensive literature would explode the framework of our exposition and must be reserved for another investigation. I would, however, like at the least to point to the thoroughly clear exposition by Werner Sombart, "Das Wirtschaftsleben im Zeitalter des Hochkapitalismus" (*Der moderne Kapitalismus*, Volume III, 1), (Munich and Leipzig, 1927), 66ff; as well as to the above-mentioned essay by Carl Brinkmann; and Heinrich Triepel, *Hegemonie* (1938), 185ff (Imperialism and Hegemony).

241. "The *Reich* rose first in Babylon" (*To babilonie irhur sik irst dat rike*), *Sachsenspiegel* III, 44, §1; on the medieval concept of *Reich* see Otto Brunner, *Land und Herrschaft* (1939), 217, 234f.

242. According to, for example, Friedrich Apelt, *Das britische Reich als völkerrechtsverbundene Staatengemeinschaft* (Leipziger rechtswissenschaftliche Studien, Volume 90 [Leipzig, 1934]). The alternative between interstate and intra-state designations cannot be overcome by the state itself. This fact owes itself to the decisionistic structure of the concept of state, which leads all questions concerning a concrete order of international law into a hopeless dead end. In contrast to this, it is an attention-worthy sign of progress that Santi Romano (Corso di Diritto Internazionale, 4th edition [Padua, 1939], 79) recognizes from his "institutional" thinking that certain closed "state" connections outfitted with their own institutionalizations are neither intra-state nor interstate connections. He counts among such entities confederations, royal unions, and colonial protectorates. Paolo Biscaretti di Ruffia further elaborated on this question in the *Festschrift* for Santi Romano (Padua,1939) in an essay on "non-international unions between states, distinct from interstate unions" ("Sull'esistenza di Unioni non internazionali tra Stati, diverse dagli Stati di Stati"). He treats in particular the British "Commonwealth of Nations" as an example of such a connection that is neither interstate nor purely intra-state state. Unfortunately, he does not succeed at convincingly solving the difficult questions of such topics because he remains stuck in the decisionistic concept of state and cannot therefore overcome the dilemma between the intra-state and the

interstate. What does "Unioni non inter*nazionali* tra Stati?" mean, then? As long as "international" law is fundamentally an "interstate" law, then it is nothing more than a simple mix-up in the terminology, namely "Unioni non inter*statali* tra Stati"! Much would have been gained had we grown used to precisely differentiating, at least in our language, between "international" and "interstate" relations and avoiding the designations of "international" community and "community of international law" as names for interstate law, since these designations only blur the lines and confuse things. The state-centric conceptual view that Biscaretti di Ruffia retains makes it impossible for him to think outside the two alternatives of interstate and intra-state. International relations that are neither interstate nor intra-state and connections between states that are not interstate must appear impossible, indeed, totally absurd, to this state-based way of thinking. Those entities named by Santi Romano can only be understood in their legal and scholarly context proceeding from an analytic category higher than that of the state – for example, from that of the federation (which *precedes* the conceptual alternative of state federation or federal state), or of the *Reich* or of the *Großraum* – if their unique legal character, which cannot be comprehended using the two alternatives of interstate and intra-state, is not to be destroyed.

243. Carl Bilfinger, "Zum Problem der Staatengleichheit im Völkerrecht," *Zeitschrift für ausländisches öffentliches Recht und Völkerrecht*, Volume IV (1934), 481ff, and "Les bases fondamentales de la Communauté des États" in *Recueil des Cours de l'Académie de Droit International*, 1939, 95f (Equality and Community of States).

244. H.H. Lammers, "Staatsführung im Dritten Reich," in the Lecture Series of the Austrian Administrative Academy (Berlin, 1938), 16: "Unifying the idea of state and nation, the term '*Deutsches Reich*' seems to me to be of deep meaning for state law and, for the first time, to be the proper designation for the German state." This comment was repeated in the *Völkischer Beobachter* from September 2, 3 and 4, 1938. See Wilhelm Stuckart, first in the lecture "Party and State," *Deutscher Juristentag* (1936), 271–3, on the *Reich* as a *völkisch* life form and order of life.

245. Fritz Berber, *Prinzipien der britischen Außenpolitik*, Schriften des Deutschen Instituts für außenpolitische Forschung (Berlin, 1939), 20f.

246. Christoph Steding, *Das Reich und die Krankheit der europäischen Kultur* (Hamburg, 1939); see also Carl Schmitt, "Neutralität und Neutralisierung," in *Positionen und Begriffe* (Hamburg-Wandsbek: Hanseatische Verlagsanstalt, 1940), 271f.

247. "Conflicting Social Obligations," in *Proceedings of the Aristotelian Society*, New Series XV (1915), 151. Cole's theory of society goes back to Lewis Morgan's theory, outlined in *Ancient Society* (1877).

248. *Air Power and Cities* (London, 1930) (the continuation of *Air Power and*

War Rights [1924]). Remarkable and characteristic here is Spaight's follow-ing sentence: "Air power will clear the way of the acceptance of the new order of ideas." (*An International Air Force* [London, 1932]). James Molony Spaight (1877–1968) was an English lawyer who wrote on the legality and ethics of aerial warfare in the early twentieth century.

249. H. Wohlthat, "Großraum und Meistbegünstigung," *Der Deutsche Volkswirt*, December 23, 1938; Ritter von Epp, Speech of February 23, 1939, available in *Hakenkreuzbanner* 56, 2.

250. See p. 78; for more, consult the *Zeitschrift für Völkerrecht* XXIV (1940), 146f.

251. One should only compare – in contrast to the English and French protests of 1/15/1940 and 1/22/1940 – the German declaration from 2/14/1940 on the American security zone (14th Resolution of the Pan-American Conference from 10/3/1939). On this, see *Zeitschrift für Völkerrecht* XXIV (1940), 180f., Ulrich Scheuner, "Die Sicherheitszone des amerikanischen Kontinents," as well as (in the same issue), Carl Schmitt, "Raum und Großraum im Völkerrecht," 172.

252. Roberto Sandiford, *Brevi note sull'analogia tra Diritto Marittimo e Aeronautico*, Studi di Diritto Aeronautico VI (1933).

253. See the concluding section on the "Concept of Space in Jurisprudence" on p. 181.

254. It is a noteworthy symptom of the spatially revolutionary effect of the mastery of the air that already the idea of a border zone (instead of mere areal borders and linear borders) is represented in aerial law: Kroell, *Traité de droit international public aérien* (1934) I, 71 ('frontière volume" instead of "frontière surface"); see further (rejecting this position) Friedrich Giese, "Das Luftgebiet in Kriegszeiten," *Archiv deutsches öffentliches Rechts, N.F. 31* (1939), 161.

255. Carl Schmitt, "On the Relation of International Law and National Law," *Zeitschrift der Akademie für Deutsches Recht* (1940), 4; see further the discussion of H. Triepel's book, *Hegemonie* (1938), in *Schmollers Jahrbuch*, Volume 63 (1939), 516, and, finally, the *Festgabe* for Georgios Streit (Athens), (1940), in *Positionen und Begriffe* (Hamburg-Wandsbek: Hanseatische Verlagsanstalt, 1940), 263f.

256. See also Böhmert's discussion surrounding the 1st and 2nd edition of this piece of writing, "The *Großraum* Order of International Law with a Ban on Intervention for Spatially Foreign Powers" (also in the collection *Politische Wissenschaft*, published by Paul Ritterbusch [Berlin: 1940], 27–69), in *Zeitschrift für Völkerrecht* XXIV (1940), 134–40.

257. It is for these reasons that the attempts to portray this Congress as an authoritative model (Guglielmo Ferrero, *Reconstruction*, 1940) or to allow several figures of this Congress, Metternich, Talleyrand, or Alexander I, to be shown in a glorified light are all the more naïve.

258. Carl Schmitt, "Die Auflösung der europäischen Ordnung im 'International Law,'" *Deutsche Rechtswissenschaft* (Quarterly Journal of the Akademie für Deutsches Recht), Volume V (October 1940), 267ff.

259. The Belgian Congo colony was a later shady deal characteristic for the overall situation of international law of the time and could not, of course, have formed a *Reich* and therefore could not have formed a *Großraum*.

260. See further, Giorgio Cansacchi in the *Scritti giuridici in onore di Santi Romano* (1940), 393f, and Carlo Costamagna, in *Lo Stato* VII (1936), 321ff.

261. Karl Brandi, "Der Weltreichsgedanke Karls V." in *Europäische Revue* XVI (May 1940), 277.

262. Carl Schmitt, "Inter bellum et pacem nihil medium," *Zeitschrift der Akademie für Deutsches Recht* (1939), 594; *La Vita Italiana* XXVII (December 1939), 637f, *Positionen und Begriffe*, 246f.

263. Julius Evola, "La guerra totale," in *La Vita Italiana* XXV (1937), 567; Carl Schmitt, *Die Wendung zum diskriminierenden Kriegsbegriff* (Schriften der Akademie für Deutsches Recht, Gruppe Völkerrecht Number 5) (1938); G.A. Walz; *Nationalboykott und Völkerrecht* (Schriften der Akademie für Deutsches Recht, Gruppe Völkerrecht Number 7), (1939); Theodor Maunz, *Geltung und Neubildung modernen Kriegsvölkerrechts* (Freiburg, 1939); H. Pleßner, *De huidige Verhouding tusschen Oorlog en Vrede* (Groningen, 1939); Franz von Wesendon, *Der Kriegsbegriff im Völkerrecht* (Dissertation, Bonn) (1939).

264. Fritz Berber, *Prinzipien der britischen Außenpolitik* (Schriften des Deutschen Instituts für außenpolitische Forschung) (Berlin, 1939).

265. The first example of such a "friendship line" was certainly the (verbally agreed) agreement from the Spanish-French Treaty of Cateau-Cambrésis, 4/3/1559, in F.G. Davenport, *European Treaties Bearing on the History of the United States and Its Dependencies to 1648* (Publications of the Carnegie Institution 154, I), (Washington, 1917), 208, 219ff. Along with this, see Adolf Rein's exposition, which has not yet been sufficiently appreciated by international jurisprudence, *Der Kampf Westeuropas um Nordamerika im 15. und 16. Jahrhundert* (Stuttgart-Gotha, 1925) (Allgemeine Staatengeschichte 2, 3), 207f; on the sentence "Beyond the Equator there is no sin," see p. 292. See also Ulrich Scheuner, "Zur Geschichte der Kolonialfrage im Völkerrecht," *Zeitschrift für Völkerrecht* XXII (1938), 466; Wolfgang Windelband, "Motive europäischer Kolonialpolitik," *Deutsches Adelsblatt*, November 14, 1939.

266. Henri Hauser, *La Modernité du XVI siècle* (Paris, 1930).

267. Friedrich Ratzel, *Der Lebensraum* (1901), 67.

268. Gunter Ipsen was the first to use the expression "field of meaning" in the *Festschrift* for Wilhelm Streitburg (Heidelberg, 1924), 225. The words of Ferdinand de Saussure, Leo Weißgerber, and Jost Trier also belong

here from recent linguistic and semiological research. The expression is, however, still strongly spatially determined in the sense of a mere areal.

269. Carl Schmitt, *Die Wendung zum diskriminierenden Kriegsbegriff* (1938), 7f; Kindt-Kiefer, *Fundamentalstruktur der staatlichen Ganzheit* (Bern, 1940), Introduction.

270. The designation "spatial theory" (for more on its most important representative, see note 187 on p. 219) is an example of the "monstrous adaptive ability of the mathematical way of expression" (G. Joos). A spatial theory for international jurisprudence worthy of its name would have immediately to guard itself against the differences and unique characteristics of the status of space and ground – differences and characteristics that would dissolve any general theory of space into nothing; consider, for example, the unique nature of the ground status of protectorate, colony, state territory, national soil; see further Friedrich Klein's most attention-worthy approach here on the difference between territorial eminence and spatial eminence and the attempts of Italian legal scholars to differentiate between *territorio statale* and *spazio imperiale*.

271. Credit for the first stab in this direction belongs to Walter Hamel's work, *Das Wesen des Staatgebietes* (Berlin, 1933).

272. Fr. Ratzel, *Der Lebensraum* (1901), 12.

273. Max Planck, *Das Weltbild der neuen Physik*, 1929, 25ff. See further, the interesting essay by Hermann Wein, "Die zwei Formen der Erkenntniskritik," *Blätter für deutsche Philosophie*, Volume 14 (1940), 50.

274. Viktor von Weiszäcker, *Der Gestaltkrise. Theorie und Einheit von Wahrnehmen und Bewegen*, (Leipzig, 1940); for our context, p. 102 is especially important.

275. Otto Brunner, *Land und Herrschaft, Grundfragen der territorialen Verfassungsgeschichte Südostdeutschlands im Mittelalter* (Veröffentlichungen des Österreichischen Instituts für Geschichtsforschung, 1939), 219.

276. Otto von Gierke, *Das deutsche Genossenschaftsrecht*, II (1873), 575f. Otto von Gierke (1841–1921) was a German legal historian.

277. On the opposition of land and sea in the international law of the modern period, see the treatise named in the preface, "Staatliche Souveränität und Freies Meer," in *Das Reich und Europa* (Leipzig: Koehler und Amelang, 1941), 79f.

The International Crime of the War of Aggression and the Principle "Nullum crimen, nulla poena sine lege" (1945)

278. The statute determines that whoever is convicted of stealing horses is to be punished with death. As judges no longer found the death penalty sufficiently modern, they judged that the statute did not concern those who had stolen only *one* horse and not, as it was stated in the text of the law, hors*es*

(in the plural), and recognized only the punishment for normal robbery in the event of the theft of only one horse, or more than one individual horse.

279. The formulation comes from a speech of *Sir Austen Chamberlain* in the House of Commons from November 24, 1927; the decisive sentence reads: "I therefore remain opposed to this attempt to define the aggressor, because I believe that it will be a trap for the innocent and a signpost for the guilty."

280. See p. 213.

281. See p. 191.

Index

Made in the USA
Columbia, SC
26 May 2020